LEAD BY
GREATNESS

LEAD BY
GREATNESS

*How character can
power your success*

DAVID LAPIN

To

Ashira, Livia, Bruria, Hedva, and Moshe,

my beloved children

ACKNOWLEGEMENTS

I feel indebted to so many people for their influence on me through my life's journey so far. Beginning with both my parents, and continuing with my mentors and my teachers, many people have been living examples to me of human greatness. Everything I think and innovate, both in business and in general philosophy, contains within it the seeds of my father's teachings and those of one of my most influential teachers, R. Hayim Lifschitz. My thanks to my patient and supportive editor, Miriam Shaviv, both for what she helped me write and for what she forced me to omit. Carmel Pelunsky, David Feldt and his team, and Steve Gottry and his team of editors, designers, and proofreaders were all immensely helpful in preparing this work. I deeply value the contributions of my colleagues at Lapin International, Clint Parry, Jocelyn Sanders and Adena Philips who support me, challenge me, and encourage me every day. I am especially indebted to our president, my friend and trusted business partner, Desi Rosenfield, without whom this book would never have come to light. Since we met eighteen years ago, Desi has steadfastly believed in me and in the value to the world of what I teach. She has supported and inspired me every day since then, partnering with me in the development of my ideas and their delivery to our clients, whose success is her passion. Through the many years of preparing this book, she consistently encouraged me, preserved and grew our firm through challenging times, and spearheaded our move from South Africa to the USA.

From my heart's depth I thank my beloved and accomplished children—Ashira and Ohran Gobrin, Livia and Jared Dunkin, Bruria and Yaacov Martin, Hedva and Eitan Sender, and Moshe Lapin—for their constant and unconditional love and their profound wisdom so beyond their years. My thanks also to their mother, Serena Gould, for her support and the many lonely days and nights she spent taking care of our children while I studied, traveled, and worked.

I am grateful, as well, for the time and help given to me towards my research for this book by many CEOs of fast-growing companies. Their personal experiences, insights, and values influenced me deeply. I am humbled by and indebted to my many students and wonderful clients around the world who trusted me enough to embrace my ideas, implement them and measurably demonstrate their economic and human value long before these ideas became fashionable.

Lastly, I thank you for taking the time to explore this new leadership framework with me and to apply it to your own life and leadership. I hope it will help you to ever-new levels of personal and professional accomplishment.

"Great men are not born great,
they grow great..."

- Mario Puzo
The Godfather

CONTENTS

PART ONE: THE CASE FOR GREATNESS

Your Competitive Edge

PART TWO: UNLOCKING YOUR CORPORATE SOUL

Applying Spiritual Fundamentals to Business Practice

PART THREE: THE NEXT ERA OF LEADERSHIP

Taking Corporate Soul Across Continents, Cultures, and Generations

CONCLUSION

TWO GENETIC STRAINS

*Greatness is not a skill set, but a way of being
that expresses a person's sense of destiny and purpose.*

"DO MORE!" a large blue and red IBM billboard seemed to be shouting out at me as I walked through the concourse of Los Angeles International Airport. It was well past midnight, and I had just had a very long day of consulting and lecturing. "Do more? When, exactly?" I shouted back at it in my head. Can you imagine doing any more than you currently do? I can't.

There had to be a way, I thought, while walking to my car, to *accomplish* more without having to *do* more. And I don't believe we can rely on technology alone for that. Curt Doolittle, CEO of Seattle-based Ascentium,[1] once told me he believes that computing as we know it has already extracted all possible business efficiencies from technology and that we now need exponential innovation. So if it won't be technology, what will it be that will drive this exponential innovation? If most of us can't continue doing more and more, what will power the next wave of economic growth?

Business visionaries already recognize that the next wave of growth won't come just from a focus on profits and process. It will come from leaders who successfully set their organizations apart by infusing them with innovation, energy, and heroic performance. These leaders will be individuals who are able to connect, inspire, and instill in people a passionate sense of purpose. The next wave of growth will be driven by leaders who are not only functionally competent, but who are also people of character and true human greatness. Greatness of character powers leadership success more than any other single factor.

Greatness is not a skill set, but a way of being that expresses a person's sense of destiny and purpose. When great people lead with a sense of destiny and purpose, they become great leaders. Consider Winston Churchill's reflection as he lay awake at 3:00 a.m. on the morning of his first day as Britain's prime minister during the Great War: "I felt as if I were walking with Destiny, and all my past life had been but a preparation for this hour and for this trial."[2]

Leaders who live by their purpose and values are people of authenticity and integrity; they do not need to bully others with the power of their status. Instead, they lead people with the authority of their stature; they *Lead by Greatness*™.

Terms like *purpose* and *greatness*, now accepted in business, are inextricably linked to a spiritual foundation. Purpose is about so much more than money, and greatness goes far beyond power. When I recognized this, the powerful connection between business performance and human spirituality, I knew I had stumbled upon a truth that would deliver the kind of exponential growth so many business leaders sought.

To many people the idea of linking business and spirituality appears an oxymoron, but to me, business and spirituality are natural, ideological siblings.

I was raised in a family that valued both the spiritual and the business worlds. Both my grandfathers were businessmen who immigrated to South Africa from Lithuania at the beginning of the last century. My paternal grandfather's brother, Rav Eliyahu Lopian, was one of the most revered spiritual teachers of the twentieth century. My father was a leading rabbi in South Africa, and later in the U.S., his brother, my uncle Joseph Lapin, was a businessman who in the 1950s pioneered the market in South Africa for Japanese consumer electronics. The businessmen of my family understood how their spirituality enhanced their business success. Those of my forebears who were spiritual leaders admired honest, hardworking business people, and they understood that business could teach many deep and meaningful religious lessons. They often applied business principles to explain some of the more complex ideas of their spiritual teachings.

I inherited two genetic strains: one from generations of spiritual guides, and the other from generations of businesspeople. Perhaps that is why I was never satisfied pigeonholing myself in either the business world or the spiritual world alone. I needed both. And I wanted them in my life simultaneously. I wanted to prove how much more influential business leaders could be when they know not only how to manage people's labor and talent, but also how to connect with their essence; to unlock their spirit and liberate their genius. I also wanted to bring the lessons I could learn from great business leaders into the world of spirituality.

So I became a rabbi, unveiling the wonders of the Torah[i] and Kabbalah[ii] for business leaders, professionals, and educators around

i The Torah is not just the Bible; it is the aggregate compendium of all ancient and contemporary Jewish wisdom of life.
ii Kabbalah is the science of ancient Jewish mysticism and spiritual teachings. It deals with the workings of the cosmos and the principles governing the interface between the material and the spiritual worlds. The Kabbalah based on the Zohar, ascribed to second-century Shimon Bar Yochai.

the world. At the same time, I joined an international commodities trading company. As global head of the Metals, Minerals, and Energy Division of Raphaely International, I came to see the world and learn how its different peoples think, act, and work. Thirty-odd years later, I am both a spiritual teacher and a bottom-line-focused leadership and strategy consultant helping some of the world's best companies become even better and training leaders to use their greatness to grow economic value. I started my consulting firm, Lapin International,[3] in South Africa twenty years ago and expanded it to the USA in 1997. We serve companies and their leaders in many different industries internationally. Having straddled the business and spiritual worlds for decades, I have now found a way to combine human values and economic output to achieve astonishing results. In this book, I will share with you how my clients have achieved these results.

This book is not about great corporations, but about the greatness of leaders who make their corporations great. Other authors have correlated *corporate* greatness with financial results. In this book, I set out to demonstrate the correlation between the greatness of *human character* and business results. I suggest that most people have the components of human greatness, and that with the help of this book you will more easily access these components and hone them for success.

Most management models deal with how to change the behaviors of others. This book argues that the only person we can truly change is ourselves, and that when we know what to change in ourselves and how to do it, the impact on others is exponential. For this reason, Part One deals with knowing ourselves and the forces that drive our choices at the deepest of levels. We will map our own unique *Spiritual Fingerprint*, discover our *Personal Purpose*, and learn to access our vast reservoir of inner wisdom.

Once we recognize ourselves as our most powerful instrument of change, in Part Two we learn how to impact the people around us, our teams, and our organization. In Part Three, we expand these ideas for building lasting impact across both cultural and generational divides, a competency vital to lead into the future. During all this time, we will use our own human greatness as our tool for change.

The leadership strategies detailed in this book are all *driven* by human, ethical, and spiritual imperatives, but their success is *measured* by the financial performance they deliver. As we begin to implement these strategies, we find our effectiveness increasing, both as individuals and as business leaders. We rethink our products and services, our customers, and our employees in ways we never have before. We re-imagine ourselves: who we are, what values drive our choices, what sacrifices we are willing to make, and *why* we are willing to make those sacrifices. We discover how to build our customers' sense of worth and satisfy their craving for meaning.

The methods detailed in this book are not merely theoretical; they have proven to inspire people to exceptional performance. Using the *Lead by Greatness* method, leaders in the finance, mining, retail, and manufacturing industries have profited, improved efficiencies, and increased productivity. U.S. law enforcement agencies[4] have used *Lead by Greatness* to develop new strategies to combat hate crime and terror. Companies like General Electric, whose global resourcing team used our strategies, improved their trading effectiveness in emerging economies, saving millions of dollars in the process. The Standard Retail Bank used principles from *Lead by Greatness* in the redesign of its operating model. At that time it dramatically improved its level of customer satisfaction and achieved an astonishing four-year compound earnings growth in excess of 16 percent. Truworths International, a large fashion retailer, applied our fundamentals and grew at annual rates well in excess of 20 percent consistently over fifteen years, with returns on equity in excess of 50 percent. It was rated as the second-best fashion retailer in the world (after Abercrombie & Fitch) for return on investment and margin.[5]

There is also another, different side to this powerful equation of character greatness and business success. Not only do human and spiritual imperatives enhance business results, but I have also learned how business is a near-perfect environment for character growth. A business environment, filled as it is with its paradoxes and challenges, provides a unique opportunity for us to learn and develop our characters with immediate feedback. The ever-present temptation in business to sacrifice sustainable growth for short-term gain separates people of character from those driven by greed. The business world can be viewed as one of the finest "universities" of greatness for those of us who choose to see it that way. I certainly do.

We are at the threshold of a newly dawning era in business, where offerings that contain a rich intangible component are worth far more to customers than those that do not. This era is about more than making and selling commoditized products and production-line labor. This era in business is also about creating experiences for people that inspire and uplift them, both at work and in the process of their buying, selling, and using our products. In this new era, leaders who combine their tangible assets and financial acumen with the greatness of their character will easily and consistently outperform those who do not. In *Lead by Greatness* we'll disover how.

PART ONE

THE CASE FOR GREATNESS

Your Competitive Edge

CHAPTER ONE

NOT A SOUL IN
THE BOARDROOM?

*A company's competitive advantage can only be
sustained if it is an authentic manifestation of that
company's unique essence, its corporate soul.*

LIKE INDIVIDUALS, groups of people—sports teams, families, and even corporations—have souls, too: a personality and an essence that makes them unique. The difference is that whereas people are *born* unique, the unique essence of an organization needs to be uncovered and cultivated.

One of my first duties as a young rabbi, before I was ever involved in the business world, was to officiate at a bris, the ritual circumcision of an eight-day-old Jewish male.[6] Poor little chap, I thought, very soon he will need to carve out a space for himself in a large and accomplished family and compete with his many siblings for attention. This led me to reflect, as I looked at his proud parents and watched the mohel[iii] perform this mitzvah,[iv] that from the time we are born we strive to differentiate ourselves in some way. I was caught off

---

iii *Professional trained to perform the circumcision.*
iv *Commandment of God.*

guard when the boy's father asked me to give his son a blessing. What was I to say? I had never given blessings before. "Go out and make a difference in the world," I said, with my hands gently on his head, "but always, always be yourself, because there is no one else in the world who is just like you; no one else who has a soul the same as yours; no one else who can accomplish what you can."

If we are true to ourselves, our uniqueness will always be valued, because there is no other in the world just like any one of us; no one who can make the difference we were created to make. We all carve out special places for ourselves that add value to who we are and to what we do. Kids want to be like other kids, but they also want to be different, special, and unique. We all want to fit in and at the same time to offer something valuable and unique in our business, professional, or social lives. This unique offering is our "competitive advantage" in society, and it provides us with much of our sense of social self-worth.

The idea of competitive advantage is usually associated with businesses rather than with individual people. A business has competitive advantage when it does something valuable for its customers that others cannot do in the same way or for the same price. The key to competitive advantage in business, though, is the same as it is for individuals: it is about being ourselves. When Herb Kelleher, former chairman, president, and CEO of Southwest Airlines, was asked the secret to building a great organization, he answered in two words: be yourself.[7] When, as an organization, you are yourself, no one can be quite like you. This is because when companies (or individuals) are true to their essence, they embrace their most unique qualities: the ones that get to the core of who they are and distinguish them from others. This authentic essence is what I call the *corporate soul.* A company's soul is its spirit, its personality, its culture, and the values by which it firmly stands, no matter what the cost. A company's soul is the reason why its customers stay loyal to it, and why its best employees never leave.

Many corporate leaders worry about how quickly competitive advantage can be eroded by the instantaneous diffusion of information on the Internet, which rapidly transforms innovation into commoditization. However, when a company's competitive advantage is rooted in its *corporate soul*, it is protected from the threat of imitation and can more easily be preserved. A company's soul is an intangible gold mine, and the real secret to developing its worth lies with great leadership—men and women of exceptional character.

Southwest Airlines, one of the most notable case studies in the world, is a company with soul. I will refer to Southwest (and to a few other well-known companies with soul) frequently in this book, both because of the availability of data and anecdotal information about it, and because so many people have experienced Southwest's customer service firsthand. Southwest competes in what would appear to be a commoditized industry, yet, despite every effort, no other airline has successfully replicated the Southwest experience and business model. This is due to Southwest Airlines' *corporate soul*—or what Herb Kelleher calls its personality—and the way the company uses it strategically.

"Personality is a strategy," Kelleher says. "Despite what the experts say, air travel is not a commodity business. We market ourselves based on the personality and spirit of ourselves."[8] No other airline can replicate the particular soul of Southwest. You can copy everything that other people or companies have, but you cannot copy who they are. Who you are is deeply embedded in your DNA and cannot be

3

replicated. No business needs to be a commodity business competing only on price. Every business can market itself based on its personality and spirit—in other words, its soul.

A company's soul is authentic when it resonates with its leaders and employees not only as a business strategy but also as an all-encompassing way of life. Kelleher used to say, "My hope is that when [our employees] are talking to their grandchildren, they say that Southwest Airlines was one of the finest experiences they ever had."[9] In a similar vein, Alan Pullinger, CEO of Rand Merchant Bank, told me that their leadership brand (a set of character traits built on *Lead by Greatness* principles that RMB cultivates in each of its leaders), "is a brand for life, not just for work. If our leadership brand doesn't resonate enough with our leaders that it embraces their whole life, they shouldn't be working here. The way we are at work must be authentic to who we are at home. This is basic to character."

Leaders of character are authentic. They know who they are and what the values and beliefs are that drive their choices. Their actions align with their values both in business and beyond as they courageously lead by their own greatness. Rather than imitating the "best practices" of others, they set the bar for best practice and leave their competitors striving to emulate them. They do not look over their shoulder at what their competitors are doing, because that just places limitations on what they themselves could be doing. Leaders of character inspire their organizations with something of the spirit of their own authenticity. An organization can only authentically be itself when it is aligned with the beliefs and passions of its leaders. The spirit of Southwest still reflects Herb Kelleher's spirit and his own beliefs. The same applies to Richard Branson and his Virgin Airlines— so different from Southwest but just as unique.

Branson did not conceive the Virgin experience in a clinical strategy session. His passion for flying is in his blood, and by infusing this passion into the Virgin experience he has given Virgin its *corporate soul*. On a Virgin flight you experience some of Richard Branson's personality. No other airline gives or can give the particular Virgin experience, because no other airline has Branson's soul. The Virgin competitive advantage is both lasting and unassailable for this reason. Branson's edge—his love of life and his willingness to push boundaries to challenge convention—seems to be core to his soul and permeates everything he does, not just his airline.

Consider Virgin's competitor, British Airways. British Airways is staffed by competent people and offers a good product, but it lacks soul. Because Virgin competes with its *corporate soul*, not just its commoditized product, it seldom needs to discount its fares. Yet Virgin doubled its profit in 2009, one of the worst years in airline history, while British Airways posted a record loss for the same year.[10] When a company reflects the passions and the purpose of a great leader, it maintains its competitive advantage and never needs to compete on price alone.

Great leaders live the purpose for which they believe they were put into this world. Their greatness describes much more than their competencies; it describes their characters. Great leaders effectively blend measurable accomplishments with spiritual aspirations, and they inspire that blend in others. A great business leader satisfies people's needs for the tangible things that make them feel secure, as well as their cravings for higher intangibles, like a sense of purpose, human dignity, and a feeling of being valued as an individual. Above all, a great leader can work successfully both in the world of operational effectiveness and in the world of human and spiritual values.

But how does one develop the skills to operate in these two realms at once? Can "human greatness" be learned? Indeed, it can. It starts with leadership character and, as it turns out, there is no better place to build it than in business itself.

CHAPTER TWO

CHARACTER SCHOOL

Leaders of character build great businesses, but the converse is true, too: great businesses are the ideal place in which to build great character.

HAVE YOU EVER wondered why, if so much conflict comes from trade and relationships, an intelligent Creator designed the world in a way that people have to trade and have relationships with each other in order to survive? I pondered that question for years as a child. Much later, after my own successes and failures in relationships and in business, I discovered that there are no better schools for character development and human greatness than relationships and business. This is because to succeed in either of these areas, one has to put the needs of others before one's own, and this is the essence of character greatness. One needs to be generous and humble; one must be willing to trust others and be able to cultivate the trust of others in oneself. One needs the backbone to stand by what one believes to be true and right. David Ogilvy, the "father of advertising," once said that there is no shortage of people with brains, but "the spinal column seems to be in much shorter supply."[11]

Not only is great character the key to success both in business and in relationships, but these two areas also provide us with instant feedback about our own character. In business, as in relationships, we get immediate feedback about how authentically we care about others and how effectively we add value to their lives. Do we lead and mentor people with humility? Do we inspire people with a higher sense of purpose and meaning? If we lose the trust of others in our company or team and are perceived to be acting without integrity, we feel the result personally. Sustainable business success is a mirror reflection of our growth as human beings and as leaders.

People who have achieved human greatness radiate a palpable aura. You sense it when they walk into a room. They have presence and charisma. You feel their energy and respond to it—and so does the universe. When you are imbued with the clear sense of your own purpose, the reason for which you were created, you radiate a transformational energy. When your purpose is clear and vibrant, others will align themselves to your purpose and support its realization, sometimes without even knowing it. But how can you access this energy and radiate it?

Jim Collins, author of *Good to Great*, believes that most people have the capacity to become great leaders. He says, however, that although he would love to be able to give a list of steps for people to develop themselves into what he calls Level 5 leaders—the key leadership component for taking companies from good to great—he has no solid research data that would support a credible list.[12]

There is no "list of steps," which, as Collins rightly says, would trivialize the very idea of leadership greatness. But the character traits of leadership greatness are identifiable and there are ways to develop them.

In my work with leaders and through the research I conducted for this book, I have identified eight character traits that define great leaders. These eight are generic and apply across the board. However, they can be modified, adapted, and expanded to fit the leadership needs of any given organization.

1. **Authenticity**: Exceptional leaders are vehemently *authentic* to their own beliefs and values, but are agile in the way they adapt to changing situations and diverse people.
2. **Destiny**: They have a sense of *personal destiny*, a role they believe they need to play in the world and a purpose for which they believe they were put here.
3. **Mastery**: They *master* their defensive instincts and are always able to choose an appropriate response to the most trying challenges.
4. **Humility**: They are *humble* enough to know they are part of something bigger than themselves, and they surround themselves with people who are each, at least in some way, better than they are.
5. **Vulnerability**: They courageously admit and confront their own *vulnerability*.
6. **Generosity**: They show sensitivity to the vulnerability of others, crafting environments in which people feel safe enough to give of themselves *generously*.
7. **Awareness**: They are *aware* of the different lenses through which people of different cultures and generations experience the world, and they know how to build trust and respect across cultural and generational boundaries.

8. **Wisdom**: Finally, exceptional leaders know how to trust their *inner wisdom* and access their greatness, and how to unlock the greatness in others.

Leaders of character display a remarkable similarity in possessing these traits. Because of this, they see value and opportunity where others do not. They foresee trends, but are not enslaved by them. They can buy when others sell and sell when others buy, because they are persuaded by value and opportunity, not by fad or frenzy. They recognize talent, inspire it, and nurture it. They are guardians of their organizations' futures, and they build trusting teams and sustainable reputations. They care, they innovate, and they deliver.

Leaders of character build great businesses. It seems intuitive, doesn't it? So much so that you might find yourself wondering why so few leaders seem to do what appears so obvious. But the fact that so few are willing to embark on a journey to their own greatness creates a brilliant opportunity for you to distinguish yourself and your business.

Some people miss the opportunity to become great, and thereby to inspire greatness in others, because they fear being great. As Marianne Williamson says in *Our Deepest Fear*:

> *Our deepest fear is not that we are inadequate. Our deepest fear is that we are powerful beyond measure. It is our light, not our darkness that most frightens us...As we are liberated from our own fear, our presence automatically liberates others.*[13]

There is another reason why people often fail to pursue a passage to greatness despite its obvious payoffs. This is because instinctively we tend to focus on solutions to problems *outside* ourselves rather than focusing *within*. It is very hard to look in the mirror when we don't like what we see. We are quick to make external changes: fixing structure, operations, marketing, and public relations; we implement technology, drive innovation, manage employees, and incentivize managers. But these are all symptoms of problems, not causes. We ourselves, and the choices we make, are the root cause of our challenges, and often of the challenges that face our organizations. We ourselves are also the key to change and to new opportunity. Great leaders recognize this. And greatness is something any of us can choose. It only takes one person to start the process.

The Power of One

In the Post-Information Age of abundance and freedom, leaders who inspire have the edge over those who intimidate others into servility and obedience.

I lived in South Africa during its dramatic transformation from a repressive regime to a vibrant democracy. That is when I learned how the power of a single individual can change the world; how responding to circumstances can define his or her own reality. Working with business and government leaders in South Africa during and after its transition from apartheid to democracy, I came to have a real understanding of President Nelson Mandela and watched how he, one man, affected millions of people. In observing his profound impact, I realized how it is nearly always *individuals* who change the world—not societies, governments, or organizations. In fact, whenever I think of prime movers in the world, I think of individuals: Bill Gates and Steve Jobs; Roosevelt and Churchill; Newton, Einstein, and Marie Curie; Mother Teresa, Martin Luther King, Jr., Pope John Paul II, and

Mahatma Gandhi. But more important than learning that a single individual can change the world, by observing President Mandela I learned *how* a person does this, and moreover, that one doesn't need to be a president or a CEO to make a remarkable impact on countless others. Anyone can do it.

Like most South Africans, I knew very little about Nelson Mandela, a man imprisoned for twenty-seven years before he was finally released on February 11, 1990. Since Mandela's initial imprisonment, we hadn't seen him, heard his voice, or read his writings. Raised on South African government propaganda, we feared the banned African National Congress (ANC) and its jailed deputy president. They had "planned revolution," they were "allied with Communism," and they were "radicals." Upon his release, however, this so-called "radical" was poised to take up a leadership role on a national and even an international scale.

I will never forget the day Nelson Mandela walked out of the Victor Verster Prison, an hour later than scheduled, into the hot Cape afternoon. We were tense with anticipation. Will this be a man to fear or to admire? Will he be in touch or remote? Will he command respect, wield force, or lose control? Will he polarize people or will they rally around him? What does he really know about leadership, politics, and government after nearly three decades in captivity?

His first steps were a little tentative, but his charisma was instantly evident. Standing tall, smartly dressed in a brown suit and tie, he waved to us and smiled. Taking his wife's hand, he walked deliberately and purposefully to a waiting car. An electric wave of relief shot through the crowd and the nation: this man appeared to be a new type of leader; different from anything we had seen in recent history. I can remember feeling then some degree of reassurance that there would be no revolution in South Africa. Nelson Mandela could unite a divided nation; he could heal a broken people, perhaps he could even bring our differences into harmony. And he did. He did it through the authority of his personal stature as a human being, rather than through the power or status of the government he led. He did it with compassion, wisdom, and persuasion. People followed him out of respect, not fear, because people follow leaders whose authenticity they trust and those whom they believe put the interests of the people ahead of their own. Mandela did not coerce; he inspired.

In this remote country at the foot of Africa, it was becoming evident that in the Post-Information Age of abundance and freedom, leaders who could inspire would have the edge over those who could only intimidate others into servility and obedience. Mandela was blessed with great character, which he nurtured and grew throughout his time in prison. Great character easily translates into great leadership prowess. The Mandela phenomenon only cemented my understanding of greatness: once you possess it, your reach is unlimited.

You Are Nuclear

We are powerhouses of incalculable spiritual energy capable of transforming others with a single action, a word, a gesture, or sometimes even just a feeling.

Early in my rabbinic and business career I was privileged to be introduced to a great Jewish spiritual figure known throughout the world simply as The Rebbe.[14] His kind face exuded warmth and great humanity, but his piercing blue eyes projected the profound brilliance for which he was known and seemed to look straight into your soul. I waited outside his Brooklyn office until the early hours of the morning for my turn to see him. In talking about the potential of individuals to make a difference in the world, my vision was clearly not ambitious enough for him. The Rebbe himself was known for his intense passion for making a difference in individuals and communities throughout the world.

"You see, you are thinking of your interactions with others like a chemical reaction, changing one molecule at a time," he chided me. "But humans don't function that way. We are not mechanical, and your connections do not follow the laws of mechanical physics and chemistry. You are a spiritual being, and every time you meet someone a nuclear reaction occurs, not a chemical one. A nuclear chain reaction can release several million times more energy than a chemical reaction. Each person on whom you have some impact can in turn affect the lives of countless others. The effect is exponential."

Thirty years after this conversation, the *British Medical Journal* published the results of a twenty-year study by a Harvard social scientist, Dr. Nicholas Christakis, and his political science colleague, James Fowler, at the University of California, San Diego. The study showed that emotions can pass among a network of people up to three degrees of separation away. As *Time* magazine commented, your own joy can affect "how cheerful your friends' friends' friends are, even if some of the people in this chain are total strangers to you."[15] Think about the number of people you engage with in a week, and how many people each of them mix with, and how many people there are in that network three degrees of separation from you. The number could be well into the millions!

Christakis and Fowler were not even talking about the effects of your *actions* on others; they were just talking about the way you *feel*. But consider how easily a small action can change the way another person feels: a smile, a pleasant comment, an affectionate touch. When other people feel in some way uplifted by your act of caring, they in turn are likely to act more caringly with the people they meet. This just amplifies the extent of the chain reaction you trigger each time you engage with someone, however briefly.

The Rebbe was right. I was overwhelmed by the possibility of it. Physically we only affect the people we touch. But with our spiritual energy we can impact the lives of millions of people, and he told me this long before the era of e-mail and the Internet! I hadn't previously thought of human interaction as nuclear reaction. I thought of it as a form of linear causality where, other than by means of publication or celebrity, a person could only impact another with some form of direct contact. We sell ourselves short when we think of ourselves as objects rather than as powerhouses of incalculable spiritual energy capable of transforming others with a single action, a word, a gesture, or sometimes even just a feeling.

The fact that you can have an effect on such vast numbers of people is exciting, but even more exciting is how quickly you can do it. Changing other people's behaviors is nowhere near as complicated as you think and can be done much more quickly than you imagine. We think that changing other people is hard because we approach it the wrong way. When we fail, we try again and again, but we often do so without changing our tactics. As with any task, if you use the wrong tools, it can be difficult or impossible. Changing the behaviors of others is no different. Using the wrong tools doesn't work, but if you modify your tactics the results are profound.

Think of it this way: Imagine you are a pilot flying a large aircraft. You notice that the altimeter reading is dropping. No amount of effort you put into forcing the altimeter to display a different reading will make any difference to your altitude. The altimeter is just an instrument, like a compass, that tells you when you are on or off course. When an instrument gives you an unexpected reading, you need to change your course, not your instrument. You need to know what lever to move in order to get a different reading on your panel of instruments. The moment you move the right lever, the instruments reflect the change and give you the reading you want.

Think of people's reactions to you and the way they behave around you as a set of instruments that reflect your mood, attitude, and actions. Trying to change others is like trying to change the instruments on your cockpit panel instead of moving the levers. You control the levers by changing yourself; they are just the dashboard indicators that will reflect the changes you make in yourself. The only way to get *them* to change is to change *your* course; then they will give you the reading you want. So much of our training in management and the literature written about leadership is about how to change the behaviors of others. It is much more important to know what levers within yourself will elicit the changes you want in the people around you. You can only change others by changing yourself, and when you do, the change in others is almost instantaneous.

Many people believe that they are in this life on a journey of learning, self-discovery, and growth. If this resonates with your belief system, then consider that every person you interact with crosses your path in order to help you on this journey. As your dashboard indicators, they reflect to you what you are projecting to them, both consciously and subconsciously. Assume that the things you see in every other person— their behaviors, attitudes, and reactions—all mirror you in one way or another. Sometimes they reflect something you are doing; at other times they show you the opposite of what you are doing, in order to draw your attention to it.

If you walk into an elevator on your way to work on a Monday morning and notice that all those inside look dour and burdened, think of their expressions as reflections of yours. Check whether you are radiating a similar negative energy, and see what happens in the elevator if you change your expression and make a cheerful comment to someone. In all likelihood, you will be able to immediately change the attitudes of an elevator full of strangers. You will do it without managerial authority and without trickery. You will have changed them by changing yourself.

Your actions directly correlate to the response you receive. Nothing you do or say, and no attitude you exude exists within a vacuum. Every action, expression, or mood gives rise to a reaction in others. The effect of the moods and gestures of leaders on their teams is well-documented, but this is the case not only with leaders but with anyone interacting with others.

This is part of the "power of one." You are a nuclear reactor emitting powerful energy. You emit energy all the time, and it travels far beyond your geographical confines. At its core, leadership is less about how well we manage others than how well we manage ourselves. The quickest—and perhaps the only—way to change others is to change ourselves.

The Change Challenge
When leaders make a choice to change themselves, it will inevitably transform their team, too.

Traditionally, we manage people by promising them rewards for reaching their goals and penalties for failing to. If this doesn't work, we often replace the individual or change the team. Many times though, after the change the team is as dysfunctional as it was before. This is because the only thing that hasn't changed is the only thing that needed to change: the leader!

A client of mine told me about a military unit in which he once served. He was embarrassed by its reputation for ineffectiveness and poor discipline. Nothing the lieutenant did made any difference to the unit's performance, and the unit was ridiculed and shunned. Then a new lieutenant was appointed. With no other apparent changes, the unit transformed and became one of the finest. Changing a leader changes a team, but "changing a leader" does not necessarily entail replacing him or her. Changing a leader could simply mean that a leader makes a choice to change him or herself. This will inevitably transform their team, too.

If you are experiencing difficulties with the team you lead, see what happens when you begin to handle yourself more effectively, controlling your emotions and treating others with more respect. Show your team members a new trust. You know intuitively that the team will change. They will respond by trying to prove themselves worthy of your trust. We are wired not to disappoint the people who have faith in us. When you show your faith in your people, they will almost always rise to the occasion. The response you get from others naturally mirrors the energy you exude.

Chief Ethan Brenner (the names in this story were changed to protect privacy) had just been appointed chief of police in a large city in the U.S. Northwest. He had competed for the job with a colleague named Scott. After losing the position, Scott became impossible to work with. Chief Brenner made Scott head of traffic, but he was often tardy, and failed to deliver results. Every attempt the chief made to discipline him and manage his performance was met with greater mistrust from Scott, who took every opportunity to undermine Brenner and sabotage his efforts. That's when Brenner turned to me.

At the time I met Chief Brenner, I'd been working with law enforcement leadership in the U.S. for over a decade in an effort to increase their interpersonal effectiveness, both internally and externally, and to reduce their dependence on the use of force. By then, more than one hundred thousand police officers in California alone had been influenced by *Lead by Greatness* methods.

In Brenner's situation, the solution was clear. Scott was disgruntled and clearly in no state of mind to support the efforts of his new boss and former peer. He needed to change—but it was not only his *actions* that needed improvement, it was also his state of mind. So I urged Brenner to change his tactics. Soon afterward, the president was due in town. The chief knew he could not afford any mistakes, but it was then that he made his bold move.

Brenner called Scott and said, "I'm under tremendous pressure, and I'd really appreciate it if you took complete command of the president's visit and the smooth operation of his motorcade. I have faith in your ability, and while I am only a call away if you need me, I trust you to handle this on your own."

Brenner stepped back, and Scott rose to the occasion. The presidential visit went smoothly, and Scott became the chief's biggest supporter, never needing to be disciplined again. The chief had tried to change Scott for years and had accomplished nothing but failure and heartache. How did the chief finally change Scott? After trying to change him in every way possible within the conventional parameters of human resource management, he ultimately succeeded only when he changed himself. By trusting himself to trust Scott and removing any manifestation of defensiveness and anger toward Scott, he began to *Lead by Greatness*. Scott responded with a greatness from within himself that had never before been evident to Chief Brenner.

Your own greatness is your best, if not your only, tool with which to change the way other people live and act. Your power to change people with your own greatness extends far beyond your family, team, and even organization. Each of us has the power and the ability to change the world and leave it a little different, a little better than it would have been without us. This principle is foundational to the Kabbalistic view of the purpose of humankind. "He [the Creator] did not create the world to be a wasteland; rather He formed it so that humankind would develop and impact it."[16] This is true not only of the world as a whole, but also of each individual's life, as it is lived every day. We can, and we do, leave every person or group of people we touch a little different every day.

By honing your leadership character and building your human greatness, you will generate higher, more focused energy and impact the people around and beyond you in ways you could never before have imagined. In the next chapters, we will learn how to project our own authenticity, master our instincts, and harmoniously balance the competing tensions of our life. However, to effectively accomplish this and to truly get to know the power of your being, you will want to learn how to access your inner wisdom—the source of your subconscious insight. You will be surprised how much knowledge about yourself and your role in the world you actually possess when you tap this inner wisdom.

CHAPTER THREE

THE INNER GURU

*You were born with all the intelligence you need
to fulfill your inner purpose.*

THE FIRST STEP in implementing change towards achieving real greatness is to know both who you are and who you could become. You need to discover your authentic self and the purpose for which you were created. Revealing who you are at the very core of your essence—and the purpose for which you are here—will help you to access vast reservoirs of inner wisdom. This wisdom will not only guide you in living out your purpose and in realizing your dreams, but will also guide you in every decision you will need to make to develop your corporation's soul and ignite the life force of your team.

Where does this concept of "inner" or innate wisdom stem from? Isn't it true that wisdom and knowledge are learned, gleaned from life and study? Aren't we all born blank slates, to be filled every day with more information and experience?

Simply, the answer is no. We were born with all the intelligence we need to fulfill our purpose. There is a tradition in Kabbalah that has its parallels in many other ancient cultures. Before a baby is born, while still in its mother's womb, its soul is taught all the wisdom of the universe. As it pushes its way through the birth canal, an angel touches it above the lip, forming its infranasal depression and causing it to forget everything that it learned. From then on, the process of learning is one of rediscovery. This is why wisdom and truth often resonate within us when we hear them for the first time. It is as if we are being reminded about something we intuitively know to be true. This is why we can so often rely on our intuition to guide us about the truth and authenticity of the things we hear and learn. Our souls know what is true; our souls recognize that which is authentic.

Of course, there are still many skills we have to acquire and information we need to gather as we grow. We have to accumulate experience and learn from it and further develop the talents we already have. However, all these things we need to learn do not detract from how much wisdom we naturally have within us, irrespective of our educational level. Think of the wisdom an infant possesses, enabling it to learn the complexities of language so young. Infants have an innate capacity to recognize grammatical patterns and the meaning of vocabulary. But not only do they recognize vocabulary and grammatical patterns, they innovate them too. There is no reason why adults, even with little or no formal education, should not also be able to exhibit this same capacity to intuitively grasp complexity.

I have so often been both humbled and inspired by the brilliant insights I have received from people who had no formal education, and in some cases, who were even illiterate. I have seen people use their innate wisdom to develop profoundly innovative strategic ideas for the companies that employed them.

A good example of this was at a large Coca-Cola bottler, Amalgamated Beverages (ABI), now a subsidiary of SABMiller. The company was planning significant downsizing and closure of plants some years back as a result of a recession. This was made even worse by the anticipated aggressive entry of Pepsi into a market in which, until then, Coke had held a virtual monopoly. ABI's labor relations at the time were strained, and the strike by workers had reportedly even resulted in loss of life. ABI feared that the inevitable layoffs were going to make things much worse, and asked my consulting firm to assist.

We worked not only with management but also with lower-level employees at ABI, many of whom had no formal education. Despite severe hostility from the unions toward management, we took a chance and bet on the inherent integrity of the workers, their desire to do the right thing, and the possibility that they possessed more inner wisdom than management had ever given them credit for. And we were right.

After working through their grievances and developing new attitudes and relationship skills in managers, we began the work of building sound bridges of trust between employees and management. We guided the workers and taught them some universal principles of business and strategic thinking with which they could culturally identify. We trusted them and encouraged management to share company information with them that they had never before been privy to. We discussed budgets and targets, some macro-strategies, the threat from Pepsi, and the impact of impending plant closures.

Applying the framework we gave them, and without management participation, the workers designed their own strategy to grow sales, avoid plant closures, and keep Pepsi at bay. Their strategies were brilliant in their simplicity and effectiveness. They included building close personal relationships with the thousands of small mom-and-pop stores they served and persuading them to make Coke far more accessible on the shelves than Pepsi. They used their informal but extensive personal networks in their own communities to market Coke aggressively to families and schools. They also had some new ideas to improve efficiency and raise productivity levels. Their own improved morale inspired the company with new energy. They executed on their strategies flawlessly and delivered astonishing outcomes. No plants were closed, workers were not laid off, Pepsi withdrew from the market, and ABI embarked on a path of aggressive growth and acquisition.

Senior management and people with higher education do not hold a monopoly on strategic thinking. Sometimes, using nothing more than their inner wisdom and their knowledge of the day-to-day business, employees with limited or no formal educational qualifications can contribute untold value, not only to the execution of strategy, but also to its formulation. In fact, Roger Martin, Dean of the Rotman School of Management at the University of Toronto, argues that it is time to drop the distinction between the formulation of strategy and its execution, a distinction that makes employees into "choiceless doers." Instead, he argues for the model of "strategy as a choice cascade" where "employees toward the bottom, make… concrete, day-to-day decisions that directly influence customer service and satisfaction."[1] The employees at ABI transformed from choiceless doers into active creators and executors of corporate strategy, and according to Trent Odges, CEO at the time, this saved the company.

Bob Christie is the head of 3E in Carlsbad, California. After an impressive career of exponentially growing successive companies in the financial information industry, including Standard and Poor's, he moved to 3E to help its clients improve their compliance with global environmental health and safety (EHS) requirements. Bob shared his belief with me that the key to his success has been mining the brilliant thinking of ordinary people in the ranks of the companies he has been tasked to lead. "My receptionist at the door is my most important salesperson. She is our first point of contact with customers. She knows my revenue numbers, our expansion plans, and all our strategies. She has to know that in order to contribute optimally."

As in the case of ABI, Bob believes that strategic innovation and sales acumen do not always reside only at the top. Bob told me how he learned this attitude from Harold McGraw, his mentor at McGraw-Hill, which acquired Standard and Poor's in 1966. He has lived by this philosophy and implemented it ever since. Everyone on his team is given insight into the bigger picture, and is able to contribute toward that bigger picture due to his or her inclusion.

It is not only junior employees or those without formal qualifications who have deep resources of wisdom that we seldom tap. Each of us has hidden intuitive knowledge, deep insights, and innovative ideas that, once unlocked, can generate significant energy and value.

In the West, we tend to confuse academic achievement with brilliance and information with wisdom. But these academic achievements and information do not always correlate with brilliance and wisdom. I often marvel at how Nelson Mandela, for instance, who had no formal leadership training and for many years was in prison, isolated from the evolution of political thinking, became a leader of international repute just by accessing the resources within himself.

I am sure you have often noticed leadership qualities in little children in grade school or younger. Not only can children sing, paint pictures, and create stories—they can lead. They can follow. They respond to authenticity and detect the lack of it. Where do these little children learn all this, and why do they so often lose these talents after a few years of education?

The reason is because our educational system is geared to convince students that everything they need to know is outside them. They need to learn from textbooks and from teachers. And while the *information* they need is outside them, of course, imagine what they could achieve if they learned to access and use the vast *wisdom* that already exists within them. Children naturally know how to ask questions. Textbooks and most schoolteachers know how to provide answers, but are our children being taught to ask the right questions? For my part, I would rather have my children know how and what to ask and where to seek the answers, than to have all the answers in hand. In any event, the answers they learn today will probably be irrelevant tomorrow. "Where is the wisdom we have lost in knowledge?" asks T. S. Eliot (1888–1965). "Where is the knowledge we have lost in information?"[18]

When I was a student, I was preparing for the entrance exam into the class of one of the great Talmud[v] teachers of our times. The exam was to be open-book, and I was given as much time as I needed to prepare for it. When I was ready, I felt completely confident and knew that I had the answer to every conceivable question I could be asked. Imagine my shock when, instead of confronting me with the barrage of questions I expected, my examiner asked me what questions I had for him! He explained to me that he had no interest in my prepared answers. He preferred to hear my questions because those would show him how I could think; answers could at best show him how well I could memorize. Teachers like that are great; they are also rare.

v Encyclopedic body of rabbinic law, philosophy, and methodology of inductive and deductive reasoning.

More recently, I was studying Veda philosophy in the beautiful foothills of the Himalayas, just above the town of Rishikesh, the "world capital of yoga." I was interested in similarities between certain Kabbalistic ideas and the ancient Vedas, and how they could be applied to modern leadership challenges. When I asked my teacher, a brilliant young chemical engineer, for some references I could follow up on when I got back home, he looked at me quizzically and asked, "Why would you want to study what other people have written? Wouldn't you be better off thinking your own wisdom through?"

Authentic Asian education focuses on accessing your inner wisdom rather than cramming you with the ideas of others. Accessing our own inner wisdom versus learning what others have taught and said is not a choice we need to make. We can and should do both. We can learn knowledge, information, and skills from others, and discover wisdom within ourselves.

The wisdom within each of us is profound. Used correctly, it can help us to resolve some of our most difficult dilemmas, to make the tough choices we often have to make, and to maintain a positive attitude. This inner wisdom is like an inner compass pointing us in the direction we ought to go. It is also what I call our inner prophet or guru.

Many people find it hard, and sometimes impossible, to access their inner guru. This is not because they do not have one, but because the confusing noise of our ego often drowns out the voice of our inner prophet. There are many voices out there that you can hear, but only one is your authentic inner wisdom. Some of these other voices say things like, "I want," "I need," or "I am afraid to." Others could be the imaginary voices of admonishing parents: "you have to," "you should," or "how could you?" Some voices are just assumptions built on other people's opinions that our subconscious mind has indiscriminately collected, and that we carry around with us. How are we to recognize the voice of our inner wisdom among all the clatter? What if we do not hear a voice at all? How do we find our inner prophet?

Think of it like a radio receiver. A radio can pick up a range of frequencies, but you can dial in to the one particular frequency you want to listen to. In the same way your "inner receiver" picks up many frequencies, including some that are not your own. Those are the frequencies on which you will hear the fears, assumptions, and addictions that have been collected over time. They are not authentic to your own soul. You need to tune in your receiver to your own frequencies and ignore the others. You can best do this when you are living your own life; when the choices you make are not in response to the expectations of others or mimicking the lives of other people. You must live *your* life, not theirs, or your inner prophet will be silenced. This is because when you live someone else's life, you are tuned in to his or her frequency, not yours. Your inner prophet cannot communicate with you, nor can you know anything with certainty, if you are not tuned in to your own frequency—to whom you really are.

To tune in to our own inner wisdom, we need to focus on two fundamental things. The first is what we will call our unique *Spiritual Fingerprint*. The second is a clearly articulated statement of the purpose for which we believe we were put in this world, our *Personal Purpose*. In the following chapters we will learn how to craft both of these instruments, starting with our *Spiritual Fingerprint*.

CHAPTER FOUR
SPIRITUAL DNA

*Not only are no two individuals alike, but
no individual is identical to any other human being
who has ever lived or ever will.*

EACH INDIVIDUAL is uniquely distinguishable from every other. William James (1842–1910) expressed human uniqueness beautifully when he wrote: "In every concrete individual there is a uniqueness that defies formulation. We can feel the touch of it and recognize its taste, relishing or disliking as the case may be, but we can give no ultimate account of it, and we have in the end simply to admire the Creator." Individual uniqueness was first discovered as a scientific fact in 1902 by Alfonse Bertillon (1853–1914), a French detective and biometrics researcher who used this discovery to solve a murder case in Paris. His work led to the universal adoption of fingerprinting as a reliable method of forensic identification. By 1910, United States law enforcement agencies and the military were using fingerprint technology to identify people.[19]

The knowledge of the uniqueness of human features, however, is not new. In ancient Japanese pottery art, a fingerprint pressed into the clay was used to identify the potter. The Talmud[20] (circa 100 CE[vi]) says that although every person is created in the Divine image, no individual resembles another. There is evidence that ancient Babylonian contracts dating back to nearly 2000 BCE[vii] were authenticated by fingerprint impressions in clay tablets. There is even a prehistoric Native American petroglyph (stone drawing) on a Nova Scotia cliff face depicting a hand with exaggerated fingerprints.[21]

What is the origin of human difference? Our understanding of the origin and extent of human difference only began to emerge after the solution of yet another murder.

In November 1983, an attractive teenager named Lynda Mann was raped and strangled in Narborough, a quaint Leicestershire village in central England. In July 1986, the rapist struck again, murdering another teenager, Dawn Ashworth, close to where he murdered Lynda. Richard Buckland, a local boy, confessed to the crime. For the first time ever, the forensic DNA technique of thirty-four-year-old Leicester University genetics researcher Alec Jeffreys was applied in a criminal case, to compare the boy's blood with semen found on the two dead girls. "Prove he murdered Lynda as well," the police told Jeffreys, who took semen samples from the girls' bodies and blood from Buckland. The results showed Dawn and Lynda had been raped by the same man, but not Buckland. Colin Pitchfork, a local baker, was eventually caught trying to avoid taking the DNA test after police asked all local men to give a sample. He admitted his guilt—later confirmed by DNA profiling—and in 1988 was sentenced to life imprisonment.

Even now we only have begun to understand the full ramifications of human individuality. Not only are no two individuals

vi *Common Era; matches up with AD.*
vii *BCE is recognized as before 1 CE.*

alike, but no individual is identical to any other human being who has ever lived or ever will.

Individual difference, genetic in its origin, is therefore the product of an individual's history. Isn't the paradox strange? We inherit our uniqueness from our parents. "Each gene is a message from our forebears and together they contain the whole story of human evolution. Everyone is a living fossil, carrying within themselves a record which goes back to the beginnings of humanity and far beyond."[22] However, genetics are not the only source of individual uniqueness; other factors influence our uniqueness too.

Human difference goes beyond fingerprints and features and extends to taste and preference. The Kabbalah[23] relates how God created every individual with unique tastes and preferences to avoid the jealousy and dissent that would result from everyone liking the same things. This means that every person has a unique way of making choices. Some of those choices are just inexplicable intuitive responses determined by what one person finds appealing and another does not. But people also make moral and strategic choices differently. In a similar situation, two different people will often choose different courses. Neither one is necessarily right in an absolute sense. The important thing is that the choices you make are authentic to who *you* are; that they are right for *you*. What informs your moral and strategic choices is not a biological genetic influence, but a spiritual influence. This is what I call your own unique *Spiritual Fingerprint*, a fingerprint that is as real as the concentric ridges in your fingers. Sometimes discovering your *Spiritual Fingerprint* alerts you to truths about yourself that can be hard to hear but crucial to confront and master. I was shocked to my core when I first looked at my own *Spiritual Fingerprint*.

The "DNA" that makes up your *Spiritual Fingerprint* comes

from the intertwining of genetic and epigenetic factors. Some of it is inherited from our culture and background, some from our learning and life experience. Unlike our physical DNA, our spiritual "DNA" is not static. Rather, it continues to evolve throughout our lives. Knowing what our *Spiritual Fingerprint* looks like makes it easier to develop and grow as human beings and become leaders of stature. Our *Spiritual Fingerprint* is also an invaluable tool in making hard choices, in explaining our viewpoint to others and in understanding theirs. It provides you with the moral compass you need to lead authentically, and once you get to know your team's *Spiritual Fingerprint*s too, you will gain unparalleled advantage in directing their activities and inspiring them. With far less effort and fewer resources, you will get better results from the people you lead than you ever have before.

So how can you identify your spiritual "DNA"? Much like our physical DNA, our spiritual "DNA" is not recognizable to the naked eye, but it does reveal itself through our behaviors; it informs our decisions and guides our choices. Recognizing your *Spiritual Fingerprint* requires some serious soul-searching, but doing so will ultimately help you navigate your pathway through life. And although we are dealing here with matters beneath the level of our conscious minds, it is possible to physically map your *Spiritual Fingerprint* and begin to understand how it works.

Mapping Your Spiritual Fingerprint

How different my life might have been if someone had taught me how to identify and map my Spiritual Fingerprint earlier.

To learn about your own *Spiritual Fingerprint*, you will need to identify your *value-drivers*. *Value-drivers* differ from *values*; they are a more specific set of beliefs than the beliefs typically referred to as *values*. Our values are the sum total of all the things we believe to be good or bad, right or wrong. However, among this set of beliefs are beliefs for which we have made, or would be willing to make, significant sacrifices. These beliefs are what I call our *value-drivers*: values we have actually used to drive hard choices and resolve difficult dilemmas.

Try making a list now of the values in which you believe and for which you have made a meaningful sacrifice at some time in your life. Consider, for example, that education is one of your values. Ask yourself when you made a sacrifice for education. If you have made a sacrifice for education and paid a price for it at some time in your life, then education is a value-driver for you. If you cannot recall making a sacrifice for education then it is still one of your values, but for the purpose of this exercise it is not a value-driver. Be very honest with yourself in this process even if you only emerge from it with a handful of *value-drivers*. Most of us have a small set of *value-drivers* even though we probably have a much bigger set of values for which we have not yet had to make a sacrifice or pay a price.

Identifying your *value-drivers* is essential to beginning the process of self-discovery, but it is not sufficient in itself. Many people share the same or similar *value-drivers*, like honesty, truth, and fairness. What really differentiates one person from another is not so much our sets of *value-drivers*, but how we employ them.

There are two factors we can use to understand the differences in the way people employ their sets of *value-drivers*. First, how high a "price" are you willing to pay to sustain your *value-drivers*? When honesty entails the loss of a fortune, a job, or a family home, and dishonesty in that case would carry no penalty, not everyone who believes in honesty will act honestly. Some may pay the price for their value of honesty, and others may not be willing to pay so high a price. In this case, although both people consider honesty a value, it is a value-driver for one but not for the other.

The second factor that differentiates us is the way we prioritize certain values over others when necessary. When the values of loyalty and fairness conflict with one another, for example, which of these values do you cling to, and which would you trade off if you had to? Would you stand by one friend because of your loyalty to her even if doing so entailed an act of unfairness to another? Your *Spiritual Fingerprint* answers these questions for you.

Consider the example of Larry and Emma, who share the same two *value-drivers*; they both believe uncompromisingly in **human kindness** and in **honesty**. However, Larry and Emma will not necessarily make the same value-based choices. This is especially so in situations where their two values clash with one another, and they may need to exchange one value-driver for another. So, imagine that both of them are managers needing to give tough feedback to an employee. Emma might say, "I am going to give it to him straight up. He will appreciate my honesty, and even though it will be painful in the moment, in the long term he will benefit from my forthright approach." Larry may say, "I could never be so brutal and cause another person such pain; I prefer to be gentler. I will sugarcoat the message, and he will get the point just the same. Meanwhile, he will appreciate that I have preserved his dignity while, at the same time, delivering a hard truth." Emma is the purist, and Larry the diplomat.

Both of their choices are value-based, and they both share the same *value-drivers*: kindness and honesty. However, even though they both share the same *value-drivers*, their *Spiritual Fingerprints* are different. In Larry's *Spiritual Fingerprint*, human kindness is at the core of his system of *value-drivers*, and honesty is further out. In Emma's *Spiritual Fingerprint*, honesty is at the core, and human kindness is further out; it is slightly subjugated to honesty. What is important is that, although Larry and Emma have different styles, provided they both act in ways that are aligned to their own *Spiritual Fingerprints*, they will both be behaving authentically, and the person to whom they are giving the feedback will trust them.

Now, getting back to your own *Spiritual Fingerprint*; having listed your *value-drivers* (values you have made some sacrifice for at some time in your life) and having separated them out from a large list of your more generic values, think of your *Spiritual Fingerprint* as your set of *value-drivers* laid out in concentric circles. The idea of the concentric circles is not about ranking them for importance. Rather, it is about seeing your *value-drivers* as a dynamic system where the inner values nourish and drive the values that are more peripheral to them.

The next step in this process of mapping your *Spiritual Fingerprint* is to identify the single value-driver that is most central to you. This value-driver may jump out at you from your list as being essential to your essence. Your core value-driver is the one you are least likely to compromise—ever, unless your survival or that of your family is threatened. This core value-driver nourishes your other *value-drivers* and sustains your system. If you compromise your core value-driver, your entire system of *value-drivers* collapses. You will have compromised your very essence, your soul.

Now draw a set of seven or eight concentric circles and place your core value-driver in the center of your set of circles. Here is an example of three different people with the same three values: family, working hard to add value, and the importance of receiving and giving recognition. They differ from one another because they place a different value-driver at their core.

Even though all three of these people share the same *value-drivers*, they, like Larry and Emma, have very different *Spiritual Fingerprints*. It is the *Spiritual Fingerprint*, rather than a given set of *value-drivers*, that governs the choices individuals and organizations make, and the cultures that organizations build. One list of *value-drivers* can generate many different systems of *value-drivers*, or *Spiritual Fingerprints*. There are multiple variations in how a person's *value-drivers* could be laid out in a *Spiritual Fingerprint*. Even if an individual or organization had only six values in their set, they could combine them in 720 different ways to produce 720 different *Spiritual Fingerprints*. Then, when you get into describing what each value-driver means to you personally and how the linkages between them work for you, the subtle variations are infinite. Merely knowing your values without building them into your unique *Spiritual Fingerprint* is not very helpful.

We can take a look at how these three people with the same three *value-drivers* have very different *Spiritual Fingerprints*.

The core of a person's *Spiritual Fingerprint* (the value-driver at the center) and its outcome (the value-driver in the outer circle) are equally important. The core tells you what you must nurture every day of your life and nourish constantly in order to achieve your outcome value-driver. The outcome value-driver is the value-driver that most influences the way you interact with others. It naturally becomes manifest when your other *value-drivers* are functioning properly, and it is likely to be the way many other people experience you. Your core drives and energizes the next value; the second one drives the value that follows it; and so on. Without a healthy core, there cannot be a fully functioning dynamic system of *value-drivers* influencing your life choices.

Consider the individual who has family as his core value. This means that every other value-based choice he makes is driven by the importance he places on his family. When he is committed to, and therefore fulfilled by, his relationship to his family, he has the energy to commit to his work.

Figure 1

Because he works hard to add value, he gets the recognition he needs for his self-esteem, as well as the financial reward he needs to support his family.

If this individual does not spend quality time with his family (his core value-driver), his entire value system destabilizes. This leads him to resent his work, and in turn to put less into it, resulting in him ultimately receiving less recognition. This damages his self-esteem and his capacity to provide for his family. It can spiral into unhappiness, deplete his energy, and even lead to poor physical health.

Now, take a look at the individual who places "working hard to add value" at the center of her system. She is nourished by her work and loves to be making a difference. She believes the recognition she receives

Figure 2

for her contribution at work provides for her family (her outcome value-driver) and makes them feel proud of her. She is motivated by increased responsibility, provided she is recognized for it. Under normal circumstances, she will even put her work (her core value-driver) before her family's needs, believing that ultimately it will be best for them too.

Both the first and second individuals have family as one of their *value-drivers*. Since *value-drivers* are not ranked by importance, family is equally important to them both. However, in one case, the value-driver of family is the core value that motivates and drives him. If his family is struggling, he will find it impossible to dedicate his attention to work. For the other person, however, family is an outcome, the result of everything else she does. The value-driver of family makes her work, and the recognition she receives for it, more meaningful, but it isn't the driving force of her life.

Now, let's look at the third individual who values the recognition shown to her as the core of her *Spiritual Fingerprint* and is driven by

Figure 3

her need for recognition. Whereas the person in Figure 2 wants recognition to follow her contribution, the individual in Figure 3 enjoys up-front recognition, to which she responds with even more engagement in her work. For her, recognition is not the outcome of her performance; rather, it actually drives her performance and inspires her to give her very best.

As in the case of the second individual, this person sees her family as the ultimate beneficiary of the hard work she does and the value she adds. The differences between them stem from their core *value-drivers*. The individual in Figure 2 is driven by an inner need to make a difference, whereas the individual in Figure 3 is driven by her desire and need for recognition.

So these, then, are the three different *Spiritual Fingerprints* all made up of the same *value-drivers*.

If you were leading these three individuals, it would help you to know their respective *Spiritual Fingerprints*. This is because you will get the most value from your investments in people when you invest in what is at the core of their *Spiritual Fingerprints*. If you nourish people at their core, their other *value-drivers* will thrive as well, leading them to function optimally. This applies in personal relationships, too. Usually, each of the partners in a relationship is inspired by a different value-driver that sits at the core of his or her *Spiritual Fingerprint*. In such cases, each partner should nourish the other according to what is at their partner's core, not with what is at his or her own core.

In the cases of the three individuals above, since you will get optimal benefit from each of them by nourishing the specific value-driver at the core of their *Spiritual Fingerprints*, you may at times need to treat them differently. In one case, you might make sure to recognize how important their family is to them, and make it easier for them to take care of their family's needs. If you do, you will get far greater output from this individual. In the second case, you will make sure the individual is challenged with responsibility and autonomy at work. In the third case, you will tend to show a great deal of appreciation and offer praise up front, knowing that this will drive better performance afterward. Knowing your team's *Spiritual Fingerprints* in this way can help you maximize their potential by rewarding them with things that nourish their cores in order to deliver a better outcome. However, the first step in working with *Spiritual Fingerprints* is to know your own.

It is not important how many or how few *value-drivers* you have. Some people only have three *value-drivers*, others may have seven or eight, but most people have five or six. Now you will place one of your *value-drivers* in each of the concentric circles, beginning with the center. Ask yourself which of the remaining *value-drivers* would most logically follow if your central value-driver were well nourished and well. Then do the same for the third and the fourth until your outcome value-driver appears on your outermost circle. Check your system by making sure that in the event of a conflict between two of your *value-drivers*, you would always sacrifice an outer value-driver in favor of the one closer to the core. When you are satisfied with the way you ordered your *value-drivers*, and you feel it is authentic, you will have successfully mapped your *Spiritual Fingerprint* (or at least the first iteration of your *Spiritual Fingerprint*). The logical connection between your different *value-drivers* and the way they synchronize to form a single dynamic system makes it easier to manage them as one idea, rather than six or seven. As a single, integrated individual, your ethical choices should indeed be informed by a single worldview, your *Spiritual Fingerprint,* and not by a multiplicity of disconnected ideas or values.

It is very important that the *Spiritual Fingerprint* you work to uncover is truly yours. It needs to come from deep within you and to resonate with you at a level deep within your soul. Often people construct systems that they would *like* to have or believe they *should* have, rather than systems that are authentic to them. These artificial systems depict false fingerprints, and cannot help people to resolve dilemmas or *Lead by Greatness.* To get a quick, although somewhat superficial feel for it, try using the tool we have provided for you at leadbygreatness.com/tools/. To perfect the mapping of your *Spiritual Fingerprint* and gain more useful insights about yourself, consider using a certified *Lead by Greatness* coach (you can access one at leadbygreatness.com/coaches). You may be quite surprised to find how different and more authentic your *Spiritual Fingerprint* is when a coach works with you.

By investing yourself in this process, you can sometimes reveal things about yourself that were previously dormant. This happened to me when I first mapped my own fingerprint.

I love my family very deeply and always have. But when I looked carefully at my own *Spiritual Fingerprint,* it struck me for the first time that family was not the true core of my value system. In fact, it hardly featured in my *Spiritual Fingerprint* at all. The value of family had not been a driving force in my choices and decisions until that time. There was a reason for this: I was raised with the conviction that my destiny was to serve my people and community, and to make a difference in the world. My family always knew this. They knew that, due to my vocation as both a rabbi and a business leader, my life was public and dedicated to public service. They supported me in my endeavors unwaveringly. Public service was my core value-driver. However, I failed to realize that family had lost its central place among the values that drove my choices and decisions, and that they and I were paying a heavy price for this omission.

Even though I understood why family didn't feature prominently in my *Spiritual Fingerprint*, I still felt despondent at that realization. I often wonder how different my life might have been if someone had taught me how to identify and map my *Spiritual Fingerprint* earlier. Of course, I would have had to be completely honest with myself in order to recognize what I considered to be a shortcoming in my *Spiritual Fingerprint* and take steps to rectify it. While this kind of unflinching self-reflection is not as easy as it may seem, it is essential if your *Spiritual Fingerprint* is to be of any use. In fact, it is fatal to make yourself feel good by window-dressing a *Spiritual Fingerprint* to align it with who you would like to be. Rather, you need to look at it squarely, and align your life to your true *Spiritual Fingerprint*, not the other way around. The journey of character growth requires that we understand our *Spiritual Fingerprints,* own them, and use them to manage our interactions with the world more effectively while remaining true to them. The good news is that, unlike a real fingerprint, you can, within reason, engineer your *Spiritual Fingerprint* or, over a period of time, cause it to evolve. You do this by consistently making choices that reflect the *value-drivers* you would like to merge into your *Spiritual Fingerprint*. Eventually, if these additional values become natural to you, you will see them appear in your *Spiritual Fingerprint*.

After recognizing that family was absent from my own *Spiritual Fingerprint*, I resolved to slowly transform my own spiritual "DNA" and work hard to make my family much more core to who I am and what drives my choices and decisions. I learned to empathize more deeply with my family and experience their lives, their joys, and their struggles. I strove to engage with my family in a more mindful and present way, to invest in them and to enjoy every precious moment with them. I began to make choices that put them before many of my other priorities. This resolve changed my life and theirs.

Upon this revelation in my own life, I realized the implications this kind of self-reflection could have, not only on individual lives, but also on companies, organizations, and even government agencies. Using the power of your *Spiritual Fingerprint* to access your authentic essence, the very soul of your character, you can change your own life and the lives of countless others. You will be astounded by the results you get in your personal life and your business circle when you use this tool.

CHAPTER FIVE

THE FINGERPRINT ADVANTAGE

*The daily nurturing of your core value-driver
is the most important thing you will do
in your quest for greatness.*

BIDVEST IS a seventeen-billion-dollar international services, trading, and distribution company that employs over one hundred thousand people worldwide. Founder and CEO Brian Joffe is Bidvest's secret weapon. He adds an energy, resourcefulness, and brilliance to his organization that others cannot copy. His genius lies not only in his selection of investment opportunities and identification of competent management teams, but also in the value he personally adds to each of the companies he acquires. He and his team are known for turning ordinary companies into extraordinary performers. Yet, as you will see from his *Spiritual Fingerprint*, he believes that "people create wealth; companies only report it."

Brian drives fast cars and flies jets, but at heart he is a simple, warm man of deep faith and solid family values. Accustomed to speed in all aspects of his life, there was a point when Brian became worried about Bidvest's relatively sluggish performance after a nearly twenty-year run of staggering growth. Understanding the principles of leadership, Brian showed me how his own personal level of focus and commitment at any given time impacted Bidvest's performance. With the company's stock lacking its old pizzazz, Brian wanted to look inward and address whatever was blocking his own energy.

Brian knew he was not feeling fully centered and balanced, and believed this was influencing his performance as CEO. So instead of the usual strategic analysis we might have undertaken in order to identify the causes of Bidvest's suboptimal performance (in Brian's estimation) at the time, we began instead by focusing on Brian's own *Spiritual Fingerprint*. When we use the *Spiritual Fingerprint* as a diagnostic tool (as in this case with Brian), we approach it from the outside in. We look at issues on the peripheral rings and track their root causes to those nearer the core. This is how Brian's *Spiritual Fingerprint* looked as we began to diagnose his challenges by "unpeeling" it, starting from the outer value-driver and moving inward.

By checking in with one's outer value-driver, the one I call the outcome value-driver, one can gain insight as to how well a *Spiritual Fingerprint* is functioning and how much nourishment it is receiving. In Brian's case, he knows that if he is not in a general space of well-being, his core value-driver is being compromised in some way. No one around him gets the full benefit of his energy and brilliance when this is the case.

When the outcome value-driver is not working well, it is helpful to first check the value-driver that is one level below it. Brian needed to check the level of positive feedback and recognition he was getting at that time. Clearly, with a relatively weak performance, the market was beginning to question Bidvest's strategies and Brian's future role. Brian was used to well-deserved acclaim and hardly ever being questioned, because his results always exceeded expectations. This was the first time in his career that he was not getting the accolades that powered his energy to achieve. Knowing there was valid reason for this and that it reflected lower levels of success (his next value-driver, moving inward), Brian's sense of well-being was somewhat shaken. He was determined to get to the bottom of this, and intuitively knew the root causes were within himself.

So we probed further. The next value-driver inward in his *Spiritual Fingerprint* was independence. Was he feeling that his independence was being hindered? This was where we got to the heart of the issue. We found that Brian was feeling too encumbered with bureaucratic activities, caused by a growing regulatory environment of solid corporate governance. Corporate governance and its attendant administration were important, but they were not part of what fueled Brian's energy and drove his success. How had he gotten sucked into it?

Brian believes that overstaffed head offices do not generally add sufficient value to organizations to justify their costs, so he runs a very lean head office. But that very leanness left Brian himself having to perform functions that others could have done just as well. There was no advantage for Bidvest to have Brian buried in administrative tasks. This impeded his ability to get deeply involved in the individual companies in his portfolio, and it kept him from using his brilliance to add value to them. His head-office costs were impressively low, but the savings did not compensate for Brian's wasted time and intellect, which would've been better applied to his businesses for optimizing their success. Even worse, Brian was not living authentically, he was not actualizing the purpose for which he was put here, and he was no longer bringing his soul into Bidvest's boardroom. In fact, people in Bidvest were beginning to question what Bidvest's soul was. Brian had made structural and operational changes to his company without checking in with his own inner wisdom, his inner prophet.

From his *Spiritual Fingerprint,* it was clear that Brian needed to reclaim his autonomy if he was truly going to add value to his company, rather than merely manage its corporate affairs. I facilitated a meeting between Brian and his global executive team where he presented his *Spiritual Fingerprint* and addressed each aspect of it publicly. He told them directly what he needed from them to help him function independently and add more value to each of their businesses. In turn, they told him how he could be involved with their businesses in the most valuable way and which of his behaviors they found disruptive. Brian delegated some of his bureaucratic responsibilities to the managers of his businesses and got the support he needed to manage the rest. Brian's engines began to rev at full throttle again, and the company could feel it.

After sharing his *Spiritual Fingerprint* with his team, they understood aspects of Brian's management style in a way that many of them had never before grasped. Family is at his core, and he regards his team as members of his family. He radiates genuine affection for them, responds to their loyalty and commitment with amazing generosity, and gets deeply hurt and disappointed if they let him down. Brian puts his real family first, too, despite the demands of his business. He worries about them, provides for their future in every way, and loves them deeply.

I met Brian again a few months later. He appeared to be much more relaxed; a joyful sparkle had returned to his eyes. Since our previous meeting, he had marched back onto the global leadership stage, taking his company forward with new focus and energy and successfully navigating through times of turbulence. He was smiling, light, confident, and happy. His life had turned a corner. Brian was using the inner wisdom gleaned from his *Spiritual Fingerprint* at every juncture, and Bidvest's share price appreciated by 30 percent in the two years following our work with him. In that same period, the Dow Jones Industrial Average lost more than 10 percent of its value.

Banking Dignity

Founded in 1862, the Standard Bank has a long history, and with over one thousand branches, it is counted among the fifty-two largest banks in the world. With 20 percent of its equity owned by ICBC (China's and the world's largest bank), the Standard Bank is a formidable banking force in Africa and other emerging global markets.[24] When the bank appointed a brilliant young black South African, Simpiwe (Sim) Tshabalala, as CEO of its Personal and Business Banking Division (PBB), it sent shock waves of fear and insecurity through PBB's all-white executive team. South Africa was emerging from the shadows of apartheid and the government was aggressively promoting its version of affirmative action. Sim's awesome leadership qualities were not yet widely known to many senior executives who worried that he would rapidly replace them with black executives in line with government direction. They feared for their own jobs, and their fear held them back.

But Sim's appointment was no mere gesture of affirmative action, and Standard Bank, as sensitive as it is to the socio-political needs of the countries in which it operates, is not an organization that would sacrifice competence on the altar of political correctness. Sim is a man of international stature and formidable intellect. He has since risen to the position of CEO of Standard Bank South Africa, which is responsible for 73 percent of the group's earnings. Soon after he took over at PBB, I was privileged to work with Sim, helping him to put his own authentic leadership brand on the division and take it to new levels.

In less than two years, Sim not only refashioned his team into a cohesive, focused powerhouse of energy, but together with them raised his branches to unprecedented levels of customer satisfaction. One of our first exercises was to deeply probe Sim's own *Spiritual Fingerprint*. Once articulated, we would share it with his team and build the division's strategy and culture on a platform of his own leadership authenticity. This was what his *Spiritual Fingerprint* looked like.

Simpiwe Tshabalala

The uncompromising core of Sim's *value-drivers* is his own humanity and his belief in, and admiration for, the humanity of every other person. This leads him to treat all those around him with respect and dignity, and drives him to run his business with this value in mind. Not only does the value of humanity push him to perform at the frontier of his industry, but it also allows him to be truly honest with himself and with others in business and in his personal life. The resultant self-respect and respect for others ensures that all who encounter him feel their dignity enhanced and are encouraged to follow him.

After we determined Sim's authentic *Spritual Fingerprint*, his challenge soon became apparent in a strategy session we held with him and his executive team just after his appointment. The Standard Bank is a powerful and efficient machine, with brilliant operational systems and an experienced management team. Led by Jacko Maree, an intellectual titan and a humble man, Standard Bank measures its fifty thousand employees strictly by performance criteria; it isn't a touchy-feely kind of a place. Would Sim set his deeply human *Spiritual Fingerprint* aside to focus his leadership on the purely operational business criteria that the bank traditionally valued so highly? What would that do to his authenticity as a leader? Could he actually use his *Spiritual Fingerprint* to uncover resources of human energy in the bank and turn those into exponential growth of shareholder value and organizational sustainability?

Sim, forever stretching himself, strives to *Lead by Greatness*, and he chose the latter course. He decided that if he were true to his *Spiritual Fingerprint*, the bank would learn that if you focus on people, trust them, and value each person's capability to make a unique contribution, they will deliver. And they did. Sim is the first to admit that this was achieved as a result of the strong team he built around him, including Jacko's leadership of the whole bank and the ingrained ethos of teamwork within the organization. With his soft, human core, Sim achieved impressive, irrefutable, bottom-line results. Within the first year of Sim's leadership of SBSA, it improved its cost-to-income ratio (a measure of banking efficiency) from 48.3 percent to just 44.1 percent. Through the banking industry's hardest era in decades, Standard Bank achieved an astonishing four-year compound growth of earnings in excess of 16 percent. With his team, he launched the bank in a new direction, unlocking human energy and converting it into measurable economic value.

Soft Values with Hard Results

Brand Pretorius is CEO of McCarthy Motor Holdings, one of the top twenty automobile retailers in the world. Brand, now in his early sixties, is an elegant, tall, soft-spoken man with piercing eyes. He has a noble bearing, but is unassuming and approachable, and mixes freely with his employees and customers.

Brand was never your typical business leader. Since starting in the car business over thirty-five years ago, he has proven himself to be an overachiever. He increased Toyota's share of the South African market from 7 percent to 30 percent, and in only three years he brought them from eighth place in customer satisfaction to become the market leader. His program, The Toyota Touch, was recognized by Toyota as "the Best Customer Satisfaction Initiative in the World." In the automobile business, Brand is considered a virtuoso.

Being a successful marketer and leader like Brand is a task that takes more than just brains, savvy, and business sense. Not everyone possesses those, but there are enough competitors out there who do. Brand stands alone among his peers because, in leading by greatness, he achieves his results by using his own *Spiritual Fingerprint* to create his leadership philosophy and to influence the choices he makes as a leader.

"Leadership is not about what you do, but about what you are and what you believe in," Brand says. "The legitimacy of my leadership is not the power of my authority, but the power of my ideas and the strength of my spirit. The heart is the fountain of leadership. I look for voluntary commitment, not forced obedience. Leading this way delivers world-class achievement."

When I saw Brand's *Spiritual Fingerprint*, I realized how well his leadership philosophy is aligned with his own *value-drivers*. And though others have proposed that it was his genial manner, his eye for the market, or his business intuition that have propelled him thus far, the foundation for his success has in fact been his authenticity.

EXCELLENCE/ACHIEVEMENT
PASSIONATE COMMITMENT AND LEARNING
CARING
OPENNESS
RESPECT
TRUST & FAIRNESS
HONESTY & INTEGRITY

Being honest and having integrity drives my behavior. When that is in place, it enables me to be fairly treated in return. This builds trust and a deep, meaningful mutual respect. These values then enable openness and a caring attitude that fuels my passion and commitment, which leads to excellence and achievement.

For Brand, honesty and integrity have been his driving forces. Treating others fairly results in others treating him with fairness in return. This mutual respect fuels his open attitude and ultimately his unmatched success.

It is interesting how, in the cases of so many of the successful business leaders with whom I have worked, their core *value-drivers* are "soft," human, and personal. They bring their unique humanity into the way they make business choices, too, and that is what makes them different. Their soft core values all convert somewhere along the line into measurable performance and delivery. In Brand's case, his passionate commitment to learning translates into performance excellence, his outcome value-driver. Sim's value of humanity in the tough environment of financial services pushes him to pioneer and perform at the forefront of his industry. And Brian's core value of family well-being ultimately drives his success in business.

Leaders with a human value at their core achieve their desired financial outcome best when they are nourishing these human cores. You can only *Lead by Greatness* when your own soul is healthy and rich. The daily nurturing of your core value-driver is the most important thing you will do in the quest to lead by your own greatness: a greatness that will inspire the people around you to the pinnacle of their own achievement capabilities.

When people's core values are undernourished, their system of *value-drivers* implodes and their *Spiritual Fingerprints* dim. They become defensive, behaving by instinct and habit rather than by choices rooted in the greatness of their souls. The voice of their inner wisdom fades, and they lose authenticity and integrity as their actions edge more and more out of alignment with their values.

Checking Alignment

Your Spiritual Fingerprint is a wonderful diagnostic tool to ascertain what in your life, if anything, needs to change.

"To what extent do you feel a clash between being the person you want to be, the values you have, and the responsibilities of running a big public company?" This is the question that Adi Ignatius put to Howard Schultz, CEO of Starbucks, in a July 2010 interview.[25] Shultz answered:

"That's a very important question. Being the CEO of a public company over the past couple of years has been difficult. And lonely. The tension you describe assumes that one can't be values-driven or values-based and achieve success or the respect of the Street. I don't think that is true. But the only ingredient that works in this environment is performance—so we have to perform. If we don't perform, either we have the wrong strategy or we don't deserve to be here. I think we've demonstrated that the strategy is right and the balance between profitability and having a social conscience and being a benevolent company will lead to significant long-term value for shareholders."

But not everyone's *Spiritual Fingerprint* is as aligned with his or her work as Howard Schultz's. Sometimes people's *Spiritual Fingerprints* evolve, and after a time they find that their work is no longer aligned with who they are. Sometimes it never *was* aligned. What happens when a leader's work and his or her own *Spiritual Fingerprint* are misaligned?

This happened to Samuel Elkin (real name withheld to protect privacy), a graduate of one of America's finest business schools and a star in the New York investment banking community. He was a high-flying socialite, both in business and socially, and winning was all-important to him. Generally, whenever he competed for something, he won. After his career in investment banking, he built a premiere media empire that eventually ranked among the highest in the world in many of the categories in which it operated. Samuel was driven, and he rose to the top because of his intuition and intellect, but he lost track of his spiritual, value-driven compass along the way. Life was good for Samuel. Business dominated his life; he knew or cared little about anything else.

However, in his mid-forties and at the height of his career, he began to explore and rediscover his spiritual roots. Life started to take on additional dimensions for Samuel as he increasingly felt a growing disconnect between the values he had built his business on, and his own shifting and expanding beliefs. Together we mapped Samuel's *Spiritual Fingerprint* to clarify who he really was at his core. We did the same with the *value-drivers* of his business. The disparity was stunningly clear.

Samuel could not simply change the company values to align them with his own. The business had developed its own *corporate soul* and culture over the years, and any change in its values now would be cosmetic, inauthentic, and could even damage trust in the integrity of leadership.

Instead, knowing the breadth and the depth of the management team he had put in place in his media company, Samuel had the courage to withdraw from leading the business that he had founded. He started a new venture in an entirely different industry. This one he would build in a way that was congruent with his own *Spiritual Fingerprint* and his *Personal Purpose*. In this way, his personal and business lives would be more spiritually aligned, and both would flourish. His spiritual and emotional life would become an enabler of his business success, rather than something separate. Samuel is a much happier man today, and is on the verge of changing the game of yet another industry by combining a number of medium-sized "players" in the retail field into one large, integrated, and entirely new model of building and retaining retail customer loyalty.

Not all who feel a disconnect between their work and their *Spiritual Fingerprint* need to change their career, though. Sometimes your life can improve radically with just some minor fine-tuning. Your *Spiritual Fingerprint* is a wonderful diagnostic tool to ascertain what, if anything, needs to change.

Diagnosing the Problem: From the Outside In

When you feel that you are not functioning at your full potential, you can use your *Spiritual Fingerprint* to diagnose the root cause. Check your outcome value-driver, the last one of your concentric circles. It is there that you are first likely to notice that something is wrong. If your outcome value-driver is not delivering optimally, check how well the value-driver beneath it is functioning. Continue to "peel the onion" until you find where in your *Spiritual Fingerprint* a value is being diluted or compromised.

As an example, let's go back to Brand of McCarthy Motor Holdings. Brand and I met in his office on a bad day. The man I saw in front of me was not the confident, high-achieving (his seventh and outcome value-driver) leader I knew. It was not hard to see through his mask of optimism and to realize that, on that day, the spark of passion (his sixth value-driver) had left him. Using his *Spiritual Fingerprint* as a diagnostic tool, it was clear that something had happened in the caring (fifth value-driver) circle of his *Fingerprint*. When I questioned him about it, he told me that only minutes before our meeting (which happened to be at the height of the 2009 auto industry crisis), he had had to lay off one of his senior executives. This, as well as having to lay off thousands of lower and middle-level employees who had served the company loyally for many years, shook his *Spiritual Fingerprint* to the core, even though these were the only options for the company at that time. Brand had been feeling for a while that the process of layoffs challenged his own inner *value-drivers* of trust, fairness, respect, openness, and caring. He felt, in essence, that circumstance was forcing him to betray his own values. And this was compromising his drive for excellence.

When the core of a person's *Spiritual Fingerprint* is compromised, the entire system is weakened, and he or she cannot deliver as effectively in the outer circles. When you become aware that you are not functioning optimally at your outer *value-drivers*, you are likely to notice deficiencies in your inner core, as well. Brand could not deliver excellence while his sense of fairness and caring was compromised, because excellence for Brand is an outcome of his inner *value-drivers*, which include fairness and caring. When this happens, the way to recenter yourself is to start repairing your life by working from your core value-driver outward. And that is exactly what I began to do with Brand.

Repair the Root of the Problem: From the Inside Out

We checked in with Brand's core values of honesty and integrity. In laying off his workers, some of which lived paycheck to paycheck, had he abandoned his own *value-drivers* as a result of shareholder pressure? Or, did he make hard, proactive choices consistent with his own *Spiritual Fingerprint* to save his endangered company in the best way he could to rebuild it for the future? Had he explored every alternative avenue to gain efficiency in those troubled times before resorting to layoffs? In dealing with the layoffs, had he betrayed the trust of his people or dealt with them unfairly? Did he show honor and respect even to the people he needed to lay off? Did he help them retain their dignity as much as he possibly could?

Talking this through, Brand realized that you do not always create the circumstances you confront. You can only choose your responses to those circumstances. When your survival is threatened, you may well make different choices from the ones you make when your survival is not at stake. However, even when you are battling for survival, you can still do so in ways that compromise your *value-drivers* as little as possible. Even when you are in a crisis, you can still use your *Spiritual Fingerprint* as a point of reference. When you do so, you come through the experience feeling that your integrity is intact. It is only when you completely abandon your *value-drivers* that you are likely to feel disappointed and off-center.

Recognizing that he never once abandoned his soul in the layoff process (even though he would never have chosen retrenchment if there were an alternative), Brand began to sit tall again. Reclaiming his passionate commitment, he prepared himself once more to achieve excellence in everything he did.

Once you have mapped your *Spiritual Fingerprint*, try these two processes: first try a diagnostic examination from the outside in of how well your *value-drivers* are functioning; then, if there is a need to strengthen them, start working with your core value-driver from the inside out. Nourish yourself at your core to deliver results on the outer rings of your system.

It is important that you occasionally check in with your *Spiritual Fingerprint* to make sure that it feels right for you and that it still reflects with who you really are; otherwise, it may not be authentic. Provided your *Spiritual Fingerprint* is authentic to who you are and not a model of how you would like to be perceived, it becomes a vital tool you use to access your inner wisdom and to inform your decision-making process. Referencing your *Spiritual Fingerprint* before you make difficult choices and checking in with it regularly is one of the ways you can access your inner prophet—your own innate wisdom.

It is not sufficient to make decisions from your instincts, because you actually have two kinds of instinct. One kind is designed to defend you from physical danger, and another kind is creative and heroic and is an expression of your ideals. To know which instinct is guiding your actions, check your instinctual response against your *Spiritual Fingerprint*. Is it aligned? Is what you are doing or about to do congruent with your *Spiritual Fingerprint*? If it is not, your inner wisdom is telling you that while your intended path may work for another person, it is not the right one for you. Check why you might be attracted to a path that is inauthentic to you. Is it outside pressure? Are you being influenced by a desire to please others? Are you being driven by instinctual fear rather than by your creative passion?

In this process, you will go deeper and deeper to discover the *value-drivers* at the very core of your being, your place of truth. When you lead from these *value-drivers*, people will follow you not out of fear of your power, but out of respect for your authenticity.

This concept of *value-drivers* originates in the work of second-century Kabbalistic master, Pinchas ben Yair.[26] He was a wise man with many disciples and was known to perform spectacular miracles, including splitting the Ginnai, a river in the Beit She'an Valley in Israel. When asked how he did it, he answered that anyone could perform such miracles if they were sure never to have harmed even so much as the *feelings* of another person.[27] He taught that values are not static; they expand like ripples in a pond when they are being energized from the core, one giving rise to the next.

I have found that this model works well to help people understand the way their own *value-drivers* function and how they make up a *Spiritual Fingerprint*. The order of each individual's *value-drivers* depends on which value lies at the core and energizes his or her system, how this core value-driver influences other *value-drivers*, and which of the *value-drivers* are outcome *value-drivers*. The resulting order of *value-drivers* is therefore unique and expressive of each person's individuality.

But your *Spiritual Fingerprint* is not the only tool you will use to access your inner wisdom on your journey to greatness. The power of your spirituality resides both in your *Spiritual Fingerprint* and also in the unique purpose of your life. Your *Spiritual Fingerprint* tells you *who* you are, but you also need to discover *why* you are. Wouldn't it be wonderful to know why you have been put on this earth and what you are meant to accomplish in your lifetime? Wouldn't you love to discover, articulate, and live your own unique purpose, one that no one else can fulfill? It may surprise you to find out that it is not beyond your grasp, and that once you know these two dimensions of your spirituality—the core of *who* you are and *why* you are here—you can put them to work, not only for your personal advantage and growth, but for your economic well-being, too.

CHAPTER SIX

IT'S NOT JUST *WHO* YOU ARE, IT'S *WHY* YOU ARE.

*The purpose of economic activity is to make
a valuable contribution to the well-being of others.*

THERE'S AN OLD STORY about a prisoner in Siberia whose sentence of hard labor required him to pull the wooden shaft of a huge millstone around in circles all day. It was similar to the work that mules were made to do in that time. Day after day, year after year, he toiled in the prison yard, keeping his sanity by imagining the value of his work to others. He thought of the farmers who, after each day of harvesting their wheat, would bring their loaded wagons to the prison for milling. He thought of the bakers lining up outside the prison early each morning to collect the bags of flour that he had milled the day before. He delighted in the thought of the wives and mothers who baked fresh loaves of bread each day for their families using the flour he had toiled to mill. He could virtually smell the bread and hear the chatter of children as they enjoyed their meals with their families. He would smile as he labored his time away.

The day he was to be released, the prisoner was overwhelmed with emotion and anticipation. At last he could walk behind the prison walls and see the outcome of his work. He could watch the farmers offload, see the bakers arrive, and know that in some small way his years in prison had been of value. His heart pounding with joy, he collected his meager belongings, left the prison gate, and turned to walk by the prison wall to the point where the flour from the mill would pile up outside. But there was no flour piling up. There was no mill. There never had been. There were no farmers and bakers. No women ever baked bread from flour he milled. His work had not been intended to be productive; it was only intended to torture him. It was all meaningless, and his life in prison had turned out to be a tragic waste. His heart broke, and he died.

Anyone who is not gratified by the knowledge that his or her work has value beyond the money it makes for shareholders dies a little each day. A person's work is more than the exchange of his or her labor and skills for cash. Irrespective of how much you earn, your life has to have meaning, and so does your work. The quest for meaning is the striving of the human soul; it is a spiritual need, but it has a place at work, too. When work is meaningful to people, they bring far more energy and innovation to it than when it is not. This is one of the most important areas where spirituality and economics intersect.

I learned the economic and human value of work that has meaning at the very beginning of my consulting career.

Bill Nairn, then CEO of JCI Gold Division, one of the largest gold mining operations in the world, faced a daunting dilemma. The price of gold had reached a plateau, but mining costs were spiraling upwards, causing profit margins to collapse. The economy in South Africa, where JCI's mines were located, was heavily dependent on the gold mines, both for revenue and for employment. The socioeconomic repercussions of the mine closures JCI was contemplating would reverberate throughout the economy. JCI had already pursued every conceivable means to improve efficiencies. Bill had to find a way for his mines to continue producing at a lower cost to maintain profitability and justify their continued existence.

Bill happened to be at a human resource conference that I was addressing back in 1994, and something I said resonated with him: "The solution to every business challenge, outside of purely technical issues, lies at the root of people's relationships with their work. Vast resources of human energy, innovation, and productivity wait to be liberated by managers willing to learn how to inspire employees with a passionate belief in their own dignity and the human value of the work they do." This was my first articulation of the ever-evolving thesis I have used since then to help individuals, leaders, and corporations unlock people's immense capacity for achievement.

Bill brought his chairman, Ken Maxwell, to meet me. Our meeting resulted in one of the most remarkable studies and subsequent programs linking human dignity to economic performance. One of my findings was that the laborers who worked the mines had no idea of the purpose and real value of their work. They toiled long hours in torturous heat and harsh conditions several miles underground to extract minute quantities of gold powder from tons of rock. But when asked what gold was used for, the miners said it was sold to the government, which then put it back in underground vaults! Imagine working so hard for such an apparently meaningless cause.

We set about teaching the miners, down to the lowest levels in the organization, the value of their work to people and society. We showed them how gold is used in technology and medicine, and the part it still plays in stabilizing economies. We also showed them how gold enhances romantic relationships. They had no previous idea about the vastness of the impact of their work on people's lives.

Before our very eyes we saw the miners' new understanding about the meaning of their work reflected in the way they perceived themselves. They stood taller, walked more proudly, and had smiles on their faces that we hadn't seen there before. Morale improved and so did productivity. They began to work with more energy and surprised management with their innovative suggestions about how to work more efficiently. Layoffs proved to be unnecessary, and the mines were spared until the gold price again began to lift, and with it, the profits at JCI.

The man in the picture below would notice and repair his leaking buckets if he saw his purpose as providing milk to people in need, rather than as a functional operation of milking the cow, which he is in fact doing successfully! Sometimes, just reframing the description of a person's job to include its purpose uplifts the person, motivates him or her, and increases the effectiveness of their work.

In thinking of business differently, it is important to remember that financial reward is the *outcome* of successful economic activity, not its *purpose*. Starbucks CEO Howard Schultz puts it so well. "What I stand for is not just to make money," he says, "it's to feel like I've done something that has meaning and relevancy and is something people are going to respect."[28]

The purpose of economic activity is to make a valuable contribution to the well-being of others; "*the world is constructed by acts of kindness.*"[29] The more rare and needed a person's or organization's contribution to others is, the more value it has and the higher the price people will pay for it.

Woodrow Wilson (1856–1924), the twenty-eighth president of the United States, put it beautifully when he wrote:

> *You are not here*
> *Merely to make a living*
> *You are here*
> *In order to enable the world*
> *To live more amply*
> *With greater vision*
> *With a finer spirit of*
> *Hope and achievement*
> *You are here*
> *To enrich the world*

I believe we all embark on our life journey in hopes of making a difference, and having our deepest spiritual needs filled each day. The reason I started my consulting firm after many years in international commodity trading was because I wanted to make a difference in people's lives in a more direct way. That is my purpose in life; not to make money, but to earn money from the difference I make in the lives of others. As Albert Einstein said, "Strange is our situation here upon earth. Each of us comes for a short visit, not knowing why, yet sometimes seeming to a divine purpose...We are here for the sake of others."

The knight shown above is bored by the operational job he has of slaying dragons. He is far more animated in the next picture when he understands the higher purpose of his work!

My friend Keyvan Zarin (name changed to protect privacy) is a physician, who has dedicated his life to improving the health of underprivileged people in developing countries. On a visit to South America, where he was working at the time, I met him for lunch and found him uncharacteristically frustrated. I asked what had him ruffled. Keyvan still practices old-fashioned medicine in the communities he

tends, routinely making house calls to understand the conditions under which his patients live. Late the previous night, he had heard a knock at his door and, upon opening it, had found a bedraggled young man standing before him, looking desperate. "Doctor, my mother is ill. Can you come now?"

Committed to this community, Keyvan grabbed his bag and headed out in his car with the boy beside him. They drove in the pouring rain for many miles through poverty-stricken neighborhoods, finally coming to a home near the end of the village. There, Keyvan stopped his car and the young man asked, "How much will you charge for this, Doctor?"

"Probably forty or fifty dollars. It could depend." (This was some years ago, and in a rural community.)

The young man pulled forty dollars from his pocket and thanked the doctor for the ride. "That was cheaper than a taxi," he said. Then he hopped out of the car and ran into his home. Keyvan was stunned to realize the boy had not needed his medical services at all, just a ride home! He felt completely exploited, and his anger and irritation showed clearly at lunch that next day.

"Why does this bother you so much?" I teasingly asked him. "From a business perspective it turned out to be a productive night. You were willing to make the house call, including the ride, for forty to fifty dollars. Well, you made the money without having to administer any treatment. You got home much sooner than you anticipated."

My point was that if the physician were in it just for the money, he might not have been as resentful of the ploy. Yes, the boy was dishonest, but it was not just his dishonesty that irritated Keyvan so deeply. Keyvan isn't in it for money. He works hard and passionately for a higher purpose. Money is simply the outcome of the contribution he makes curing people of disease and improving their health. The previous night's work may have been profitable, but in terms of the purpose of his life, it was wasteful. Keyvan would have gotten far more satisfaction from healing someone for free than from providing a duplicitous youth with a ride for a forty-dollar fee.

Like Keyvan, each of us has been put here to do something we are good at and passionate about. We are here to serve some cause that others cannot serve in quite the same way; we all have a specific and unique purpose. But whereas my friend found it easy to determine and fulfill his purpose—he was passionate about medicine from early childhood—how do the rest of us do it? How can we determine the purpose of our lives?

The Great "Why"
By analyzing our differences we uncover our purpose.

There is a reason why each of us is created differently. Our differences are more than a random coincidence of evolution; our differences are the most important clue to identifying the unique purpose for which each of us has been created. There is something divine about the way each of us has been engineered with singular capabilities designed to enable us to live our specific purpose.

The idea of *Personal Purpose* is that every person is born with the talents, intuitive wisdom, passions, and capabilities he or she will need to fulfill the purpose for which he or she was created. Each person has a different purpose here, and is therefore necessarily created differently. Thus, by analyzing our differences we uncover our purpose.

Some people are built for performing physical feats, with the ability to break records of human endurance and physical strength. Others are gifted with the ability to perform feats of intellect and spirit. They do not need the physical stature of the athlete, but rather are imbued with a rare power of thought and creative genius. A person destined to delight the world with musical compositions will not likely have the mind for nuclear physics. A physicist may not be the world's greatest orator, but can speak to the world through his or her inventions or research. Each of us is designed with the potential to play our part in the unfolding of the world's history. Knowing our *Personal Purpose* is the first step, but the choice we make to live it determines our destiny.

Some people are born with such obvious talent in a particular sphere that their purpose in life is abundantly clear to them. However, you don't have to be born a Mozart, Shakespeare, or Einstein in order to identify your *Personal Purpose* and live it. Anyone can do it. And when you do, the forces of the world harmonize to support you in the most marvelous ways. Even more importantly, knowing your *Personal Purpose* with clarity helps you to solve problems and make hard choices more quickly and efficiently. When options present themselves to you, knowing your purpose allows you to quickly evaluate which option is most likely to propel you in the direction of your *Personal Purpose*. Many times, you will notice that some of the options you are considering do not further your purpose at all; some may even detract from your focus. If you follow these alternate paths, you are straying from your *Personal Purpose* and ignoring the key coordinates provided by your internal GPS system. If you adhere to your inner voice, however, your true purpose will unfold before you.

When you are living your *Personal Purpose*, you live your life to the very fullest. Every talent and passion bubbles forth; your goals are being met; you radiate an aura of positive energy, to which people are attracted and which, in turn, attracts the generous support of the people around you. If you are alert, you will begin to notice how often seemingly coincidental events happen that powerfully move you further on the path of your purpose. You are doing that which no other person can do quite like you. Does this sound too good to be true? It isn't. It works for you as an individual in much the same way as it works for your business. Here's how it works and why.

Think of businesses that are truly differentiated and that use their uniqueness to do things for their customers that others cannot easily do. Apple, for example, uses its design brilliance to combine technology with style and marketing flair in ways that no one else has. The result? In 2010, while the rest of the world was reeling from the recession, Apple's revenue grew by 61 percent. Google, using the uniqueness of its search engine technology and its awesome corporate culture, brought in a 23 percent year-over-year revenue growth in the first quarter of 2010, when general U.S. Internet advertising revenue grew by only 7.5 percent.[30] By February 2011, *CNBC* said that analysts declared Apple "the most valuable company on earth."[31]

The unique innovative ability of Intuitive Surgical, Inc. makes it the world's sole provider of robotic-assisted surgical systems. In 2010, *Bloomberg Businessweek* included Intuitive Surgical in its top-performing U.S. stocks "of the past five years, one of the most turbulent periods in our country's economic history," second only to Priceline, Inc. Priceline, a major innovator in online travel reservations, was *Bloomberg's* number one, and its stock grew more than tenfold during the travel business's hardest era in modern times.[32]

What differentiates businesses like these that stand head and shoulders above the rest? Their leaders believe in and are passionately committed to the purposes of their own lives, and they express their *Personal Purpose* in their work. This enables them to stay true to themselves. When leaders stay true to their purpose, their strategies are focused, and their markets are defined. They attract capital, talent, and customers. The bolder their vision and the more differentiated their edge, the more powerfully they surge forward to fill unoccupied market space, redefine their industry, and build value and wealth. This ability to identify purpose attracts more than just economic success; it aligns positive forces around you and your company and brings triumph to your endeavors.

When you envision your purpose clearly, things that you thought of as mere coincidences reveal themselves as miracles, and seemingly random events may begin to appear to you as a deliberate string of fortune. Say, for example, you decided that climbing Mount Kilimanjaro in Tanzania at the end of the year is an important step in fulfilling your *Personal Purpose*. Once you have made the decision to undertake the trip, you will be surprised to see how many "coincidences" occur between now and then that can help to make that journey a reality. You may meet people who have knowledge or experience that is helpful to you; you might come across books, articles, and television programs that inform you; or you might stumble across others who are planning to be in Tanzania at the same time as you. Your clarity of purpose and vision alert you to notice things you otherwise might not have.

However, it goes further than that. When you clearly see and articulate the purpose for your business or team, things tend to fall into place to support your effort and help get your business from where it is to where it needs to be surprisingly quickly. Until your purpose is clear to you, you cannot align the forces you need to make your purpose a reality.

Living your purpose does generally attract material success. But your *Personal Purpose* is about loftier things than making money. It is about making a difference, often in a more profound way than you could have thought possible.

The exercise of discovering your real purpose is not always easy. I would caution you to allocate some meaningful quiet time to the process. It is much more than jotting down a personal mission statement or articulating what you would like to do with your life. This exercise, like the one to uncover your *Spiritual Fingerprint*, is a process of discovering something that exists already but which may not be evident to you. It is not an exercise in composing a pretty statement. It requires that you go deep into yourself and the unique qualities and circumstances you have been given to search for the higher purpose for which you were created. Like your *Spiritual Fingerprint*, your authentic higher purpose is yours alone, and you should never copy it from another, or adopt it artificially.

Even greater than the challenge of discovering your purpose is the challenge of living your purpose. It can happen that once you have discovered your purpose, you realize that the life you are living is not fully aligned with it, or not aligned with it at all. In these instances, being true to yourself might require some significant changes in your life. We will now learn the process of discovering and articulating your higher purpose, but you may find that you will reach a greater depth and authenticity if you use a certified *Lead by Greatness* coach. These coaches are trained to take you to the depths of your essence and to truly discover what makes you unique. They are also experienced in helping you align your life with your purpose; a process that can be extremely challenging and in which you can face some significant personal and environmental barriers. You can find your own *Lead by Greatness* coach at <u>leadbygreatness.com/coaches/</u>.

I always knew that a pillar of my own purpose was to teach. I particularly wanted to expose people to the principles and wisdom of universal truths I had learned, which I knew could help them to enhance their effectiveness as individuals and as leaders. This purpose was, in fact, such a passion that I did not want to be financially dependent on it. I wanted to feel free to practice my passion and live my purpose in the most authentic way, without having to worry about its financial rewards. So I took a job in business to fund my passion, first in a global corporation, and later as an entrepreneur in my own business. In this way, I could teach whomever and wherever I chose, and I could teach whatever and however I chose without having to worry about the financial implications of these choices. After a period of time, though, I found that the bulk of my day and some of my nights were dedicated to business, and I had less and less time available for teaching. I was no longer living my purpose; instead, teaching had become just a hobby to do when I had the time. So I merged my teaching and my business into a single entity— a consulting practice. At first, it was called Strategic Business Ethics, Inc., because it taught business leaders how they could leverage their strategic advantage by building and running highly principled organizations. Later, we rebranded the firm to Lapin International, Inc. Now, I am able to live my purpose while I earn my living.

Not all who choose to realign their lives with their purpose will find the process as straightforward as I did. Sometimes it may entail greater sacrifices than I had to make, as a person may need to give up something he or she does well in order to create the space in his or her life for a different purpose. It could entail a move into the unknown or a degree of financial risk. Often, we fear to do what we are created to do and are really passionate about, because we fear our own greatness. However, all fear is really the fear of loss: loss of life, health, love, money, recognition, or status. Effectively detaching our identities from the things we fear to lose can often dissolve the fear and uncover the courage we need to make the change. To move onto a new path of life, whether that requires a change of geographic location, a change of job, or any other significant life change, we might need to detach ourselves from what we know in order to discover what we deserve. When we do this authentically, living our higher purpose brings us a greater sense of well-being, and often better health, too. Are you ready?

Articulating Your Purpose

Your Personal Purpose informs and aligns every important decision you make.

Choosing to live your purpose and achieve your destiny is a decision that is yours to make. It is a decision that will affect the success of your accomplishments and the ease with which you achieve them. Your *Personal Purpose* informs and aligns every important decision you make. When you are imbued with a clear sense of your own purpose, you radiate transformational energy, and the universe collaborates in an almost magical way to smooth your path and turn your dreams into reality.

Here are the three steps to discovering and articulating your own *Personal Purpose*.

Step 1 – List Your Capabilities

At this given juncture of your life, you have a very specific set of capabilities that allow you to make a contribution quite unlike anyone else. Your assets, skills, and experience all come together to give you that unique set of capabilities. Your capabilities stem from your individual assets, such as your physical ability and skills, upbringing and education, mental capacity, personality traits, worldview, life experiences, network of contacts, and talents. None of those assets are particularly rare, but your specific blend of all of them is completely unique. There could be many people who have some of the talents and skills you have, and others may have had an education like yours, but no one else will have your whole package of assets, which together determine the precise nature of your capabilities to make a difference. Whatever your capabilities, they are indicators of what your purpose is. So why not try to identify your unique capabilities?

Here's a way to do this that has helped many of the people I have coached:

List your portfolio of assets. Assets are all the things that have value to you and that contribute to who you are at this point in your life. Include any experience, skill, or other asset that can be valuable to you in making a difference with other people. One of my coaching clients, Clive Nordell (name changed to protect privacy), created the following table as a framework for using this method. These are the actual assets he listed.

Physical Abilities	32 years old, male, good health, reasonably fit, tall, and fairly charismatic.
Skills	Good communicator, excellent with numbers.
Upbringing	Raised with strong Christian values and work ethic. A father who was a successful CEO and community leader, a warm and dedicated mom active in community philanthropy.
Education	Majored in Philosophy and Economics, Ivy League MBA.
Material Assets	Debt-free, except for manageable mortgage on a home, and some investments.
Mental Abilities	Above average, strongly analytical with an appreciation for art and music.
Personality Traits	Extrovert, sociable, empathetic, focused, driven to achieve.
World View	Personal accountability, free market.
Life Experience	Worked as a CFO of a failed start-up, lost all my savings and money I borrowed from my family. Worked like crazy to repay every dime. Helped nurse my mother through cancer. Backpacked extensively in Asia, worked for the Peace Corps in Central Africa.
Network of Contacts	Ivy League College and Business School, Venture Capital community, my father's contacts in senior positions in large corporations in the retail industry.
Talents	Teaching and coaching, cooking.

After listing your assets, articulate a few of the ways you could make the biggest difference to others. These are your capabilities. Avoid being influenced by what you are currently doing, and also ignore the need to generate income. At this point, this is a theoretical exercise, so try to look at your list objectively. If you were told about somebody with this particular portfolio of assets, what would you identify as some of the most valuable things this person could do for others?

Based on his whole portfolio of assets, Clive identified his main capability as *mentoring and developing people for success and building teams to excel.*

Step 2 – Primary Beneficiaries

Once you have identified your capabilities, you will see that many different people could benefit from your unique portfolio of capabilities. But we want to identify the single set of people or entities that could derive *the most* value from your capabilities. To discover your *Personal Purpose,* it is helpful to focus on a specific group of people where your impact could be greatest. These are your primary beneficiaries. All the other people who can, and probably will, benefit from you along the way are your secondary beneficiaries. However, by identifying your primary beneficiaries it is easier to more clearly articulate what kind of people or what groups or entities you were most likely created to serve. These beneficiaries may be your family, your employees or teams at work, your customers or clients, or underprivileged children in your city.

In Clive's case, he listed two potential sets of primary beneficiaries:

- People with capital to invest who are seeking a leader capable of identifying opportunities, building teams, and creating wealth.
- Businesses that are underperforming because of unmotivated teams and that are seeking a CEO who can turn morale and performance around.

Until this point, it seemed clear to Clive what he was put here to do. He has so many leadership qualities, particularly business leadership. It seemed to him that he should look at three potential options: a) work for a venture capital or private equity firm where he could identify and grow businesses for investors; b) seek a position as the CEO (or owner) of a business with high potential but poor performance; or c) work as a turnaround specialist. Although his talents could lead him to success in any of these three areas, none of them really engaged his passion. It was therefore unlikely that the purpose of his being, at this particular point in his life, was any one of these potential opportunities. It was when he did the third part of the exercise and probed his *passions* that he discovered a very different and inspirational direction.

Step 3 – Identifying Your Passions

You have a source of internal energy that helps drive your progress through any obstacles to living your purpose. This energy takes the form of a passion for those activities you will need to engage in as you make your unique contribution in the world. So, identifying your passions is another way to help you discover and more precisely describe your purpose.

To identify your passions, ask yourself what activities in your work or personal life energize you. What are the activities that bring you a sense of joy and satisfaction when you do them? Which activities give you a sense of all-around well-being? These are the activities that energize you and that you would do most of the time, if you did not have financial considerations to worry about. It is sometimes helpful to look at the opposites—the activities that drain you, exhaust you, or depress you. Then flip those activities around to identify their positive opposites.

When you have identified these activities, ask yourself what about them energizes and uplifts you, because this is how you will find your passions. For example, if you have a passion for cycling, ask yourself what it is about cycling that fuels this passion. Is it being outdoors? Is it freedom? Is it the wind on your face, or the people you cycle with? Probe each activity that energizes you to determine what about that activity you truly love. You may well find that there are similar passions hidden within a number of different activities you enjoy. Focus on them.

Clive identified his passions as:
- Making a difference
- Helping ordinary people surprise themselves and others with what they can achieve
- Exploiting opportunities that others don't see
- Classical music
- Performing in front of large audiences

As he wrote down the last two passions on this list, Clive nearly jumped out of his seat. In the past he had always looked for opportunities that would yield the most money. This, he figured, would provide him with the freedom to pursue his passion for music in his spare time. He would coach kids and listen to music when he wasn't working. But he found throughout his life so far that he was seldom "not working," so he hardly ever got to do the things he really loved to do. Now he thought of things differently. He would work at what he loved and trust that the money would follow. And even if the money did not follow in the same quantities as before, he would be a happier, more fulfilled, and more successful person.

Clive accepted the position of CEO of a symphony orchestra in a small city in the Midwest of the US. The orchestra was short of both funding and talent, but not of enthusiasm and passion. He decided to reform the organization into a youth orchestra. His mission was not only to entertain people, but also to develop young talent. Using his network and his charismatic sociability, Clive built a community of support beyond the borders of the city, and worked closely with a dynamic musical director who had retired from a successful career of leading well-known orchestras. He searched for unrealized talent among the youth of the city. With the director, he nurtured young men and women, trained them, and gave them opportunities they could not easily have found in bigger cities. He started attracting young talent from around the country, and his orchestra began to be noticed by serious reviewers in the media. He became quite a celebrity and a high-profile leader in the community. But most of all, Clive Nordell, exploiting opportunities that others didn't see, was helping ordinary young people surprise themselves and others with what they could achieve. Using his unique capabilities, he was making a difference to individuals and to communities. And after all, that is what he is passionate about. Clive felt he was doing what he was meant to be doing, and the forces of the universe were aligning to support his purpose.

Too often, people separate their passions from their work, seeing the one as duty and the other as pleasure. Like Clive, try to incorporate your passions within your work. Doing what you love is so important, both for your success, and for your health and well-being. Bring your passions to work and use them. Don't limit your passions to part-time interests and hobbies. Incorporating your passions into your work will add so much energy to what you do. Your passions are one of the three indicators that direct you in determining what it is that you were created to do and be. The three indicators are your capabilities, the primary beneficiaries of your contribution, and your passions. These are the three pillars that form the foundation of your statement of *Personal Purpose*.

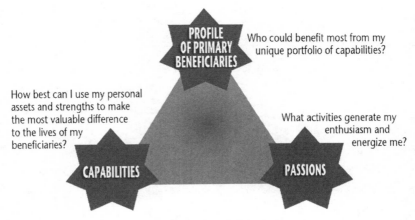

You are now ready to begin crafting your statement of *Personal Purpose*. Check how well your passions and your capabilities are aligned. Is there a match between your identified capabilities and the things about which you are passionate? Do you feel that you can express your passions in the things you are most capable of contributing to others? If you do not think that your capabilities are well matched to your passions, then revisit the exercise. Either you have not been clear enough in identifying your capabilities or you have not gone deeply enough into your passions. Referring back to your *Spiritual Fingerprint* might help you crystallize your statement of *Personal Purpose*.

Now, identify both the tangible and intangible services you could provide to the people and entities you highlighted as your beneficiaries. These services should combine the use of your capabilities with activities about which you are passionate.

Clive Nordell articulated his purpose as:

Using music, I develop extraordinary talent, confidence, and self-esteem in ordinary young people. I build community, and delight and uplift people who are burdened with the mundane nature of everyday life.

Dr. David Ridley (names changed to protect privacy) was a family medicine practitioner living in a small city with his wife Mary-Anne and their two young children. We did his purpose exercise together with Mary-Anne. Not surprisingly, his key strength was that he is a qualified physician and a good communicator. His capability is to heal people and teach them about health. So, he decided that his primary beneficiaries were any people in his community who needed medical attention.

His passions, though, are for teaching and for children. David, it turns out, had always harbored a secret desire to be a schoolteacher! He decided that the primary beneficiaries of his contribution should be children, and that to deliver his tangible service to them he should be a pediatrics specialist and not a general family physician. His intangible service could be *to inspire as many children as he could to live lives that are physically, mentally, and emotionally healthy.* This, then, he figured, was the purpose for which he was created; this surely was David's *Personal*

Purpose. It was not the life he was living at that time, though.

Mary-Anne looked him in the eye and urged him to go back to school and specialize in pediatric medicine. She would partner with him in his purpose by supporting the family while he studied. So he returned to school. They struggled financially for a few years, but they had never before been as happy as they were during that time.

By articulating his purpose in this way, he moved into fields beyond traditional medicine that he had never previously considered. He wrote books for children, gave presentations at schools, created his own newspaper column, and for a while even had a television show. These projects were all within his purpose, because he is a talented speaker and passionate about media and communication. He boosted his medical practice and was catapulted into national prominence. He even traveled to remote parts of Africa, Asia, and South America promoting child health. He is indirectly responsible for improving the lives of hundreds of thousands of children, and maybe many more. He has saved tens of thousands of lives. He has a sparkle in his eyes, and his life has unfolded in ways it might never otherwise have done had he simply continued to practice family medicine in a conventional way. Living his purpose, the forces of the universe aligned to support him and bless his efforts with spectacular success. Indeed, it impacted every area of his life; even his marriage blossomed!

So now, looking again at your own capabilities, passions, and beneficiaries, write one or two sentences that describe what tangible and intangible values you can provide, and to whom. Look for some unique element in your approach to this, ways that express your own personality and your own *Spiritual Fingerprint*. In the statement, include words that express your passions. Write your statement in the present tense, to infuse it with more energy. If you wish, you may choose to open with a phrase such as "My purpose is to…"

Here are some examples of other people's statements of *Personal Purpose* that you may find helpful.

Brian, the entrepreneur from Chapter 5:

I see value where others often do not. By reducing complexity into simplicity I show people how to optimize that value and develop their capabilities to grow their businesses and make themselves and their businesses the very best they can be.

Brian began to delegate more of his administrative work and focus his creative genius on helping his teams around the world to grow their businesses and to be the best they could be. His company's results bear testimony to the power of his contribution.

Gail, founder and principal of one of the most innovative elementary schools in North America:

My purpose is to create a school without walls in which children and adults can learn how to meaningfully express their values individually and globally, thereby finding their place both within themselves and within the world.

Gail's vision of a school without walls permeates every part of her organization. But she realized that, without noticing it, invisible walls had evolved within her school's administration and between it and her teaching faculty. These invisible walls inhibited the free flow of learning and teaching. Working closely with her faculty and board, she removed administrative layers, built a unified and trusting team with her faculty and administration, and empowered a cadre of teaching specialists with the authority to make administrative decisions. The unintended outcome was that the teachers saw no further need to be part of the teachers' union and decertified themselves. With that, the last remaining wall in the school's administration fell.

Caryn, executive VP of HR at a large investment bank:

I transform the effectiveness with which groups of bright, high-energy people I care about interact with each other and lead their teams. Bringing simplicity, clarity, human energy, and authenticity to the team, I create the space in which they can feel safe enough to be vulnerable and confront unasked questions. By taking the noise out of situations, I help them get to the heart of the issues they are confronting.

The bank valued Caryn enormously. She was, at the time I worked with her, the youngest member of the executive team and its only female member. She had felt somewhat inadequate because of her lack of technical knowledge about investment banking. Her purpose statement clarified her contribution, and she realized the important role she plays in the team's dynamic and success. She gained confidence, built a powerful team, and succeeded more than ever.

Stephen, a national sales director in a Fortune 500 company:

I enable diverse people in focused teams with a common purpose to translate important ideas into things of tangible and enduring value.

When Stephen came to see me, he was stressed and worried about some health problems. He was also upset about a job transfer he had been offered that he feared might sideline him from future opportunities within sales. Once he realized his purpose, he happily accepted the transfer to head an SAP implementation team. He realized he had been clinging to the sales position for the money he believed it offered in the future, rather than because it was where he could optimize his contribution to his company. A few months later I got the following e-mail from him:

Hello David,

Building on what we spoke about in my session with you, I also started to change my personal life. I purchased a farm property about two hours north of the city. It is quite large, with lots of space at 160 acres, and I don't think I will ever run out of wood, as most of the property is lined with trees. I have an old farmhouse, a barn, a pond, and eight cows that belong to a real farmer. I will use it for rest, relaxation, and family as a reminder that I need to leave the office.

I have started to work on the SAP project, and I am enjoying the work. Just last week, I was also asked to join a World Headquarters team to conduct some due diligence at several business units around the world. I have agreed, as the work will help my SAP project, and I will get to see a little of the world. I will need to travel to the UK, Germany, Italy, Spain, France, Singapore, Australia, and New Zealand. The gentleman who asked me to join this team reports to our global CEO.

Kind regards,
Stephen

Stephen is quickly becoming far more valued at the higher echelons of his corporation than he ever was working in sales. This is because in both his personal and his work life, he is doing what he was put here to do; he is fulfilling his *Personal Purpose*.

Now try your hand at crafting your own statement of *Personal Purpose*. Together with your *Spiritual Fingerprint*, it will guide you in making leadership and personal choices that inspire trust and enthusiasm in the people who follow you, and ultimately it will revolutionize your company, too.

PART TWO

UNLOCKING YOUR CORPORATE SOUL

Applying Spiritual Fundamentals
to Business Practice

CHAPTER SEVEN

BREATHING SOUL
INTO A CORPORATION

Our spirituality provides us with the capacity to create
ideas and products that are unique
and different from those created by others.

HAVE YOU EVER wondered why there are so many brilliant people who have not been successful at building great organizations? This is because the quest for exponential growth in business requires more than brilliance and efficiency, and more than talent, too. Exponential growth and innovation are powered by talented people who are also infused with a driving sense of higher purpose, a sense of almost divine destiny. As we've seen, great leaders understand that purpose is inextricably linked to a spiritual foundation, the foundation on which they build a *corporate soul* for their organizations.

Yes, a corporation has a soul, too. It may sound like an abstract concept, but just as each individual possesses a unique and singular soul, every corporation possesses an inimitable soul, as well—and whether recognized or overlooked, it is fundamental to corporate success. In a soulless organization, it is impossible to generate human energy, transmit a sense of purpose, or tap human greatness. Great leaders know how to access their own souls, as we saw in Part One, but great *business* leaders know how to use this knowledge to articulate their *corporate souls* to unlock powerful new waves of economic value. In January 2011, when Larry Page took back the operational reins of Google, Inc., as its CEO, he said, "One of the primary goals I have is to get Google to be a big company that has the nimbleness and *soul* and passion and speed of a start-up."[33]

Consider Kurus Elavia, CEO of Gateway Group One in New Jersey. Kurus immigrated to the U.S. from India in 1988, starting off as a security officer with Gateway and quickly moving up the ranks. The company's only nonfamily executive, Kurus convinced Chairman Lou Dell'Ermo that if he got the top job he would either double the company's business or resign. He tripled it.

What is Kurus' secret? He understands that what customers need most is no different from what any other set of human beings anywhere in the world needs. "They want to feel that they are cared for, and they want to feel this in the most authentic way." The authenticity of the caring is the catch, because you cannot fake authenticity. If customer care is just a "strategy," customers will experience it mechanically, and it won't satisfy their deep need for dignity and caring. Caring for others needs to be embedded in the DNA of the company itself, in its *corporate soul*. And for this to happen, it needs to be a real and deeply personal value, to which the leader of a company is passionately committed. For Kurus, it is.

Kurus was raised in India where, as a Catholic schoolboy, he watched church leaders clean the feet of ordinary people in the congregation. This taught him the true meaning of service. As he says, "The purpose of my company is to serve others. Ultimately, my customer is the greater good that I must serve." To Kurus, customer service is more than a strategy for profit; it is the higher purpose for which he lives. It is integral to his *Spiritual Fingerprint* and therefore embedded into his company's *soul*.

A fierce commitment to serving customers, though, is not sufficient to give a company its *soul* and create the kind of financial success that Kurus did at Gateway Group One. For employees to adopt such a strong service ethic and believe in it, they need to feel that their leaders—namely, those espousing that ethic—connect with them and care deeply and authentically about them, too. "I put both my customers' interests and my employees' interests before my own, and often even before the interests of the company," Kurus says, "because in the long run, doing this is best for the sustainable growth of the company." He is a coach to his employees, energizing his team to be successful. "You cannot build loyalty, values, and character in financial quarterly reports. You need patience."

Gateway Group One is an extremely well-run operation, but its phenomenal success is not purely a result of its operational effectiveness. What differentiates Gateway from its competitors is how Kurus identifies and cultivates his company's *soul* and aligns it both with his own beliefs and values and also with the intangible needs of his employees and customers. Everyone craves genuine human caring—employees and customers alike. This is the way Kurus manages to "keep the customers we have and get the ones we want." He adds, "We've also never lost a manager."

Kurus has the luxury of being able to patiently invest in people because Gateway Group One is a privately held company and not subject to the demanding quarterly expectations of Wall Street.

But there are leaders of public companies who have done the same. Starbucks is a publicly traded company, and its chairman and CEO, Howard Schultz, also knows the value of a healthy *corporate soul* and of a company dedicated to serving the deeper needs of its customers.

Schultz always feared that Starbucks might one day devolve into a soulless conglomerate. After several years of exponential expansion, it did. At the end of 2007, Schultz asserted that Starbucks was "losing its soul."[34] Then, in January 2008, after a year of declining profits and share price, Schultz took back the reins of leadership at Starbucks after having relinquished his influence to subordinates. He did all the conventional things, including downsizing and closing more than nine hundred stores across the U.S. But he did not stop there. He also breathed *soul* back into Starbucks.

Barely a month after his reappointment, Schultz boldly closed 7,100 stores in the U.S. for three hours to retrain and inspire over 135,000 employees with the Starbucks mission: To enrich people's lives for one moment, one human being, one extraordinary cup of coffee at a time. Systematically, he removed anything in the Starbucks experience that undermined the company's higher purpose, and introduced everything he could to support it. Since the low point of Starbucks's share price at the end of 2008, it has nearly tripled in value over the same period of time that the Dow Jones Industrial Average grew by only 20 percent.

Both Kurus Elavia and Howard Schultz have mastered the art of creating exceptional shareholder value by using their own values and worldviews to breathe *soul* into their corporations, giving new life to the connection between their companies and their customers. Being true to one's own values in this process is what gives companies like Gateway Group One and Starbucks their authenticity, an authenticity that cannot be imitated by other organizations. Countless examples have proven that the *soul* of a corporation is core to its competitive advantage. But what happens when the *corporate soul* is downplayed, or dismissed altogether? This often happens after mergers, when neither of the merging entities extends its soul to the other, nor is the new entity given a distinct *corporate soul* of its own. Companies can lose a lot of value in these situations. Hewlett-Packard learned this lesson the hard way.

William Hewlett and David Packard started their company in a garage behind Packard's Palo Alto home in 1938. By 1997, annual net revenue exceeded forty-two billion dollars, and HP had become the world's second-largest computer supplier.[35]

In 1999, Carly Fiorina, a hugely dynamic and brilliant woman, became CEO of HP. She was the first outsider, the first woman, the first non-engineer, and the youngest person ever to head HP. Her appointment triggered a major rise in the value of HP stock, but before very long, she had to face a spiraling downturn, both in the technology industry and in the company itself. HP turned to the usual strategies to cut costs and improve operational efficiency, but by September 2001, HP's market capitalization value had fallen to less than half of its level when Fiorina was hired.

Fiorina was convinced that turning the company around required more than just operational improvement. On September 3, 2001, she announced that HP would acquire Compaq in the largest-ever deal in the history of the computer industry. The new company would operate in more than 160 countries with over 145,000 employees. HP-Compaq would offer the most complete set of products and services in the industry.

The two companies lost an estimated thirteen billion dollars of market capitalization within two days of the merger announcement, and industry analysts referred to the deal as a strategic blunder. Fiorina believed the merger would offer an advantage in persuading solution providers and customers to switch allegiances and product lines, especially if the Compaq logo were to disappear. How wrong she turned out to be. But what went wrong?

When two companies merge, financial experts conduct due diligence, scrupulously studying all the mechanical and financial aspects of the merger and exploring its potential synergies. But seldom does anyone study how to merge the *corporate souls* of the two companies into a new one or how to leverage human energy for the creation of greater economic value. As in most mergers, this aspect of the HP-Compaq merger never got the up-front attention it deserved, and this may have contributed to its failure to deliver the anticipated value.

Corporate soul goes far beyond matters of culture. A company's *corporate soul* manifests itself in the differentiated design of its product offering too. Steve Jobs articulated this perfectly: "Design is the fundamental soul of a man-made creation that ends up expressing itself in successive outer layers of the product or service."[36]

When Chrysler and Daimler Benz merged in 1998, it seemed a perfect match. The *New York Times* wrote:

Chrysler was the most American and least international of car companies, known for nimbleness and low costs but not as much for quality. Daimler-Benz was the crown jewel of German industry, a producer of luxury cars with an awesome presence across Europe. What Mercedes sometimes lacked in flair, it made up in superb engineering and one of the best brand names in the world. There was very little overlap between the two, either in the nature of their products or in their geographic coverage.[37]

Jurgen Schrempp, then chairman of Daimler Benz AG and orchestrator of the merger, said: "We are not deciding whether a German or American approach should prevail. The teams are defining best practices that will shape a fantastic new company and give DaimlerChrysler a continuous competitive edge."

However, in the clinical pursuit of best practice, both companies and their brands began to lose their soul, as Mercedes executives became indignant at any hint of having their august brand tainted by a downscale name like Chrysler. The *New York Times* called the merger "one of the biggest losses of shareholder value in history."[38]

Merging two companies structurally and taking costs out of both of them is one thing, but preserving their essence and considering how the people in the new entity will connect with each other and their customers is quite another. Successful mergers happen when the executives recognize the value of *corporate soul* and take steps not to lose it in the hype of the merger process. An example of this was the merger of the highly entrepreneurial Rand Merchant Bank (RMB) with the much larger retail and corporate bank, First National Bank (FNB), to form the FirstRand Group, one of the largest banking groups in Africa and the world. RMB has always had a *corporate soul*, and its three founders—Laurie Dippenaar, G. T. Ferreira, and Paul Harris—regard it as the bank's most treasured competitive advantage. FNB, a huge organization, was one of South Africa's great banks, but had long ago lost its *corporate soul*. Apart from the merger rationale of RMB gaining access to FNB's substantial balance sheet, RMB saw a great opportunity to infuse some of its soul and culture into the highly structured and somewhat stodgy FNB. This, they believed, could unlock hitherto untapped human energy and economic value.

RMB had one fear about the merger: what if the opposite happened and the large new entity polluted the soul of RMB? Their awareness of this possibility and how much value it would destroy was key to their ensuring that it didn't occur. We at Lapin International were consultants to FNB at the time, and RMB engaged us to help make sure the RMB soul stayed healthy and, if anything, grew in its energy and power. RMB has retained its soul and continued to grow and to thrive, now extending its reach throughout the African continent and into India and China. One of the keys to RMB's astounding success was that for several years after the merger Paul Harris remained at the helm of RMB, and after he took over as CEO of FirstRand, RMB appointed CEOs who lived the bank's soul and safeguarded it. RMB invests in its soul, in its culture, and in the ongoing growth of its leaders, who are not only competent investment bankers, but also great human beings.

But why, some might ask, would an almost spiritual concept like the *corporate soul* be fundamental to economic success? The answer is that spirituality is, in fact, what makes us creative human beings, distinguished from every other living creature. It makes each of us unique and different from every other person who is living or ever did live. Our spirituality provides us with the capacity to create ideas and products that are unique and different from those created by others, and differentiation is the core of any competitive business strategy.

Consider entrepreneurs who use intangible assets like intellect, passion, spirit, and inspiration to create something tangible whose value far exceeds the cost of its components. They literally create value *ex nihilo* (out of nothing). In this way, entrepreneurs and business leaders manifest a divine spirituality, partnering with God in the ongoing act of creation. Creating something of value from nothing tangible is not only an economic activity; it is a spiritual activity, too. This is why creating value is an activity governed not only by *natural principles* of economics, but also by *universal principles* of spirituality. It is why corporations have souls.

Knowing how to use the universal principles of spirituality that we discussed in Part One to create a corporation with soul is an indispensable skill in business leadership. And the most fundamental way to instill this sense of soul in your company is to inspire it through your actions.

CHAPTER EIGHT

INSPIRING CHANGE

*Inspiration is a spiritual idea; people are
only truly inspired at a spiritual, soul level.*

THE THINGS that inspire people to go that extra mile, stretching themselves to achieve and innovate, cannot be quantified. Daniel Pink in his book *Drive*, Simon Sinek in *Start with Why*, Chip Conley in *Peak*, and many other current authors are citing volumes of research showing that it isn't the promise of a pay raise or a promotion that binds people into extraordinarily synchronized teams. As important as tangible recognition is, that isn't what inspires people to do the spectacular. Tangible reward may temporarily motivate, but it cannot inspire. Inspiration is a spiritual idea, and people are only truly inspired at a spiritual or soul level.

Even in the work environment, people crave inspiration. Inspired people put the needs of others before their own interests and give of themselves in heroic ways that exceed anything imaginable in an uninspired environment. Companies that inspire their employees and their customers on intangible, almost spiritual, levels exude soul. This unappreciated fact is what prevents many brilliant companies from achieving their true potential.

Truly great leaders don't rely on their functional expertise or technical background. Great business leaders become experts in converting the spiritual dynamics of human energy into growth and economic value. They do this by inspiring people, connecting with them in a meaningful way, and tapping into their human spirit.

To make this connection with people, however, we need to first understand what makes them tick at a deep soul level. What inspires people to go that extra mile and do those heroic things that distinguish some companies from others? What influences people to choose to do the right thing over the easy thing, and what sometimes holds them back from doing things they know are right? To channel the energy of our teams, we must be able to identify what it is that truly drives them.

Channeling Human Energy

People do what they know is wrong when they are not willing to pay the price for doing what's right.

If only we could energize people by simply telling them what to do! It's been attempted many times, but great leaders know it takes more than an imposing command from on high to inspire enthusiasm for work and a desire to live up to expectations. For the most part, people already know what's expected of them. And even though they understand these expectations, they often still fail to perform. So, repeatedly telling people what they are *supposed* to be doing is likely to be counterproductive. There are underlying causes for people's lack of effort and results, and by understanding and addressing these causes, one can change things on a sustainable basis.

As with most leadership (and life) challenges, the explanation of why people don't do what they know is right lies within us. Our own life would also be simple if we always did what we know is right, wouldn't it? The truth is, we don't always do the right thing even when we know what's right, and nor do the people we supervise and lead.

Why is this? Why do we constantly let others and ourselves down? Why do we make New Year's resolutions and not carry them out? Why do people register with gyms and not attend? Why do people promise themselves to be more attentive spouses or parents and quickly revert to old patterns? Is it because they no longer believe in the goals they set? Did they undergo a sudden transformation in their beliefs and values? Clearly not!

Across the global spectrum of cultures, educational levels, and social status, people generally have a pretty good idea of what is right and what is wrong. Their definitions of right and wrong are not very different from yours or mine. Yet, some people do what they know is right, and others do what they know is wrong.

The reason for this is that our actions are not always driven by our beliefs and values. Sometimes our instincts drive our behavior. This does not excuse bad or illegal conduct; it merely explains what is happening when we behave in ways that contradict our own values. If you choose an unhealthy dish from a restaurant menu, it does not mean that you do not believe in the importance of good health. It just means that in that moment you made a choice based on impulse rather than on values.

This is one of the things that makes humans so different from animals. Animals are driven only by their instincts; they do not have values. Instinctively they know what is good for them and what is bad for them. We have instincts, too, and our instincts help keep us in touch with our bodies and our environment. But unlike animals, we have values that we use when we make conscious choices against our instincts. For example, even when we are extremely hungry, we may choose not to eat the dish of mouthwatering food in front of us because it isn't good for our health or because it doesn't belong to us. Animals cannot make such choices. Whenever people do something creative or moral that takes effort, they are overriding their instinct with a value-based choice. However, when little Jimmy walks down the aisle of a supermarket and puts a pack of gum in his pocket without intending to pay for it, he is acting on impulse. Instead of overriding his instincts with a value choice his parents taught him, he succumbs to his immediate desire. He acts on impulse not because he doesn't know he is doing wrong, but because, at that moment, he is not willing to "pay the price" of doing what is right.

People do what they know is wrong when they are not willing to pay the price for doing what's right. It's as simple as that. We see this in other areas of life, too. You and I may both agree that an Aston Martin is the best car on the road, but neither of us may possess one. This is not because we don't accept the *value* of an Aston Martin, but simply because we are not willing to pay its *price*. The same applies to human values: we often accept and agree on a value, but are unwilling to pay its price in time, money, effort, or self-discipline. When people act on instinctual impulse and do things they know are wrong, whether because they do not have the strength of character to resist or because they were just not paying attention at the time, they exhibit what I call a *values-ethic gap*. A values-ethic gap is the gap between people's values—what they *believe* to be good and right—and their *behavior*, their ethic. For the purpose of this discussion, we'll define *ethic* as the degree to which one lives according to one's values when doing so entails discipline, effort, cost, or restraint.

Some years ago, I headed a research team to explore the effect of people's cultures on their work ethic and productivity levels. We studied a population of about twenty thousand employees from eleven different language groups and over thirty different cultures at a large mining company. The study spanned management levels from CEOs to laborers and educational levels from PhDs to people who could barely read. We found no significant difference in the values of the people we studied. All of them, for example, rated accepting a bribe as an action that is nearly as unethical as theft. However, when we asked them whether they would accept gifts from suppliers if they were purchasing managers in their company, we were surprised with the results. We gave them a range of gifts to consider, from a pen and pencil set at Christmas to an overseas vacation for two. More than 55 percent said they would accept some level of gift without checking with their supervisors, and over 36 percent said they would accept the overseas vacation.[39]

This is when I coined the term *values-ethic gap*. The employees in this study were not willing to pay the price of turning down an offer for an overseas vacation in order to uphold their value of honesty. They knew that accepting a bribe was wrong. But when refusing a bribe would entail the loss of a once-in-a-lifetime travel opportunity, they were ready to sacrifice their values for a tangible reward.

Just as people often have gaps between their values and their ethic, so can corporations. Corporations know the difference between right and wrong, but often choose to do what is wrong. They do what they know is wrong when they are not willing to pay the price for doing what's right.

Consider Enron. Enron had good values on the face of things. According to the company's 2000 annual report,[40] Enron's values were:

Communication

We have an obligation to communicate. Here, we take the time to talk with one another and to listen. We believe that information is meant to move and that information moves people.

Respect

We treat others as we would like to be treated ourselves. We do not tolerate abusive or disrespectful treatment.

Integrity

We work with customers and prospects openly, honestly, and sincerely. When we say we will do something, we will do it; when we say we cannot or will not do something, then we won't do it.

Excellence

We are satisfied with nothing less than the very best in everything we do. We will continue to raise the bar for everyone. The great fun here will be for all of us to discover just how good we can really be.

As history showed, when the rewards for transgressing their values became stratospheric, Enron's leadership was unwilling to pay the price to uphold those values. Instead, their shareholders paid. Enron's values-ethic gap destroyed more than sixty billion dollars of shareholder value.

Johnson & Johnson, on the other hand, truly confronted its soul in the famous Tylenol case of the 1980s. Tylenol was the most successful over-the-counter product in the United States, with over one hundred million users. Tylenol was responsible for 19 percent of Johnson & Johnson's corporate profits during the first three quarters of 1982, and accounted for 13 percent of Johnson & Johnson's year-to-year sales growth and 33 percent of the company's year-to-year profit growth.

During the fall of 1982, an unknown individual (or individuals) replaced Tylenol Extra-Strength capsules with cyanide-laced capsules and deposited the resealed packages on the shelves of several pharmacies and food stores in the Chicago area. The poisoned capsules were purchased, and seven people died. Johnson & Johnson chairman, James Burke, formed a seven-member strategy team. They believed that pulling the Tylenol product nationally could fatally wound Johnson & Johnson. They consulted their company credo, crafted by their first chairman, Robert Wood Johnson, forty years before. The credo is: "Put the needs and well-being of the people we serve *first*." Burke guided the team by first asking, "How do we protect the people?" and second, "How do we save this product?" Risking the future of their company, they ordered the national withdrawal of all Tylenol products until they could assure the public of their safety.

Both Enron and Johnson & Johnson had good values. Enron's demise was the result of its values-ethic gap. Johnson & Johnson lived their values despite the grave potential cost of doing so. They had no values-ethics gap. They survived the Tylenol crisis, they grew, and they thrived.

Getting People to Do What's Right

Wouldn't it be remarkable if instead of leading teams that are motivated by the desire for reward, we could lead teams that are inspired to heroic acts of selflessness?

If people do what they know is wrong because they are not willing to pay the price of doing what's right, then how do we get them to do what's right? This question is the foundation of management and motivational theory, a theory that is so obvious when we *get* it, yet for a long time we have been getting it so horribly wrong. The way we have been managing people at work and in our personal lives, has accessed only a fraction of their potential and has failed to inspire them to greatness.

Modern management theory started with Frederick Winslow Taylor's *Principles of Scientific Management* more than one hundred years ago. Taylor made a great contribution to the way industry began to think about process efficiency, but he had a pretty dim view of the worker, a view that became entrenched in management thinking for decades. He believed people work only for what they can get and not for what they can give and that they need to be tightly controlled and autocratically managed. Describing the kind of worker needed in the iron industry, for example, he wrote:

> *One of the first requirements for a man who is fit to handle pig iron as a regular occupation, is that he shall be so stupid and so phlegmatic that he more nearly resembles in his mental makeup the ox, than any other type.*[41]

Henry Ford implemented Taylor's system in his manufacturing plants and talked openly about "the reduction of the necessity for thought on the part of the worker."[42] But in 1943, American psychologist Abraham Maslow (1908–1970) challenged Taylor's view of human motivation. He postulated that once people's basic physiological needs are taken care of, they become more motivated by needs of a higher order: love, belonging, aesthetics, and self-actualization.[43] But businesses still ignored the Maslow model and continued to measure, manage, and reward people as if they operated only at the lower reaches of his now-famous hierarchy of needs; as if they were as stupid and as phlegmatic as Taylor's ox.

In 1960, Douglas McGregor of MIT, built on Maslow's theory and spoke of two management models suited for two different motivational drives; his *X-Y Theory*.[44] Some people, he argued, are much like Taylor's description of the worker: they prize security and avoid responsibility. These people are most effectively managed by an autocratic style, or what he called *Theory-X* management. His *Theory-Y* management model is more suited for people who embrace responsibility, enjoy their work, and seek opportunities to maximize their contributions in return for commensurate reward. However, even after McGregor's theories were published, businesses, by and large, continued to use *Theory–X* in the way it measured, managed, and rewarded everyone.

It is true that in management-speak we often hear *Theory-Y* ideas expressed. However, the old and ineffective *Theory-X* still prevails as the ethos of management *action*. This ethos encourages people to do what is right, either by manipulation or by intimidation (without calling it that, of course). Either we offer employees carrots—continued employment, raises, bonuses, promotions, and management approval—when they do what we want them to do, or we threaten them with a stick—career limits, sacrifice of bonus, and possible demotion or termination—when they don't. When you think about it, this is not too different from the way we train our pets; rewarding them when they do what we want them to do and withholding reward when they disobey. Humans have instincts, too, and so intimidation and manipulation, stick and carrot, generally work to motivate us. Like all living creatures, we fear pain and discomfort and we enjoy reward, so we jump through hoops to get our promised prizes. But managing behavior in this way motivates only the animal, instinctual part of people; it fails to inspire the hero in them. It gets people to do the minimum they can to avoid negative consequences and receive rewards, but it does not spark their souls or ignite their genius.

It was in the 1980s that managers were taken by surprise at the flight of talent from "brick and mortar businesses" to much lower paying and harder working jobs in Silicon Valley. Bright young people in the early days of the Internet Age were no longer interested in businesses that saw humans as mindless functions of production. They saw themselves as resourceful powerhouses of creative ideas and motivated masters of implementation. In their new start-ups, free from corporate tyranny, many of them began to unveil wave after wave of breakthrough innovation and an explosion of productivity that shattered all prior assumptions about motivation and reward. They built systems to do the ox-work of business, which freed them to do what only humans can: connect with and inspire other people—peers, employees, investors, and customers. In 2000, Geoffrey Colvin, editor-at-large of *Fortune Magazine*, wrote:

> *The message for business people at this century's dawn, just the opposite of 100 years ago, is that management is a human art and getting more so as infotech takes over the inhuman donkey work—the ox work—of the world. Most managers now seem to understand that they will find competitive advantage by tapping employees' most essential humanity, their ability to create, judge, imagine, and build relationships.*[45]

In 2009, Daniel Pink explained what he believed motivated this new cadre of worker:

> "Our current business operating system—which is built around external, carrot-and-stick motivators—doesn't work and often does harm. We need an upgrade…This new approach has three essential elements: (1) Autonomy—the desire to direct our own lives; (2) Mastery—the urge to get better and better at something that matters; and (3) Purpose—the yearning to do what we do in the service of something larger than ourselves."[46]

In a 2010 Technology Entertainment and Design (TED) lecture, Chip Conley, Founder & CEO of Joie de Vivre Hospitality took these management ideas even further. He said: "Business must create the conditions for employees to live their calling." That's a far cry from Taylor's requirement that a worker should be "stupid and phlegmatic."

When did this new trend that recognizes the humanity of management start? I believe the father of this "new" thinking articulated by Colvin, Pink, Conley, and others, was neither Maslow nor McGregor. I believe it has its roots in a quiet revolution against the very foundation not only of Taylor's thinking, but of Maslow's thinking, too. This quiet revolution started only three years after Maslow first published his Hierarchy of Needs, but its relevance to business was not appreciated until now. It was the work of famous Austrian psychiatrist Viktor Frankl (1905-1997), work that inspired so much of what I have taught and implemented in my clients' companies over the past twenty years.

In 1946, Viktor Frankl published *Ein Psychologe erlebt das*

Konzentrationslager, better known in English as *Man's Search for Meaning*. In it he shows, based on his observations of his fellow inmates in the Nazi concentration camps of World War II, how "spiritual life strengthened the prisoner, helped him adapt, and thereby improved his chance of survival." Frankl's work differed fundamentally from Maslow's, although few people recognize how profound the difference really is.

Maslow's Hierarchy of Needs

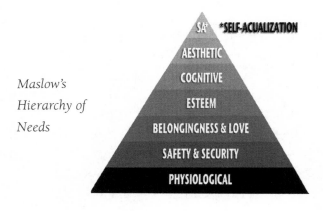

The Creative Heroic Drivers

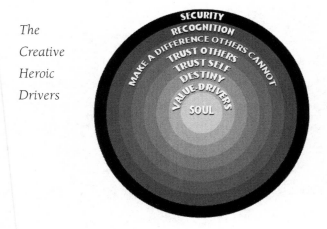

Maslow argued that people's higher needs for self-actualization, intellectual and aesthetic appreciation, self-esteem, and love can only be satisfied after the physiological security is firmly in place. People who are starving, Maslow believed, will not pursue higher goals until their basic needs have been met. Frankl disagrees.

Frankl argues that meaning, purpose, love, and self-actualization are critical not only for a sense of well-being, but also for a person's physical survival. Everyone has a soul, a spiritual life, and everyone needs a sense of higher purpose. A sense of higher purpose is so important to people, that when they have to choose, many put their higher values before their own survival. This is the phenomenon of heroism.

Frankl points out[47] that Maslow failed to explain what it is that drives even very poor people to act heroically at times, risking their survival for the sake of something higher, the meaning of their existence, their *spiritual lives*. No one, irrespective of their financial or social situation, should be managed purely by McGregor's *Theory-X*, and certainly no one ever should be treated as Frederick Winslow Taylor suggested. Treating people with human dignity and allowing them to express their purpose are not just moral imperatives. These are the conditions in which humans thrive; these conditions drive innovation and unlock economic productivity.

Wouldn't it be remarkable if, instead of leading teams motivated only by the desire for reward, we could lead passionate teams inspired by the meaning of their work to heroic acts of selflessness? The fact is we can; but only if, in addition to extrinsic reward, we master new ways of inspiring people to a higher purpose and tapping into more than their instinct for survival.

When we motivate people only with extrinsic rewards

and stimulants like motivational talks and rah-rah rallies, we are manipulating their instinctual operating systems for our advantage, and usually for their advantage, too. So long as the reward is available, and provided they need it, they will do what it takes to get it. But like an animal in a research study, they will do the minimum work needed to get the reward, and if they are offered bigger rewards elsewhere, they will leave.

Humans, however, are driven by more than their animal instinct of survival. They can make intentional choices at times *not* to follow their instinct. For example, sometimes, people choose to die for a cause in which they believe. Many men and women in law enforcement and the Armed Forces make that choice every day as they risk their lives for society's sake. Explorers and adventurers, including those who have explored outer space and walked the face of the moon, all risked their survival for something bigger than themselves. This is a choice no animal could make. It is in this choice that we find a uniquely human trait: heroism.

People are often inspired to do the most amazing things for others for no apparent reward, and choose to forgo opportunities for wealth in order to uphold a principle they believe in. Think about it. Can we really pay our astronauts or soldiers enough to justify the risks they take? Do we pay our teachers and nurses commensurately to the value of their dedication and work? And yet they continue to contribute far in excess of how we could remunerate them.

When inspired, people go above and beyond the value of the reward we offer them. People are not merely animals guided by instinct; they can be heroes. Heroism is a function of the human spirit, not a function of people's egoistic instinctual needs. To inspire heroism in the people we lead, we need to understand much more about the human spirit, and particularly about the two different, but parallel, operating systems that power it.

CHAPTER NINE

TWO OPERATING SYSTEMS

*Humankind is both an instinctual animal
and an inspired hero majestically fused into a single,
integrated, magnificent being.*

THERE ARE TWO "operating systems" that drive human behavior and that function side by side. They are our *defensive survival
instinct* and our *creative, heroic drive*, and we are free to choose which
of the two operating systems we wish to follow in any given moment
of our lives. This choice is the most significant choice we ever make,
because everything else flows from it. Both of these operating systems
are founded on a need for security and well-being. But whereas one
system protects our physical security, the other maintains our spiritual
well-being. Our defensive instinct resides in our physical bodies; while
our creative, heroic drive, almost divine in nature, resides within our
souls. (By the term *soul*, I simply mean that uniquely human quality
that differentiates us from every other living organism.) Humankind is

both an instinctual animal and an inspired hero majestically fused into a single, integrated, magnificent being.

Instinctual Animals

In some ways, we are all similar and predictable. We all get hungry when we haven't eaten, crave safety, and enjoy sex. We have the same reflexes, as well. We laugh when we are tickled, and our legs jerk upward when a doctor taps our knee with a rubber hammer. This is because we, and all animals, share the same basic reflexes and instincts. Unlike animals, though, we humans can override our instincts and make choices to act in ways that are contrary to our instinctual drives. Instinct is a mechanical response, but by conditioning ourselves to act against our instincts, we can develop habits that become virtually automatic.

The most powerful instinctual drive is the instinct for survival, a desire for protection from physical harm. Animals rely on this instinct for their survival, but humans also need the survival instinct to protect them from physical harm. When we feel threatened, our instincts kick in automatically, sometimes even subconsciously. If we are about to fall, we instantly put our hands out to soften the impact. If someone raises a hand to strike us, we lift our arms to protect our face. Sometimes our protective instinct causes us to strike out at the person threatening us. We use instinct not only for our individual protection, but also to protect those we love.

However, if we default into survival instinct when our physical safety is not under threat, instinct can get in the way of our heroism, introducing fear where there is no need for it. When we are not physically threatened, we function far better if we make proactive and creative choices based on our values instead of defaulting to instinctual defensiveness. Here is a good example of this: When we make a sales call, we might feel a fear of rejection. We are not threatened by any physical harm when we make that call, yet our fear can paralyze us. The outcome of the call will be better for us if we are driven by our sense of purpose and values in knowing that we are offering our prospect a product or service that will meaningfully improve their lives, rather than being driven by fear of failure or rejection.

We generally default into instinctual defensiveness when one or more of the three *value-drivers* that are nearest the core of our own *Spiritual Fingerprints*, are attacked, challenged, or undermined. These *value-drivers* are so foundational to our identities that when they are attacked, we feel as if we are being physically attacked and we respond accordingly. We confuse the emotional pain of this situation with physical danger. Just as our ancestors fought or fled from physical danger, we fight and flee from emotional danger. The problem is that, while fight or flight is appropriate in the face of physical danger, this same behavior in the face of emotional danger causes deep problems in relationships and in the journey to personal and leadership greatness. Emotional pain is an almost inevitable outcome of personal growth and development as a human being; by holding on to our emotional safety we can sometimes miss an opportunity for deep fulfillment. This is what happens when a boy won't call a girl for fear of rejection, or when someone refuses to make a comment in a public forum for fear of ridicule. Unless we have achieved a level of self-mastery, fear of pain triggers defensiveness, irrespective of whether it's physical or emotional pain. Even an imaginary threat can trigger fear and cause defensive behavior that shuts us down.

When we become defensive, we close ourselves to other people and block the channels of authentic communication between us. When someone criticizes us, we might shut down to avoid the discomfort of the criticism, or we might get aggressive, turning our anger toward the person criticizing us. Because we don't give ourselves the time to check the other person's intentions, we become incapable of hearing what the other person is really saying to us, and communication breaks down.

Inspired Heroes

Considering how powerful the survival instinct is, the existence of human heroism has baffled researchers for centuries. In 1871, Charles Darwin wrestled with the problem of heroic acts when he said, "He who was ready to sacrifice his life, as many a savage has been, rather than betray his comrades, would often leave no offspring to inherit his noble nature."[48] What instinctive force, based on Darwin's theory of natural selection, could drive someone to do that? The answer is that heroism has nothing to do with instinct.

Darwin's theory of natural selection and Maslow's hierarchy of needs explain the instinctual self well, but neither explains what drives heroes to acts of magnificent self-sacrifice. These theories seem to set forth that human beings have only one operating system, an instinctual one that sometimes sublimates to higher instinctual needs like self-actualization. But this is simply not true. In addition to our survival instinct, we are driven by a separate force that is not instinctual. This is the force of creative choice and a heroic urge to make a difference to others even, sometimes, at the expense of our own immediate interests. This second force is spiritual in nature, not physical, and this is why it is unique to humans.

Unlike our bodies that are fragile and can be easily damaged or destroyed, our souls are not as fragile and do not need to pursue survival and security. Impervious to physical harm, our souls are naturally secure in ways that our bodies cannot be. This frees our souls to strive for loftier things; for the fulfillment of a purpose higher than our own survival, the fulfillment of our divine destinies, and the pursuit of our values. At all times, even when hungry and tired, our spiritual strivings are present, and they require satisfaction right alongside our physical needs. In fact, when our spiritual needs are being satisfied, our prospects for physical survival and material success are also much, much higher. Hela Blumenthal is a living testimony to this.

Mrs. Blumenthal is the mother of a client of mine, and one of only three people still living who survived a Nazi gas chamber during World War II. She is a sprightly and elegant lady in her nineties, who survived both the Warsaw Ghetto, destroyed by the Nazis in 1943, and later the Nazi death camps. I asked her what kept her going through those dark years. "I knew that God had a purpose in keeping me alive when everyone around me, including my entire family, had perished. My purpose was to keep my young niece alive and to survive to tell the world what happened."

Each night in the camp, she would break her only slice of stale bread into two pieces. One she ate; the other she kept under her head when she slept, and gave to her niece (if it wasn't stolen or eaten by rats by then), whom she knew would have finished her own ration by morning. By helping her niece each day, Hela gave a meaning to her life that was higher than her own survival. Paradoxically, as Viktor Frankl observed in those very camps, people who shared their minute rations with others lived for a higher purpose and had a higher survival rate than those who stole other people's food.

Both the instinctual and heroic operating systems have the quest for security as their common foundation, but whereas the need to protect our *physical security* drives our survival instinct, we feel *spiritually secure* when we make a meaningful difference to others. The human soul does not need protection; it needs nourishment. *Meaning nourishes the soul. Purpose drives it.*

The problem is that we cannot be inspired heroes all the time; we have physical survival needs, too. On the other hand, we are not solely made up of an instinct for survival, we also crave higher goals: to inspire and be inspired, to make a difference in the world. Our two "operating systems," instinctual and heroic, function side by side, and both need constant nourishment. When we lead others, we need to lead both of their operating systems to greatness. We need to *motivate* their mechanical, instinctual operating system with extrinsic reward and recognition. We also need to *inspire* their human, creative operating system with a sense of meaning and higher purpose.

The Great Motivator

This is the art of leadership: to create in people a feeling that inspires them to heroic acts of self-sacrifice for a purpose bigger than themselves.

Sean Barry (name changed to protect privacy) was VP of sales in a large insurance company. He was a driven man overflowing with energy and had delivered phenomenal results throughout his career. When we met, he was already looking forward to his retirement and wanted to leave his company and his team on a high. He had good people skills, was liked by his customers, and was revered by his team. One of his largest teams, however, was underperforming. Not only were they failing to hit their targets, but they were also selling products that were not in their customers' best interests. "They're using customers to push products, not products to satisfy customers," Sean complained to me. He asked if I would give them a "high-powered motivational session." Before doing so, I told Sean that I wanted to be sure I understood what the problem was; I wanted to check whether the low level of motivation was truly the cause of the lackluster performance or whether it was the symptom of something deeper. The benefit of a motivational talk would be short-lived if the problem was more fundamental.

"Is the problem that they are unmotivated or that they are uninspired?" I asked Sean. "What's the difference?" he asked. "Well, think about it," I explained. "You motivate people by promising them some form or another of reward for reaching certain goals. You can make them more motivated by introducing some fun and competition into the process."

"We've done all that; that's the 'ABCs' of sales," Sean said, with a touch of irritation in his voice.

"Oh, then," I said, "so perhaps what you are complaining about is that they are *uninspired*, not that they are *unmotivated*. *Motivation* is **ex**trinsic; it comes from wanting something outside you, like reward and recognition. *Inspiration* is **in**trinsic; people can be inspired even when there is no reward for what they are doing. This being the case, there is no need for me to even meet with your team yet. They are not the whole problem, and even if they are, *you* are the solution! We have a leadership challenge here, not a motivational one."

Sean took the critique well, and we started working together on how he could quickly improve his competence as a more inspirational leader.

I shared with Sean the story of the very first major consulting project I ever pitched. I had to present to a group of some two hundred senior executives, mainly engineers and accountants, at a large multinational company. I grappled with how I could ignite their interest. This challenge got much worse when I realized that my pitch was scheduled to follow a presentation by another consultant, Ian Thomas. Ian is a brilliant presenter and his material is captivating. Before going into the field of corporate training, he was a game ranger and photographer in Africa and had developed a series of dynamic audiovisual presentations. One of these presentations, "The Power of the Pride," magnificently depicts the interdependence between individual lions and their teams on wild hunts in the jungle. How was I going to capture the interest of an audience who had just experienced the energy of Ian's safaris into the African jungle?

At the podium, I struggled to get the excited audience to settle down. When they did, I asked them to share with me some of what Ian had taught them. Pandemonium broke out as all of them began talking at once about different aspects of Ian's powerful presentation. Picking up on his "pride" theme, I talked about how lions emote pride to master territory and dominate competitors and asked them whether they believed that lions can make each other feel proud—or better yet, whether a lion could make a monkey feel proud. Now, I had their attention. They fidgeted in their seats and shook their heads. "You see," I explained, "you didn't see lions do that in Ian's presentation, because although lions can show pride, they cannot make other animals feel proud, too—only humans can make others feel proud. Only humans can create a specific emotion in others and transmit feelings to others that move them to action. This is the art of leadership: to create in people a feeling that inspires them to heroic acts of self-sacrifice for a purpose bigger than themselves. Lions cannot inspire others, only humans can. And that is why we should never learn leadership skills from animals."

We got the project, and Sean got the point.

One does need motivational programs of reward and consequence in place, and one does need to manage people's performance. But performance management alone should not be what drives one's teams. This is somewhat akin to the fact that we need laws in society and punishments for transgressing them. But wouldn't you be disappointed if your child told you that the reason she doesn't cheat or steal is because she doesn't want to go to jail? When people feel uninspired, the carrot and stick keep them focused on doing the right thing. But as often as possible, we would like to know that they are doing the right thing for a greater reason, not merely for the desire of a reward or for fear of consequences. We are at our best, not when our actions are triggered by our instinct to survive, but rather when we act from our values, inspired heroism, and a sense of higher meaning.

Meaning in Work

Money can motivate, but no amount of money can inspire. People are inspired by ideas and by ideals.

People find meaning in what they do when there is a worthy reason *why* they are doing it, a purpose. *What* they do and *how* they do it is mechanical; a job. The *why* should be an ideal, a calling, a mission. People do not find meaning in making money for shareholders, even if they get a share of that money themselves. Money can motivate, but no amount of money can inspire. People are inspired by ideas and by ideals. They are inspired when they are doing something for a purpose beyond any individual's or group's own egocentric interests. The money physicians make might motivate them, but it will never inspire them. They are more likely to feel inspired by the breakthrough technology they are using to save people's lives. Politicians can be motivated by the promise of power, but they are inspired by the difference they can make to the lives of millions and the legacy they can leave for future generations.

One thing to remember is that not everyone will be inspired by the same things. Individuals inspired by teaching may not be inspired by working in the business world. Things that inspire doctors may not inspire politicians. People feel inspired when the *why* of what they do is aligned with their specific *Personal Purpose* and *Spiritual Fingerprint*. You will only feel inspired when you are dedicated to something that is authentic to you, not to someone else. The higher purpose of your work should occupy an important place in your own personal understanding of life. This is where leadership becomes a true art.

Let's go back to Sean and his uninspired team. Lapin International's *Lead by Greatness* coaches were now ready to work with the team directly. Each member of Sean's team mapped his or her own *Spiritual Fingerprints*, and explored their own *Personal Purposes*. Then we worked with each of them individually, probing the essence of what inspired them and what kind of difference each wanted to make in the world. Sean pulled out various letters written to him by customers who had appreciated his company's work. These came from widows who got life insurance payouts when their husbands died, an individual who, through disability insurance coverage, could afford home care for several years after a debilitating illness, and families whose homes were gutted by fire. Thanks to Sean and his team, each of these people had been fully covered by their insurance, so they could now afford whatever they needed after a time of loss.

Not all of Sean's team members were inspired by the feedback he shared with them. For some, this positive feedback aligned with their own *Personal Purposes* and *Spiritual Fingerprints,* but for others it didn't. Two members of Sean's team found that there wasn't an alignment at all; their values were not about making a difference to others as much as they were about making the money they needed to support their own families. They didn't care much how they made that money, as long as it was legal. The follow-up conversations led one of these individuals to transfer to another part of the business, and led the other to move into a different industry altogether. They were happier after their moves, and so was the team.

We worked with Sean and his team to articulate the team's higher *corporate purpose* and then to build a team culture that supported that purpose and kept people focused on it. We made sure that everyone on the team was excited by the *ideas* the team was generating and inspired by the *ideals* toward which it was now working. Reward systems were aligned to the new culture, which now reflected a very unique *corporate soul*. The team became cohesive and began to perform exceptionally.

When I met up with Sean again some six months later and asked him about the team, he told me that he no longer needed to motivate them. "We watch the numbers and the targets like crazy, but our conversations are no longer about numbers. Our conversations are now about how focused we are on our purpose, and whether our first priority is really to take care of our customers' needs. We talk about whether we are living the team's values and whether our conduct is aligned with our behavioral expectations of one another. The numbers, incidentally, have never been better."

Know Yourself to Know Others

By elevating the way you see yourself and changing the way you see others, they will follow you, not out of fear or manipulation, but be inspired by the greatness you radiate.

Through our conversations with Sean and our workshops with him and his team, he got to know himself more deeply. The ancient Greek maxim, "Know thyself," should be rewritten as, "Know both your selves." Know your instinctual self, which is much like the instinctual self of any other person. But also know your heroic self, the one that is uniquely you. Know your *Spiritual Fingerprint* and your own *Personal Purpose*, because knowing your heroic self and living accordingly will elevate your stature as a person and make you an inspiration to the people around you.

As you become more accustomed to seeing yourself through the lens of your heroic, more spiritual self, you will come to see others through that same lens, too. Looking at people, you will begin to see that they are not always needy creatures trying to get what they can out of you. You will begin to see all people as spiritual beings (who, of course, also have physical needs), who more than anything want to make a difference and be recognized and loved for the contributions they make to the well-being of others. As you appreciate people, show them the recognition they crave and provide them with opportunities to shine, they are certain to become your followers. They will follow you, not out of fear or manipulation, but inspired by the greatness you radiate. They will follow you because they admire you and see the heroic in you, and they will sense that you see the heroic in them, too.

By elevating the way you see yourself and changing the way you see others, they will respond to you differently, too. You will see a reflection of yourself in the people around you. You will see reflections of your leadership in the new ways they respond to you.

Individuals are not the only ones who have two operating systems and can liberate so much human energy by unlocking their inner hero. Teams of people and entire organizations also have these same two operating systems. In a culture based on instinctive defensiveness, everyone wants to take as much as they can and give as little as they have to. The culture of a company or a team is often to blame for this, rather than a lack of accountability. In an inspirational organizational culture, people support one another, share knowledge and information, take responsibility, and accept accountability. The role of a leader in a defensive culture is to manage and control people. In an inspirational culture, a leader motivates and inspires, measures and mentors, and recognizes and rewards people generously for their sacrifices and contributions. Converting a culture from defensive to inspiring is the most exciting and rewarding role of a leader; and it's not just emotionally rewarding. The rewards come in a vibrant, new flow of economic value and human energy. But what is a culture really, and how do you change, build, and nurture it?

CHAPTER TEN

CRAFTING A
GOLDEN CULTURE

*The next big wave of growth will come from businesses
whose leaders know how to convert low-cost intangibles
like culture into high bottom-line value.*

IMAGINE A PERSON from another planet with no prior human experience turning up at a funeral here on Earth. Without having to be told, he would know that a funeral is not an appropriate place to tell jokes. This, Professor Michael Tushman tells his class at Harvard Business School, is the meaning of culture. But culture does more than inform every individual in an organization what attitudes and behaviors are expected of them. Culture also reflects an organization's soul and is responsible for generating human energy. Culture even permeates the customer experience.

The unique experience of a visit to a Disney theme park is created as much by the magical Disney culture as it is by Disney's flawless business process. The same applies to companies like Virgin Atlantic, Whole Foods, Apple, or Starbucks, the uniqueness of whose offerings you have probably experienced. Employees in these companies share a unique culture and use it to create a customer experience that is different from any of their competitors. It is harder for competitors to imitate a deliberately crafted business culture than it is for them to copy a product. And when your business culture underpins your offering, as it does in the cases of these and many other companies, you build unrivaled differentiation for your business and your product.

Like a garden, organizational culture develops whether or not you design it. If you ignore it, it continues to grow, just not necessarily in the ways you might have hoped. Without attention to culture, office politics can proliferate, becoming cancerous and blocking the free flow of information. Fear can inhibit innovation, and people may try to do as little as they can in return for as much as they can get. An unhealthy culture is a pervasive, invisible force that undermines what you do and drains your leadership energy. If you build your culture with care and you nurture and sustain it, it will help you to engage the best talent and lure the most loyal customers.

Although cultivating a great culture demands a lot of emotional investment, leadership wisdom, and a genuine care for people, it is a financially low-cost investment with a high economic return. This is why great leaders pay attention to it. An authentic culture, at the very soul of a business, is something competitors cannot imitate. Like soul, culture is intangible. Yet given a little inspiration, this intangible commodity can be converted into untold wealth. Incredibly, the next big wave of growth will come from businesses whose leaders know how to convert low-cost intangibles like culture into high bottom-line value.

The idea that intangible, spiritual commodities can be converted into tangible wealth is an ancient Kabbalistic concept illustrated in a famous Midrashic[v] story[49] about a Kabbalistic master whose students were very poor. One of them decided to leave the academy and try his luck in business. After some time, having accumulated great wealth, he returned to visit his colleagues and teacher. The other students felt resentful. One said, "We dedicate our lives to matters of the soul and we live in poverty, seeing no reward for our effort. Perhaps like our friend, we too should rather travel and engage in trade to earn money."

The master replied, "If it is money that you value, then come with me to the valley." There, he asked the hills to open up their stores of gold coins and to fill the valley for his students. He explained that when people generate vast spiritual energy, that energy either remains invested in their souls to be drawn upon at any time, or it can immediately be converted into economic value. They could choose to leave their investment in its spiritual currency or they could cash it in for gold and leave.

We are accustomed to thinking that the intangibles of life exist separately from tangible things; material things separated from spiritual, personal things distinct from commercial. This is not so. The knowledge economy has taught us how intangibles like intellectual property and design can be converted into money. Consider how much of the cost of a computer covers its tangible components versus how much you are paying for its technology and software. Tangibles and intangibles are often interchangeable. Material wealth can buy intangibles like lifestyle, time, rich human experiences, and education. In the same way, intangibles like knowledge, wisdom, culture, and caring can generate tangible wealth, too.

Southwest Airlines is probably the greatest success story in

American airline history in terms of turning intangibles into monetary value. Southwest's decades-long dominance of its segment of the airline industry was the product of more efficient operations, flying only one model of aircraft, and removing the frills of travel such as food and pre-assigned seating. However, if those factors alone were responsible for its astounding success even in the toughest of times, then others could have successfully replicated it. Southwest's success was possible because although it stripped the *tangible* commodity of its offering (airline transportation) down to a "no-tangible-frills" minimum, it gave customers something equally valuable in return: a superior *intangible* experience. Southwest gave its customers fun, entertainment, and some genuine human care that compensated for their loss of the tangible features and benefits. The secret, though, is that for this experience to feel authentic, the company's leader, Herb Kelleher, had to build an airline culture that had the properties of fun, entertainment, and genuine care at the very core of its soul.

Southwest converted its intangible culture into tangible benefits, including market share growth. In the two years between 1991 and 1993, it increased its market share in California from 26 percent to 45 percent. The energetic commitment of Southwest's employees achieved a flying cost of 7.1 cents per mile compared to over ten cents for other major airlines. They used only eighty-one employees per aircraft compared to more than 150 needed by competitors. They handled 2,443 passengers per employee compared to only eight hundred to nine hundred by their competitors.[50]

Business school case studies often focus on Southwest Airlines and its founder. However, they seldom acknowledge the most important key to Kelleher's success: his commitment to building intangible competitive advantage with as much vigor as he built tangible operational efficiencies. He invested relentlessly in his company's culture, and guarded and protected it like a fortress. Southwest's competitors cut corners that saved costs but eroded their cultures. Herb only cut those corners that did not impact the culture inside his company. In fact, he invested even more in the Southwest culture when the airline industry was struggling. He knew a safe flight was a commodity that others provided just as well as he could. So he made sure that he offered something they couldn't.

Why could other airlines not do what Southwest did? Because the intangible offering that truly differentiates a company resides in its *corporate soul* and is created by the company's culture and its values, not by its products, process, or structure. Products, process, and structure can be copied, but authentic culture and values cannot. Any company can build its own culture; one that is unique and innate to its people and strategic objectives. But when a company tries to copy another company's culture, it usually fails because culture, as part of the soul of a business, cannot be replicated. Southwest's competitors have at times tried to imitate instead of innovate by copying Southwest's processes, but they haven't been able to replicate its soul. They cannot imitate its values.

A strong culture emerges when leaders consistently act according to their own beliefs, living by their *Spiritual Fingerprints*, no matter what the cost. A strong culture emerges when leaders inspire the heroic in their employees and trust them to excel.

Although there is gold to be found in a good culture, "gold-digging" is not the purpose of great leaders who successfully build *golden cultures*. Southwest's caring for people, both employees and customers, was not conceived merely as a strategy for success. Southwest cares for its people because it believes that is the morally right thing to do. People are not a means to an end (profit), but an end in and of themselves (satisfied customers, happy employees). And, like the piety of the Kabbalistic master's disciples that could be converted into gold, Kelleher's "morality" was changed into gold, too. Success was the *outcome* of caring, not the *reason* for it. Kelleher explains:

> *"Actually we didn't have the notion of people as strategy. It was actually people as morality. We always felt that people should be treated right as a matter of morality. Then, incidentally, that turned out to be good business, too. But it didn't really start as a strategy. It began with us thinking about what is the right thing to do in a business context. We said we want to really take care of these people, we want to honor them, and we love them as individuals. Now that induces the kind of reciprocal trust and diligent effort that made us successful. But the motivation was not strategy; it was core values."*[51]

Southwest consistently stuck to its core values even through hard times.

"We've never had any layoffs in our history, and we will do our best to avoid them," Southwest Airlines CEO Gary C. Kelly said in a *New York Times* interview in January 2009.[52]

Many lesser-known companies have a similar philosophy. Robert Sutton, president of ATS Electric, Inc., told me how, when the economy hit hard times a few years ago, his staff offered to take pay cuts. Robert's response was: "No, I am the only one who takes a pay cut around here."

Leadership philosophies like these build up a large accumulation of trust and respect between employees and management. When time and time again management demonstrates its trust in and respect for its people, they in turn put the company first. This two-way trust and respect unblock channels of communication and liberate the human energy that can make a company succeed.

Organizational "Chi"—Unblocking the Free Flow of Human Energy

The free flow of human energy and information that keeps a company vital, adaptive, and resilient becomes blocked when trust is absent.

Organizations are complex human organisms whose different parts function together in much the same way as the parts of the human body do. Chinese medicine has long recognized that people function best when their energy flows freely throughout their bodies. In just the same way, an organization performs optimally when there is a healthy flow of human energy between the people and the different groups within it. When organizational energy flows freely, people connect to one another and effortlessly align themselves with the organization's purpose and objectives.

Most conventional approaches to organizational effectiveness view the organization in a similar way to how Western medicine studies and treats pain. Western medicine, successful in the instant relief of pain and discomfort, often fails to eliminate the energy blockages that caused the pain in the first place, and so the relief is temporary. Chinese or Asian medicine, on the other hand, believes that most disease and pain is caused by physical or emotional blockages of energy, called *chi* (pronounced *chee*). Rather than treating pain and disease symptomatically, it uses methods like acupuncture, reflexology, yoga, and meditation to unblock these energy passageways. Leading with greatness requires that we view our organizations in a way that more resembles Chinese medicine.

Organizations have their own form of *chi*. The free flow of human energy and information that keeps a company spirited, adaptive, and resilient becomes blocked when trust is absent.

Trust evaporates quickly when employers micromanage their teams because they do not trust them to do the job and make the right decisions. It also happens when managers withhold honest information about the company from their team, or when they fail to share truthful feedback about their team's performance. When people have to cover their backs constantly because they fear office politics and the unbridled ambition of colleagues, the information flow becomes filtered, then distorted, and sometimes grinds to a halt. When trust is low, politics, manipulation, micromanagement, and bureaucracy seep into the organization's culture and dampen its spirit. Mistrust thwarts an organization's entrepreneurial capacity to innovate and quickly adapt to changing conditions.

Building a culture of trust starts with how well one trusts oneself. In the last chapter we talked about how knowing yourself means knowing both your selves: your instinctive, defensive, ego-driven self as well as your creative, heroic self. Do you trust your heroic self? Do you listen to your inner wisdom and make your choices according to your own *value-drivers*, or are you swayed by the expectations and judgments of others? How often do you follow your own *Spiritual Fingerprint*, even when the result could make you unpopular among people who are important to you? Would you switch careers (perhaps for far less money or status) in order to fulfill the purpose for which you believe you were created?

You will notice that every decision you regret was probably made not by your own *Spiritual Fingerprint* and *Personal Purpose*, but by a desire to meet the expectations of others, or to elicit some desired response from them. When we make a decision from our own soul and manage the consequences afterward, we never, ever regret that decision, even if it led to hardship.

Amy Rees Anderson reminds herself of this every day. She has a note to herself on her office wall: "Do what's right, let the consequences follow."

Amy is CEO of MediConnect Global, a company that acquires and digitizes medical information for health and life insurance companies and lawyers. Most of her success came despite tremendous obstacles. She was a single mother of two for a good portion of her career and the sole financial support of her family. She doubled her company's sales year after year, was given the Ernst & Young Entrepreneur of the Year Award in 2007, and went on to become the first woman to receive the MountainWest Capital Network (MWCN) Entrepreneur of the Year Award in 2008. She believes you have to do the right thing irrespective of what other people's reactions might be. You cannot feel responsible for other people's reactions; you have to do what's right and manage the outcomes afterwards. "Sometimes people's reactions can be very hard on you," she says, "but whenever I do what is right, I feel better afterward, no matter what the outcome."

Once you are living and leading by your own *value-drivers* and purpose, make sure that your nonverbal messages are also aligned with your *Spiritual Fingerprint*. It is important that the messages that people in your company pick up from your daily actions are properly aligned with the values that you and your executive team espouse. When an organization's implied values (the behaviors people see in their leaders even during difficult times) align with its espoused values (the values that leaders talk about), the resulting trust not only improves its culture, it also drives its efficiency. However, often, quite unintentionally, leaders send out a different message to their employees by their actions. Leaders may be saying one thing but acting differently under pressure. This undermines trust and blocks the passageways of organizational communication. This is precisely what we found at Superior Plant Manufacturers of North America (name changed to protect privacy).

CHAPTER ELEVEN

ESPOUSED EXPECTATIONS VS. IMPLIED ONES

*Great leaders access the heroic in people and
inspire them to greatness while, at the same time,
holding them accountable for performance outcomes.*

IT IS BETTER for an organization not to espouse its values at all than to flaunt its values but fail to apply and practice them. When employees perceive a disconnect between their organization's espoused values and those that it practices, they lose trust in management, and management often doesn't know the reason why.

Superior Plant Manufacturers of North America is an organization with a long history. It employs nearly fifty thousand people across the country. New CEO Alex Nohaff, a tall, imposing, silver-haired man, was ambitious but gentle; people respected him. Having risen through the ranks, he understood Superior's history and its culture, but he also recognized the urgent need for change. Alex took over at a time when China and other Asian economies were becoming significant players in the manufacturing industry, and it quickly became clear that Superior had to reengineer itself to compete. Superior was already doing some manufacturing in its own plants in Asia and had also subcontracted other manufacturing out to independent Asian companies. Alex was committed to strengthening the U.S. business, both because he was a patriotic American and because he believed that U.S. innovation and the proximity of the U.S. plants to its biggest markets were crucial to Superior's sustainability.

Superior prided itself on its loyal employees, who often spent their entire working careers there—and they were treated well. Alex realized that new technology alone was not enough to save the company; it also needed new standards of efficiency and more flexibility from the staff that had, over the years, become stuck in their routine. The company needed fresh attitudes and a different culture.

Alex and his team simultaneously began to address process improvements and cultural change. As they re-engineered and restructured the company, they incessantly reiterated their mantra that their people were their most important asset. But no matter how hard they worked, they continued losing their best talent and retaining only the mediocre performers. Morale plummeted, process changes were slow and did not deliver the desired efficiencies, customer service deteriorated, and the future of the company looked bleak. Alex was perplexed by this turn of events. Where had they gone wrong?

The Four Implied Employee Contracts

Alex's executive team asked us at Lapin International to figure out what they could do differently. To help Alex and his team I needed to determine which *implied employee contract* prevailed at Superior. *Implied employee contracts* are essential to building a company culture, and there are four of them. We use the term *implied employee contract* to describe the way employees experience and interpret management's expectations of them. The four *implied employee contracts* are:

- We value our people unconditionally.
- We value our people *for what* they contribute to the company.
- We value our people's contributions.
- We value our people *so that* they will increase the contributions they make.

1. We value our people unconditionally.

This *implied contract* means that people in the organization feel valued by leadership as human beings, irrespective of their performance levels. They experience and demonstrate high levels of interpersonal respect, and there is a low tolerance for disrespectful conduct at any level. If the organization employs highly motivated people who are self-starters and driven, then this *implied contract* can create a superb environment. If this is not the case, then a complacent culture of entitlement develops, with low levels of accountability and no sense of urgency.

2. We value our people for what they contribute to the company.

A culture where the implied message is *"we value our people for what they contribute"* makes people feel valued and respected as human beings, provided they do make a meaningful contribution in their work. Non-contributors feel less respected and unrecognized. High performers are not only recognized materially, but are also respected as contributive and valuable human beings. This culture usually generates high performance and accountability levels and nurtures excellence. It is the hardest of the four *implied contracts* to achieve, because it requires the consistent balancing of sharp numeric measurements with genuine human appreciation and respect. Once achieved, however, this contract has no downside.

3. We value our people's contributions.

In a culture where contributions rather than people are valued, fear is the prime motivator. Morale is low, and people who can leave usually do. This *implied contract* is often deliberately used in production plants where skill requirements are relatively low and employees are easily replaced. It is a numbers-driven environment where nothing much matters except hitting targets. A surprisingly large number of companies actually use this contract in their culture, even if management never intends to.

4. We value our people so that they will increase the contributions they make.

In this scenario, management does not truly value people, other than as vehicles of production. However, management realizes that making people feel valued improves their productivity, so they act as though people are valuable as a strategy to improve performance. Their efforts undoubtedly create a more pleasant working environment together with some performance expectations. But it lacks authenticity, and no matter how enthusiastically and consistently management demonstrates their appreciation, the employees sense the absence of authenticity and management's efforts fail to build genuine respect and trust.

At Superior, we found that leadership believed that in the past their *implied contract* had been: *We value you unconditionally.* This had produced a happy environment but not one that was able to meet global competition. They believed that by introducing tougher performance expectations and controls while continuing to emphasize the importance of people, they would successfully change the culture to the second *implied contract*: *We value our people for what they contribute to Superior.*

Unfortunately, the cultural migration that Superior's leadership intended was different from the one that actually occurred. Employees did not experience a cultural shift from: *We value you unconditionally* to *We value you for what you contribute to Superior.* Some employees experienced the culture as: *We don't care about our people at all; we only value their contributions.* Other employees believed that the company's care for them had become nothing more than a soulless, insincere strategy to increase productivity. Alex and his team were espousing: *We value our people for what they contribute to Superior,* but they were acting in ways that implied no genuine care for people's well-being at all. The gap between the espoused beliefs and the actual experiences

147

of the employees was responsible for the erosion of trust and morale.

The management at Superior Plant Manufacturers was right to introduce tighter measurement controls in the business. However, they used these controls to drive the business rather than just to measure it. This was evident by how all their performance-related conversations were about data, never about principles and values. The *why* of the business was never questioned or even referred to, only the *what* and *how*. They should have balanced their tough control measures with inspirational leadership; that would have inspired the employees to greatness while also holding them accountable for performance outcomes. Although it was unintentional, management's single-minded focus on measurements caused the attempted culture-shift to fail.

By inadvertently using the "wrong" *implied contract*, Alex and his team lost the trust of the people of Superior. Processes were becoming more efficient, but the people were not, and customers could feel it.

Is there a "right" *implied contract* for *you* to lead by?

Which Is Right for You?

There is a time and place for each of the four *implied contracts*. In a small professional team of highly motivated, like-minded, competent people, who know what is expected of them, the most appropriate environment may well be *the first implied contract: We value our people unconditionally*. Some great companies have adopted this implied contract at least during certain phases of their evolution. Google operates by this *implied contract*, as do many other successful companies that employ people who share a common passion for the company's work and its products. Southwest Airlines, under Herb

Kelleher, lived this *implied contract* in the belief that most people respond well to it. This does not mean that people in companies like these are not disciplined for poor performance—they are. However, when people are disciplined or even fired, the process is governed by a tone of deep respect, and every effort is made to keep those people's dignity intact.

The third implied contract, *We value our people's contributions*, is sometimes used during a temporary turnaround from one culture to another. It may be necessary to use this contract to undo counterproductive attitudes of entitlement by introducing an environment where the focus is entirely on performance and results. When a company opts to use this contract, it will, at some point, need to shift its focus from performance and results back into valuing people for the results they produce.

The fourth implied contract, *We value our people so that they will increase the contributions they make*, also has its place. Sometimes, when talent is scarce or when there is a need to further train and develop the members of a particular community through on-the-job training in a business, a company must invest in people who may not yet be fully qualified for a given job. In family-owned businesses, sometimes a member of the family will be given a job in the company, even though he or she lacks the qualifications for the position. The intention of this contract is that people will mentor the new employee and invest in him or her with the expectation that he or she will perform well in time. This moral contract was also used in South Africa in the years following the dismantling of apartheid, when there was a need to accelerate the entry of black Africans into management positions long before they were fully qualified. They were then trained and mentored on the job, and many turned out to be exceptionally capable leaders in a very short space of time.

Nearly always, especially when a business is healthy and growing, the *second implied contract, We value our people for what they contribute to the company*, delivers the highest levels of performance and accountability. To propagate this culture, you need to balance and juggle two leadership imperatives. The first is to lead by high principle (*we value our people*) and to make sure that the conversations in the business are chiefly about principles. The second is to relentlessly track performance numbers and to share those numbers so that both managers and employees can measure their contribution (*for what they contribute to the company*). The single most vital skill to building a *golden culture* is an organization's ability to balance its focus between quantitative performance measures and qualitative business and ethical principles.

CHAPTER TWELVE

MEASURES AND PRINCIPLES

*Great leaders focus on the things
that make a business successful,
not the things that measure its success.*

PRINCIPLES, whether strategic or ethical, are qualitative business building blocks. Results are their quantitative output (the completed structure). You can *drive* behavior using principles, values, meaning, and purpose. However, there is only one way to measure the *outcomes* of business, and that is by using quantitative metrics. Great leaders drive by principle, and they measure without sacrificing either the focus on principle or the requirement of measurable delivery. Hany Girgis, one of the many exceptional leaders I know, gets this balance right. Hany was the founder and former CEO of SGIS, a San Diego-based technology solution provider to the intelligence, homeland security, defense, and space communities that was recently acquired by Salient Federal Solutions and owner/partner of SkillStorm, Inc. Both SGIS and SkillStorm have won many national awards, with SGIS ranked tenth on *Entrepreneur Magazine's* 2008 List of the Fastest-Growing Businesses in America. Hany has a fairly simple management philosophy, to which he credits much of his success:

> *"We don't only measure people's financial performance; we measure their adherence to our values, too. In a table of four quadrants, with values as the Y-axis and producing as the X-axis, we get rid of you if you are in the bottom left (low production, low values), we work with you if you're in the bottom right (low production, high values), and we manage you—out of the company, if necessary—if you're in the top left (high production, low values). We have at times had to let top performers go because they didn't live our values."*

The conversations that Hany has with his teams are not only about numbers and measures; they are equally about principles and values.

It might be helpful for you to consider where your team might place your leadership style on the *principles-measures* grid. What

portion of your conversations with them are about measurement, targets, budgets, and numbers, and how much of your conversations are about strategy, vision, values, and principles?

Consider organizations (for example, some not-for-profit organizations) that do very little measuring because there are no consequences for non-performance. Even though these organizations may have a high sense of idealism and a passion for principled purpose, they also run the risk of cultivating *complacency* and limiting ongoing improvement. Even worse are organizations (like some government agencies) where there is a focus neither on measures nor on principles. In these organizations, people's jobs are unconditionally secure and remuneration is not performance-related at all. The culture in this environment is likely to be *apathetic*, with low levels of accountability.

Often, when new leaders come into a poorly performing company and attempt to turn it around, they focus on measurements and consequences in order to instill a culture of accountability. In doing so, they tend to focus on numbers to the exclusion of principles. This tactic often results in instilling *fear and anxiety* in the staff, but not necessarily accountability. When there is fear, people seek scapegoats for errors, hide bad news from management, and create a culture of *culpability*.

Accountability happens when people feel safe enough to take ownership of errors. Some turnaround specialists deliberately move to the bottom right quadrant of the *principles-measures* grid. Their intention is, once they have the measures in place, to introduce principle and shift the culture up into the top right quadrant. The danger with this tactic is that by the time they do this, they may have lost their employees' trust, and a new leader may be needed to re-instill it. The art of leading in the top right quadrant, the quadrant of accountability, is in managing the tension between principle and numbers, between levers of performance and their instruments of measurement. This is the perfect balance of great leadership, and it takes leaders with exceptional character to succeed at it.

Numbers Focus Can Be the Cause of Death

Employees believed that management saw safety as a compliance issue, not an ethical one.

An unbalanced focus on numbers without a simultaneous focus on a principled culture and leadership style is not only financially unsustainable, it can even cause fatalities. I saw this happen in the area of safety in two different industries, mining and electrical utilities, on two different continents. In both cases, the companies appointed new leaders to address the worrying increase in accidents, some of them fatal. The new leaders, seasoned managers and respected professionals, tightened safety policies and procedures, introduced new measurements for safety compliance, and created severe consequence for infringements. In both cases, this resulted in a decrease of reported incidents, but an increase in the number of serious injuries and deaths.

What went wrong? Well, for a start they didn't analyze the root causes for the poor safety records deeply enough. If they had, they would have found that the safety issues had more to do with flawed organizational culture than with inadequate systems and measures. Even the 2010 BP oil spill in the Gulf of Mexico was blamed on "a culture of complacency" by co-chairman of the Presidential Commission of Enquiry, William K. Reilly.[53] In the cases of the mining and utility companies, we found that employees believed the company's interest in safety was more about public image, market perceptions, and saving money than about a genuine care for employees and their well-being. They believed that management saw safety as a compliance issue, not an ethical one.

Leadership had never really created a culture of caring about people and their safety. The new leaders, initially not recognizing the issue as a cultural one, simply tightened the measurement screws; the people responded by underreporting minor incidents to bring their accident records down. The managers were pleased and rewarded those who were reporting fewer incidents. But management was not getting accurate forewarnings of safety infractions; they weren't seeing the warning signals. By the time red lights started to flash and sirens began to wail, it was too late. More serious cases occurred than ever before, and people were losing their lives.

Introducing disciplined measurement and consequence was not a bad thing, in itself. To improve anything, you need to determine the right things to measure and measure them vigilantly. However, everything you measure has a principle that drives it. In these cases, the companies should have balanced their measurement focus with an equal emphasis on the principle of caring about people and their well-being, in the same way as Jay Dorris does in the large Native American

155

enterprises he so successfully leads.

Jay Dorris is a man of exceptional character and is acknowledged as such by his executive team and employees. Jay, an architect by training, has dedicated his working life to helping Native American tribes in the U.S. succeed in their business enterprises and diversify them beyond gaming. Ever mindful of his stewardship of the tribes' valuable assets, he watches the numbers of the enterprises he leads, vigilantly making sure that he not only builds wealth for the tribes but also preserves it and helps them funnel it into social programs and prudent investments. Jay always seems to have a spreadsheet in his hands. He pores over the numbers almost hourly to see where there are opportunities for improvement. In every meeting Jay runs, he uses numeric reports as the framework for conversation. It is interesting though that Jay has never instilled a culture of fear and culpability in the organizations he has led, only a growing awareness of the importance of accountability and a fierce loyalty to the principles by which he leads.

How has Jay achieved the balance between accountability and inspired commitment to principle? He invests as much time and effort on culture, corporate soul, and leadership character as he does on numbers. Jay's team knows that they are accountable for reaching and even exceeding targets, but they also know that no matter what, Jay will support them when they make principled decisions that are aligned with the corporation's values, even when those decisions may result in financial or political cost for him. With his balanced focus on numbers and principles, Jay has built loyal, committed, and engaged teams. But more than that, he also has a track record of delivering results to the tribes that employ him as their CEO beyond the most ambitious targets they could ever have expected. Most recently he and his team grew EBITDA (earnings before interest, taxes, depreciation, and amortization) fivefold in less than four years.

The more you focus your attention on measurements, the more you need to balance that focus with conversations about human and strategic principles, and the more you need to demonstrate authentic human caring.

Once I pointed this out to both the mining company and the utilities organization I was consulting to, they began to speak in earnest publicly about the paramount importance of human life, and to demonstrate authentic compassion for people and their well-being. This gave a new significance and human value to their safety measurements and procedures. People began to follow procedures because they believed in them, not because they feared them. They understood the reasons for procedures and identified with them. They made recommendations for improvements in safety procedures and found countless safer ways to do things throughout the organization.

Management responded to their recommendations and encouraged them. They began to coach and mentor people who were responsible for safety lapses rather than punishing them. They punished them only when their mistakes were repeated or egregious. People started to take more responsibility for their actions and to alert management of potentially dangerous errors. When an accident occurred, management began to investigate root causes from a multidisciplinary perspective, looking not only at the policy infringements but also at possible cultural and leadership flaws. They examined the extent to which people were buying into leadership's principles, not just whether they were complying with their rules.

Not only did the safety record at these companies improve, but so did morale and general levels of employee engagement and productivity. Instead of instilling fear into people, these leaders were now accessing people's higher sense of purpose, humanity, and caring. They had identified the true levers of human behavior and were using them. The results were apparent in numeric measures, too. These numeric measures were authentic and enduring; they were not fraudulently manipulated to give leaders the results they were looking for.

How a Numbers Obsession Can Cause Fraud

Wall Street's obsession with ever-growing short-term numeric results was at the source of the 2008 collapse of financial markets.

One of my clients discovered fraud in one of his business units. He leads a large public company with a great reputation for both integrity and performance. He and his executive team had managed the problem well and communicated openly with the market. The fraud did not entail theft or embezzlement; it simply involved some false reporting about customer satisfaction, which was designed to make a particular department and its manager look better than they really were. Still, the company took it seriously and asked Lapin International to help them determine whether similar activity could possibly be happening elsewhere in the company, and if so, how they could prevent it.

To answer the question, we probed the root causes of the fraud. Was it simply a few rogue individuals (hardly ever the case), or was there a flawed culture and poor leadership (almost always the case) in that particular unit? We found the latter: the leader of the unit, with good intention, was focusing so vigorously on quantitative results that no matter what the true numbers were, his team, who feared him, was determined to give him the numbers he demanded. And they did.

Except that the numbers they gave him were false. The manager was so eager to believe these false numbers that he communicated them up the levels of the organization. The organization trusted him; after all, he was a good performer and always delivered the numbers expected of him. Later, the CEO and his management team based a string of decisions on these fictional numbers.

We checked to see what other units in the company were led in similar ways. We found that the numbers drive was coming from the top, and that inadvertently the senior executive team was creating an environment that was so numbers-driven that it encouraged people to exaggerate financial results, which at times led to false reporting. We worked with them to design the set of *value-drivers* and strategic principles that correlated best with the business outcomes they sought. We taught these values and principles to all levels of managers down to team supervisors. We were careful to make sure that they embraced the correlation of these values and principles with the business results for which they were accountable. These new *value-drivers* and strategic principles became the cornerstone of all management conversations, and the company recovered its soul.

Quickly and clearly, everyone understood that these principles could never again be compromised, not even if that was the only way to get the results. Today, this company continues to be at the very forefront of its industry by virtually every measure.

Fraudulent behavior can bring down more than a manager or even an entire company. It nearly brought down the world's financial systems. Wall Street's obsession with ever-growing short-term numeric results was at the source of the 2008 collapse of financial markets. Wall Street's numeric expectations were forced down to the sales levels of mortgage brokers. Brokers were not merely *measured* by their numbers, they were driven to achieve nothing *but* numbers—and they did. They sold mortgages to people who could not afford them, against properties that had no collateral value. They packaged this debt into deals with sexy names and sold them. The buyers either did not understand the packages they bought or hoped not to be the one left holding them when the music stopped playing. Large institutions traded in bigger and bigger parcels of this toxic debt believing it couldn't possibly all be bad. In a sense, it wasn't bad; it was exactly what they had been demanding—parcels of numbers without any business or ethical principles to back them up. A number that is not backed by principle is worthless, but no one cared to inspect the principles while the numbers kept going up. No one asked the question "Is it too good to be true?"—until the financial system imploded.

At the start of the 2008 recession, Bob Parsons, the larger-than-life CEO and founder of The Go Daddy Group, the world's largest domain name registrar, told me that he sees a recession as *"the way we migrate from one economy to another. Whereas the old economy was shareholder-centric, tomorrow's economy will be much more customer-centric. The auto industry concerned itself more with workers' unions than with customers. The financial industry concerned itself with their own bonuses, not with making a difference to clients. All of that is what needs to change."*

It would have been worthwhile if the pain of recession had resulted in the migration of our economies from their pure focus on numbers, to a focus on numbers as a measure of strong principle. It would have been worthwhile if the recession began to "reboot prosperity" as Umair Haque writes in his Internet essay *Eudaimonics 101: America Needs a 21st Century Investment Plan:*

"America needs a human potential investment plan (strategy, and vehicle): what you might call a Eudaimonia Fund. The ultimate goal of such a plan? Not merely to "stimulate" the economy (i.e., spark commercial activity)—which clearly hasn't been the best of investments. But, more vitally, to spark human potential. To redraw the boundaries of our capacity to live meaningfully good lives; to take on the globe's greatest problems, and answer them with equally great achievements; to optimize the capacity of society for investing in and igniting, renewing and rebuilding, creating and imagining, exploring and refining what elevates, inspires, betters, lasts, multiplies, matters."[54]

I fear, though, that the recession may not have hit hard enough in the right places to really reverse the obsession of some industries with numbers to the virtual exclusion of principle. In your own organization, try to remain mindful of how a relentless focus on numbers without an equal focus on principle may, in fact, deliver the numbers you want to see, but those very numbers may not be true and authentic. They may have been manipulated to give you what you want. Operating by a set of wrong numbers is like flying a plane with inaccurate instruments. The crash will happen; it's just a matter of time. Use sound principles as your levers, and the instrument readings will take care of themselves.

Levers and Instruments
If you lead with numbers you only manipulate people into acting. When you lead with principle, you inspire action.

How can you identify the levers of human behavior? Begin by thinking of business principles and values as the levers of performance and numbers as the instruments that measure them. In order to keep performance high and encourage continuous improvement, it is essential to measure people's performance and to give them feedback from those measures. Imagine playing a sport without your or your competitors' performances being measured, a classroom without scores, or flying a plane with no instruments. Measurement and feedback are how we stay on track and how we progress, and *the only way to measure anything is with numbers.* But that is all that numbers should be used for: instruments of measure. Numbers are not the levers that drive performance, and they should never become the reason *why* people do what they do.

Great leaders measure performance numerically all the time, but they never drive performance with numbers; they drive their teams with inspirational vision, a higher sense of purpose, sound business principles, and ethical values. When managers drive their teams with budgets and targets rather than with strategy, purpose, and principle, they unintentionally create an environment that conveys the idea: "*Even though we say that people are our most valuable assets, we don't really value you; we just value the results you deliver.*" Unwittingly, they undermine trust in their own leadership and instill fear in their employees. They paralyze innovation and inhibit people's inspired contributions. When you lead with principle, you *inspire* action.

If you lead with numbers you only *manipulate* people into acting. Inspired people sustain their actions; manipulated people revert to old habits as soon as the fear factor lets up. When you lead people with strategic vision, higher purpose, and moral principle, and use numbers only for measurement and feedback, you unlock their energy and inspire them to innovate. People will surprise you with their efforts.

Imagine you are a weight coach and an overweight person comes to you for help. You put him on the scale and decide that in the next fifteen weeks he needs to lose thirty pounds. You have just set a legitimate, measurable objective. You agree that you will see him once a week and measure his weight. Each time he comes for his weekly weigh-in, you have a conversation about his weight. You chastise him when he has not made progress and praise him when he has. You even set up a system of reward and consequence to keep him motivated. You are not only measuring him using numbers, as you should, but you are also attempting to drive his behavior using numbers. He is anxious about his appointments with you, and with no new insight into health and diet, at best he obeys your orders and continues to do so for so long as you are his weekly coach.

Now imagine a second approach. At your first meeting you say something like: "Joe, you ought to weigh around a hundred and seventy pounds. The fact that you currently weigh two hundred pounds indicates that your lifestyle is unbalanced. You are eating too much of the wrong things, possibly at the wrong times of the day, and you are not exercising sufficiently or appropriately. We need to understand why this is happening. It might be because you are stressed. You could just be in a bad routine, or maybe you're surrounded by others who do the same things and who set the tone for you. So we are going to have a conversation today about what in your life needs to change and how you are going to do it so that you will have much more energy and a sense of well-being every day."

Each time he comes, you then use the number on the scale to indicate whether he has in fact been making the changes you agreed on or whether he has continued with the same lifestyle.

In this second approach, you still use the numbers on the scale to measure your client; there is no other way to measure. However, in this approach, you are not motivating your client with numbers. Instead, you have identified the levers that drive those numbers, and are helping him apply these levers to get the desired result. In both of these two approaches, you constantly keep your eye on the instrument, the scale that measures the results, because you must relentlessly measure anything you want to change.

The difference between the approaches is in the conversation. In the first approach, all you talk about is the numbers. In the second approach, the conversation is not about numbers, it's about lifestyle, health, and a feeling of well-being, because they are the *values* that you really want to reinforce. Health and well-being are the reasons why we are interested in the numbers at all. They are the levers that, if changed, will change the readings on the scale.

The same applies in business. There are a variety of business, strategic, and ethical principles that will influence the numeric outcomes you need to achieve. These principles are the levers; the numeric outcomes are the measurements. It is important to identify which levers will optimally deliver the desired numbers and then focus on those principles. In the case of Southwest Airlines, one of the principles management focuses on is a care for the employees. The leaders believe unshakably in the correlation between that lever and the business results they need to achieve. That is a unique dimension of their strategy and is embedded in their culture.

A leader is much like a pilot. Remember the pilot in Chapter 2? When the altimeter reading falls unexpectedly, he doesn't try to fix the instrument. He identifies the appropriate levers that will influence altitude. He increases the thrust and perhaps lifts the plane's nose to increase its altitude. Then he watches the instruments to check the effects of his corrective actions. When great leaders want specific results from their organizations, they identify the right levers—those that will optimize results—and focus on them, not on the instruments. Often the most efficient levers of performance are the universal principles of business and human behavior discussed throughout this book. In many instances, "soft" issues having to do with culture, *corporate soul*, and business values can do far more to sustainably deliver the right numbers than a singular focus on the bottom line.

People Are NOT Your Most Valuable Asset

People are not assets to be managed. People manage assets to make them productive.

Knowing that it isn't wise to focus on numbers alone, some leaders camouflage their focus on numbers by often repeating that "people are their most valuable asset." This popular management mantra can in fact become one of the greatest obstacles to removing fear from an organization's culture and building trust. Although they mean well, leaders would be better advised to think about people somewhat differently.

Do you think most managers truly believe that people are their most valuable asset? When you test their claim, you will find in many cases that it is just not true. Try asking a business leader to consider a scenario where he or she could achieve the same or better outcome than he or she currently gets by replacing his or her human capital with a new generation of technology that could do people's jobs at least as well as they do. Most would do it in an instant.

If we are honest with ourselves, many of us tend to think of people as a necessary cost that we have to manage if we want to achieve results. We also know that to motivate people we need to tell them how important they are, and we do. Yet, if people are such valuable assets, why do so many companies demand more and more from them while giving them less and less resources and support? Why does a company, as soon as its future appears to be threatened, so often dispense with its most valuable asset first? For the most part, employees know that the "people are our most valuable asset" mantra isn't true, and management loses credibility by saying it.

But there are companies that, even in times of recession, do not resort to layoffs. Gateway Group One is one such company. "Letting people go is like taking the wheels off a sports car to save money," CEO Kurus Elavia told me. "When I found I had too many people, I sought opportunities overseas and expanded our company into India. How could I have done that if I had earlier laid off unnecessary staff?"

There is another reason why "people are our most valuable asset" is an unwise philosophy, even when it is sincere. An asset (in its economic sense) is something an individual or entity owns that can be managed or disposed of to produce economic value. Talking about people as assets, albeit valuable ones, unintentionally communicates the sense that people, like tangible assets, need to be acted on and managed to produce value. This is not so.

The message we want to give people in our organizations is that it is *they* who must manage assets to make them productive, whether those assets are tangibles like capital, the plant, and equipment, or intangibles like time and reputation. Assets generally cannot do anything unless a person acts on them in some way. People operate machines and they manage investments. They farm or develop land and manage cash. People are not assets to be managed; people manage assets. Every single employee in any enterprise should see himself or herself as a manager who generates value by managing assets.

Even at the lowest levels in an organization, people are far more productive when they see themselves this way rather than as passive assets to be managed and directed by others. How can we hold people accountable for outcomes if we treat them as assets rather than as managers of their time and talent? But for this to become your philosophy, you need to trust the people you lead, and give them the power to manage the assets under their control. We also need to include them in some level of our strategic thinking and make sure they understand the part they play in the bigger picture.

This idea may seem like a focus on semantics, but it is more than that. The words we choose to use, especially when we say them with sincerity, frame people's realities. By precisely wording our message, we can change people's conversations, and by doing so, change the ways they work and live. But communicating appreciation, a sense of value, trust, and dignity to the people we work with is not as simple as stating it. Communication can be our greatest asset or our biggest challenge.

CHAPTER THIRTEEN

DON'T JUST SAY IT, CONVEY IT.

The success of a communication is not measured by how much
you have said or how frequently you said it, but by how much the other
party actually heard and how accurately they heard it.

THE FOUNDATION of robust communication rests more on the ability to hear than on the capacity to speak. Communication is ineffective if it isn't heard, no matter how eloquent the speech. As leaders we need to hear our people, but equally important, we need to make sure the people we lead are hearing us. This applies on a day-to-day level, but is particularly important when having a serious conversation with an individual about his or her performance.

Almost every time a company conducts an employee survey, communication features near the top of the areas that need improvement. This is like the charlatan "guru" I know who recruits naïve followers by looking in the eye of any woman he meets and saying to her: "I can see in your eyes that you are having communication difficulties in your relationship." Who doesn't have communication challenges in their relationships?

When communication tops the list of complaints in an employee survey, I urge you to probe further. Ask employees what forms of communication they seek. They are unlikely to want more meetings, e-mails, phone calls, or memos. So what do they want? They want communication they can trust and that they can hear. The effectiveness of communication is not a function of how much you have *said* or how frequently you *say* it. The only measure of effective communication is how much the other party actually *hears* and how accurately they have *heard* it.

Children sometimes play a game known as *telephone*. One kid whispers something to the next kid and that kid whispers the same thing to the next person, and so it continues around an entire circle of kids. By the time the message comes back to the originator she laughs at how drastically it has changed. Organizational communication, or personal communication for that matter, is just the same. Many times, no matter how often you say something, the other party doesn't hear it or hears what he or she wants to hear. If they haven't heard correctly, you haven't communicated it, and repeating it or saying it louder doesn't help. You need to discover what is blocking your communication and remove it. Then you'll be heard, even at a whisper.

The purpose of communication is more than the transmission of information; it is also to convey inspiration. Communication is not just about getting people to *do* things differently; it is also about getting them to *be* different and *feel* different. When people *feel* different, they *act* differently. When people act out of inspiration rather than compliance, they do so with much more energy and innovation than when they do it just because they have been told to.

Communication is the artery through which an organization's human energy runs, but like arteries, communication can also become blocked. Fear and mistrust are the "cholesterol" that block the arteries of communication. When you mistrust someone, no matter what they say or how well they say it, you will not hear their true intent. When someone you mistrust greets you warmly, you may wonder what he or she really wants from you, and you will be unlikely to believe in his or her friendliness, even if it is genuine. Someone you mistrust could give you a thoughtful gift and you might not be able to help wondering what their ulterior motive is. Mistrust filters even the best intentions out of communication. This is why when trust erodes, the feelings we try to communicate get blocked and relationships break down. Trust takes time and effort to build, but it can be lost in an instant.

Losing trust does not only result from lying, cheating, and broken promises. People can lose trust in you the moment they begin to doubt your authenticity. People trust us less when they find us arrogant or full of ego. They trust us less when we instill fear into them, persuading them to our point of view with our positional power rather than the integrity of our intent. People lose trust in us when we become defensive or put them on the defensive by making accusations that question their intent or character. As leaders, we often do these trust-eroding things without even realizing it, and when we do, we lose the trust of our people without knowing it. Then, when we communicate with them, we are puzzled when they don't seem to hear us.

When leaders feel secure, they exude an inner confidence, and they influence others with the power of their authenticity and human stature. These leaders don't need to intimidate people. As Sun Tzu puts it in *The Art of War*, "individuals who dominate others, are in

171

fact, enslaved by insecurity and are slowly and mysteriously hurt by their own actions."[55] Secure leaders build trust and open the arteries of communication so that human energy can flow freely.

You Cannot Hear a Tyrant

Channels of communication flow more openly when you use your personal stature to get things done rather than your positional status.

Insecure managers draw their authority from the status of their positions rather than from the stature of their characters. Knowing that their only tool of influence is the power they wield, they hold on to their positions of power for dear life. When they sense their position weakening, they become defensive, political, and scheming; sometimes they get nasty and become bullies. In essence, they become tyrants. And it's hard to trust a tyrant, much less hear or communicate with one.

Soon after my son had started school, his teacher called me to ask if I was aware that he was telling people I had murdered our gardener. When I questioned my son, he admitted to the lie and said, "You told me yourself that you murdered him; you said you fired him." My little boy's image was of me as a tyrant, putting our gardener in front of a firing squad. It occurred to me then that firing people is in some ways like killing them. The fear of being fired can be almost as paralyzing to a person as the fear of execution. Managers hold immense power over the lives of others; they hold the key to the financial security of the people they lead. They have status, and with that status they have power, and everyone knows that power intimidates.

The use of intimidation is the easy default for many people in positions of authority. Following the Los Angeles Police Department

(LAPD) beating of Rodney King in 1991 and the ensuing riots, the excessive use of force and intimidation in police departments became a hot topic throughout the U.S. In an effort to stem the problem, the LAPD, through the Los Angeles Museum of Tolerance, turned to Lapin International to help its officers develop better interpersonal capabilities to diffuse tension without the use of force. This began an exciting and enduring partnership between the Museum of Tolerance's Tools for Tolerance for Law Enforcement Program and Lapin International. Since that time, this program has trained well over one hundred thousand officers to use the authority that comes with personal stature to project their "command presence," not just their uniforms, weapons, and physical bearing. They learned how better to inspire people to follow them rather than to simply intimidate them into compliance. We have used a similar approach in our development of business leaders.

Controlling people by using one's status usually entails a veiled threat of force in the event the other person does not comply. In the case of a police officer, that might take the form of physical force. In business, people are intimidated by a different threat that managers hold over them—demotion or dismissal.

When people feel intimidated they become defensive, set up protective barriers, and cease to hear. They justify and rationalize; they blame others and play victim. Their survival instinct takes over, and they shut down their creative, heroic drive to protect it from possible abuse or exploitation. To avoid pain, they shut down all the passion and innovation of their spiritual dimensions. When people are defensive, their fear blocks the arteries of communication and the passageways of inspiration. The organization's human energy ceases to flow freely.

Channels of communication flow more openly when you use

your personal stature to get things done rather than your positional status. Make it safe for people to make an occasional mistake, to take responsibility for their actions even when they are negative, and to give you honest feedback. Then, people will perform not out of fear of consequence but out of a sense of responsibility and a desire not to let you down.

"I am quick to trust and empower people," Dave Lindsay, founder and CEO of Defender Direct, told me. "It is a risk, but I have never been burnt. I believe businesses don't grow—people do." Dave has been recognized as the 2010 Ernst & Young Entrepreneur of the Year in the Retail and Consumer Products category for the Midwest region, and Defender Direct is on the *Inc. 5000* list of the fastest-growing companies in the U.S. As we have already said, most people are "wired" not to disappoint others who put their faith in them. Like Dave and many other highly successful leaders, be willing to take a risk on people. Trust them.

Expect great things from people, and give them the conditions in which they can succeed. Then wait. People usually respond well. Lead them with fear, and they will respond with instinct. Lead them with greatness, and they will surprise you with inspired brilliance.

Hard Conversations

Successfully managing a hard conversation requires that you confront and challenge the other person in a way that does not raise his or her defensive barriers.

In the instance that you trust people to perform and they don't, it might be necessary to have a hard conversation with them. Managers often find these conversations the most difficult of all their responsibilities. Most managers are not well-trained to conduct hard conversations effectively, and they tend to resort to blame or withdrawal. In doing so, they miss an opportunity to bring about meaningful change in the other person. To have a successful hard conversation, a manager needs to be willing to sacrifice his or her popularity if necessary for the sake of achieving change. This can be especially challenging for frontline supervisors, who often have deep bonds and friendships with the people they supervise.

However, having a successful hard conversation demands more than a willingness to make oneself unpopular. It also requires that you confront and challenge the other person in a way that does not raise his or her defensive barriers. If he or she does become defensive, you will not be heard, and the conversation will have failed. Again, more than a specific skill, this process calls on our human greatness. It requires high levels of *self-esteem* and *confidence* in us and low levels of *egoism*.

People are often unclear about the differences between a healthy sense of self-esteem and a destructive and inflated ego; between the attractiveness of pride and self-confidence and the repulsiveness of arrogance. There are many definitions for these terms, but for the purpose of this discussion we'll assume the following definitions for each.

Ego
Ego is an armor of mechanisms that we put in place almost instinctively to protect our sense of self. When it is fragile, we feel insecure. When we act arrogantly, abusively, angrily, fearfully, or manipulatively, we are acting from our *ego*. When we rely on our status or position to feel secure in our roles of influencing, controlling, or

managing others, we are using our ego.

Self-esteem

Self-esteem is what we feel when we know that we are valuable and unique, regardless of background, education, or privilege. It encompasses the sense or attitude of being no more valuable and unique than any other person. Those who have a strong sense of self know and honor their strengths, while recognizing the areas in which they still need to improve.

People with self-esteem also know that with growth there is often discomfort; sometimes even pain. They accept the discomfort of their own challenges as they work through them. They also understand that as leaders they will at times cause others some pain or discomfort as they challenge them to grow. A person with high self-esteem will keep himself and others intact, functioning, and growing, even when he needs to confront others and challenge them. As people grow and evolve as human beings of ethical and spiritual stature, their self-esteem increases, their need for ego becomes less and less, and their leadership effectiveness grows.

Self-confidence

Self-confidence comes from acknowledging the things you have accomplished in your life and the challenges you have overcome. Even things that now seem small were major at the time, and acknowledging them helps to build confidence. Think of what age you were when you learned to speak, learned how to walk, run, write, and do math. Think of your social and family accomplishments, school, college and university, and your achievements in your career.

In short, people with large **egos** define themselves by what they *have*. This could include money, property, family, university degrees, power, and status.

People with a healthy **self-confidence** define themselves by what they *have accomplished*.

People with high **self-esteem** define themselves by who they *are*, rather than by what they *have* or what they *have done*.

Truly great people define themselves by the gap between who they are and a realistic but aspirational sense of who they could become. This gap, as discomforting as it might be, inspires them to change, because we only change when we feel uncomfortable in the status quo. People who feel comfortable with the gap between their current performance and their aspired accomplishments may only embrace change when they experience a discomfort generated from some external source. This might be some challenging external circumstance like job loss, divorce, or bankruptcy; or it could be negative feedback given to us by a close friend or a supervisor. As hard as these feedback conversations can be, if they are done constructively, they can be powerful forces in propelling us forward to change our lives. It is not only hard for the recipient of the feedback. It takes courage from a friend or manager to risk his or her popularity by confronting us about our behavior or attitude. The level of self-esteem in the person confronting us is key to this courage and to the success of the conversation.

Leaders who lack self-esteem, even if they have high levels of confidence, tend to seek popularity and affirmation, and often make poor decisions in order to gain acceptance from others. They either avoid hard conversations altogether or they sugarcoat them to the point of ineffectiveness. A good sense of self makes it easier for leaders to make hard decisions and have difficult conversations, because they

177

don't value popularity over doing what is right. They know losing popularity is worth gaining respect. Leaders with a good sense of self genuinely desire other people's success, and that is why they can have hard conversations that yield changes in people's behaviors without wounding them.

As leaders and mentors, it is our responsibility to create aspirational gaps for our teams so that the resulting discomfort drives them to close the gap and reach the goals we set for them. One way to do this is to provide negative (but not destructive) feedback about the status quo when it is unsatisfactory. And yes, one might hurt people's feelings—though one should never damage their dignity in the process—but only discomfort will elicit a change. If you give this feedback creatively from your own values and *Spiritual Fingerprint* and not from your instinctive ego-drivers of anger and disappointment, you will have encouraged the person you are leading into a new level of being and doing. And you will have done so without damaging him or her in the process.

The Gain is in the Pain

It is a tragedy of the human condition that discomfort is the most effective propeller of meaningful change.

We damage others with criticism when we use it to feed our own ego; when we use it to make us feel better about our own shortcomings, rather than to bring about improvement in them. When we do this, the other person shuts down defensively, and our criticism has no further value to him or her. You need to really care about people before you can criticize them without making them defensive.

When people are criticized, they often feel it as a personal attack and become conscious of the inevitable pain they're about to feel. Feeling intimidated and threatened, they go into a defensive mode. They blame others and claim to be victims of circumstances beyond their control. The noise in their minds, even if they do not express it, is likely to be something like: "This guy doesn't know what he's talking about; he (or she) is not someone I need to listen to; my boss is out to get me; it's personal, not professional; I'll just act as if I am listening and keep out of his way." You'll often observe these responses by the person's closed body language.

The art to having a hard conversation is to keep other people in their inspired operating system and not allow them to shift into their instinctive, defensive system where they shut down to avoid being hurt. On the other hand, unless you create some discomfort, they are unlikely to change their pattern of behavior. It is a tragedy of the human condition that discomfort is the most effective propeller of meaningful change. There is unfortunately nothing like a disaster or a near-death experience to bring about change in individuals or organizations. Clearly, we don't want to bring about a disaster or near-death experience when we have a hard conversation. But we do want to bring about discomfort without the other person shutting down in defensiveness. How do we accomplish this?

To master the art of a successful hard conversation, one that triggers change through discomfort but does not cause a shutdown, it is helpful to clarify the differences between the use of discomfort as an educational tool and the use of fear. At times, you might choose to have a conversation with a loved one that causes him or her to feel discomfort, but you would never want him or her to experience fear. The same applies in leadership.

Fear is an instinctive reaction to either real or imagined

situations that confront us. Two people may react differently to the same situation: one will be afraid and the other will not. This is because fear is a state of mind; it is not an objective reality. Fear is a defensive instinct, an involuntary reaction; it is not a creative, heroic value. As humans, we have the choice to override our instincts with a creative response built on the values we believe in. We can overcome the instinct of fear with the value of courage, or we can choose to allow ourselves to be paralyzed by our fears. Fear is almost always about the future, an event that has not yet happened. Courage is what we feel in the present moment of a crisis when we choose action over paralysis.

Pain and discomfort, unlike fear, are real feelings; they are not just imaginings about the future. Pain is something we feel in the moment. Pain and discomfort are valuable forms of feedback from nature, from the universe, from our environment, or from God. Pain indicates that there is negativity in something we are doing, thinking, or saying, or in someone with whom we are currently connected.

When we experience pain, our instinct is to pull away from it. However, we can respond to pain with a value choice. We can choose to stay present in the discomfort or pain for a while as we deepen our understanding of it and explore its message. We can seek the root cause of that pain, identify where in our bodies it is located, what the significance of that location is, and to what emotions and feelings it seems to be attached. In this way, we can learn the reason for our pain, and address it at its root. This is how we can use pain to propel change and improvement in our lives.

In the West, we are unfortunately conditioned to flee from pain. The moment we feel any physical pain, we tend to address it with medication or some form of distraction. We do the same when we cannot sleep or when we feel depressed. When we are troubled, we escape into TV. We have been trained to view pain as something negative, to be avoided at all costs. Yet this is not true. Pain that is not self-inflicted is negative feedback that communicates to sensitive people that something in their lives needs to change. It could be negative behaviors driven by ego, negative thoughts, associating with negative people, negative eating and exercise habits, holding negative assumptions, or using negative language. Buddhism teaches that all pain results from attachment to ego. The Talmud also teaches that pain is caused by negative activity.[56] Pain is the signal that warns us to check our vital navigation indicators. Pain warns us that despite our pursuit of comfort (or because of it), there is a gap between our values (the things we know to be true and right) and our ethics (our behaviors—whether in thought, word, or deed).

Think of the discomfort of pain as a trusted friend rather than as a vindictive enemy. Pain can be the friend that holds a mirror up for us to see ourselves. Sometimes, the mirror is magnified because the friend wants us to clearly see our flaws and correct them. If we understand how pain, hurt, or even just discomfort can be tools for change, then we can use discomfort to motivate change in the people we supervise. We can sometimes also use the creation of discomfort as a tool to bring about change in the people who supervise us or in anyone whose behavior we would like to see change. It is much more constructive to use discomfort to change behavior than it is to use fear.

Most performance-management models use fear to motivate people rather than pain or discomfort. They motivate people with the fear of consequence; the fear of not reaching targets and thus forgoing bonuses; the fear of job loss; and the fear of career ceilings. Even when you promise someone a bonus for a job well done, there is an implied threat: if you do not do the job well, you will forgo your opportunity for a bonus. Managing people with fear at best accesses their instinctual defensive operating system. By masterfully using discomfort rather than the *fear* of discomfort, it is easier to touch people's *value-drivers* and their heroic operating systems.

To understand this a little more clearly, think about raising or educating a child. If a child fails to respond to guidance and rules, there clearly need to be consequences. However, using the fear of consequences to train a child can hardly be termed educational. Your children may know that you will punish them if they act deceitfully, but you would not want them to act honestly only out of a fear of punishment. You want their behavior to be driven by values, and punishment to be the safety net in the case of the child's values failing.

Consider two scenarios of your child having lied to you about a serious issue. In the one case, you deprive the child of some privilege and make sure he or she feels the painful consequence of his or her actions. You do this so that he or she associates negative consequence with lying. Next time, the fear of punishment will balance the child's instinct to gain some short-term benefit from telling a lie.

In the second scenario, you may also punish the child, but in addition to that, you tell the child how you felt as their parent when you experienced the deceit—your humiliation, disappointment, loss of pride, and loss of respect. Provided you have a good and mutually respectful relationship with your child, he or she will inevitably feel deeply hurt for having let you down. This hurt does not come from the physical nervous systems; it comes from his or her ingrained desire not to disappoint those who have placed their trust in him or her. This hurt is not a survival instinct; it's the manifestation of a value system; it is the pain of moral conscience. The hurt in this instance can propel your child's ethical and moral development. The disciplinary conversation you had with your child in this scenario was not about instilling fear; it was about transmitting feeling, albeit a negative feeling at first. This was real communication.

Mastering the art of a hard conversation at work, one that triggers change and not shutdown, is not very different from the kind of conversation you might have with your child in the second scenario.

Hard Conversations: The Talker

The key to having a conversation that creates discomfort and change without shutting the other person down is to stay in your own inspired operational system and not allow yourself to strike out instinctively from the disappointment you feel as a result of the other person's actions. The *Lead by Greatness* approach emphasizes how others reflect the energy that you transmit. If you transmit the egoistic traits of control, abuse, and attack, they will be defensive or revengeful. If, however, you act out of character greatness, they will stay in a mode of greatness, too. They will respond according to their unique *Spiritual Fingerprint* and not according to their instincts.

Here are five helpful steps in the process of having a hard conversation with an employee, boss, or partner:

1. *Check in with your true intention. Is your intention to let off steam, or do you truly desire to improve the other person? Is the intention of the conversation to punish or to mentor? If you are just letting off steam and your desire is to punish him or her, you are not yet ready for the conversation. It will at best be fruitless and at*

worst introduce additional levels of mistrust into the relationship, further blocking the crucial arteries of communication.

2. *Check whether the conversation is about "being right" and winning, or about problem solving.*

3. *Ask yourself whether you are feeling disappointed, hurt, or undermined. If you are, are you willing to share these feelings honestly with the person you are about to address? If you are not, you are not yet ready for the conversation.*

4. *Make sure you can accept that most people mean well most of the time, and that it was possibly, or even probably, not the intention of the other party to disappoint, hurt, or undermine you. If you are unable to accept this, you are not yet ready for the conversation.*

5. *Be cautious at first not to talk about them in the conversation at all. People do not shut down when you talk to them; they shut down when you talk about them! So instead of commenting on their conduct, try focusing only on how you feel when they do certain things and act in certain ways; how other people in the team feel, and how this person's actions impact (probably unintentionally) the rest of the team. This way, blame does not come into the conversation, only causality. You are explaining to the other person some of the (possibly unintended) ramifications of his or her actions in the belief that once he or she is conscious of it, he or she will modify his or her behavior.*

This approach shows how much you trust people, not how little. It shows that you trust their intentions; you trust their desire to do better and their ability to change. Using this approach you will not have eroded trust—on the contrary, you'll have built it. You will have opened channels of communication and made it easier for the other person to hear what you are really saying.

The most important determinant of successful feedback is that it comes from an authentic care for the other person and a love for him or her; it cannot be motivated by your need to assert your own power.

	EGO-DRIVEN CRITICISM	*CARING FEEDBACK*
1	Judgmental, negatively evaluative, and accusatory	Descriptive, focused on providing concrete information to help the other person to reconsider his/her behavior
2	Negative assumptions about the other person's motives	Avoids speculating on the other person's intent, focusing instead on the results of his/her behavior
3	Is general and diffuse and can include negative appraisals of the other's character or temperament	Centers on the *particular behaviors* relating to the speaker's present-day frustrations or annoyance
4	Exaggerates and over-generalizes the behavior being objected to, and liberal use is made of such hyperbolic words as "always" and "never"	Is precise and delimited, aiming attention only toward those behaviors that give offense
5	Can be unrestrained and all-inclusive and revolve around things that aren't really changeable	Engages the other person on behaviors that can be changed
6	Can sound invalidating, condescending, preachy, and authoritarian—and the person delivering it as arrogant, with a clear sense of superiority	Less likely to imply that the person on the receiving end is somehow inferior, defective, or "less than"
7	Because of the angry tone in which it's typically delivered, is frequently experienced as intimidating or threatening	Delivered in a calmer, more tentative, and low-keyed manner designed to inform rather than attack
8	Commonly includes giving advice, commands, or injunctions	Rather than focusing on how the other person should change, prompts a discussion about the benefits of change
9	Blaming and disparaging, it prompts defensiveness	Leads to self-reflection and re-evaluation of the behavior

No matter how skilled you are at having hard conversations, the other person will feel discomfort and regret. But this regret propels the change process. The other person will be subconsciously saying to themselves: "I really don't ever want to feel this way again." The hard conversation is over, behaviors will change, pride is intact, and trust is built. What a win!

Here are nine helpful indicators to help you identify when your criticism is coming from your ego and will not be heard, and when it is caring feedback that can inspire change:[57]

Hard Conversations: The Listener

What if you are on the receiving end of a hard conversation? If you are a humble leader, the person having the conversation with you may not be your boss; he or she may be someone reporting to you, a peer, a spouse, or even a child.

Here are some guidelines:

1. *Brace for the pain. This is going to hurt, but remember that that pain is a message that something needs to change. Choose to hear the message rather than escape it. If you escape it, it will confront you with greater force at a later stage until finally you get it.*

2. *Avoid interrupting the other person before they have finished. Although uncomfortable, it is an important part of empathy to feel what the other person is feeling without passing judgment in your mind about whether their feelings are valid. Later, you can process the information you received and decide what, if any, modification to your behavior you need to make in the future.*

3. *When the other person finishes speaking, acknowledge their feedback by saying something like: "What you have said is very*

important to me, and I want to be sure that I have understood you correctly. I understand that although I didn't intend it at all, my missing our appointment yesterday made you feel disrespected and undermined. It set your other arrangements in the day back, and you feel that I am responsible for a number of things that happened to you as a result, including that speeding ticket you got afterwards. Is this right?"

4. Thank the other person for their candor, and express remorse: "I really feel very sorry that I caused you so much aggravation. I hope you can accept that it was never my intention to do so."

5. Avoid defensiveness and excuses, and take responsibility for your actions. This always diffuses the other person's anger.

When we get defensive or aggressive towards a person who feels disappointed, we add negative energy into the conversation and nothing constructive can result. By taking the punch, so to speak, we absorb the other's negative energy and dissipate their anger. Always respond to negative feedback with creative heroism, not instinctive defensiveness. This is likely to cause the person giving the feedback to calm down and get himself or herself back into a heroic mode, too, and perhaps it can even get them to acknowledge that they overreacted.

Notice how by following these guidelines you determine the feelings that underpin the conversation even though the other person initiated it. You shift the conversation from ego-based defensiveness to values-based creativeness. You do this by making yourself vulnerable. Knowing how to appropriately expose vulnerability is the way to open the channels of communication and enable the free flow of human energy. But showing vulnerability takes courage, another characteristic of great leadership.

Courage and Accountability

Ego is an armor designed to protect our vulnerability. Courageous people don't need it.

In 1936, J. R. R. Tolkien, author of *The Lord of the Rings*, gave a lecture called "Beowulf: The Monsters and the Critics." In it, he identified a Nordic definition of courage as "the heroic insistence to do the right thing even in the face of certain defeat without promise of reward or salvation." Courage, defined this way, inspires trust. Could you imagine *not* trusting someone who has the courage to do the right thing without promise of reward or salvation? But the courage to unconditionally do the right thing, only manifests itself in people who are operating in their heroic, non-defensive mode, living authentically by their own *Spiritual Fingerprint*. These are people who define themselves by who they are, not by the power they wield or the possessions they have.

Attachment to objects that feed the ego, like possessions, power, or status, interferes with courage. To act courageously, a person needs to be willing to lose just about everything he or she values. Heroes are able to detach themselves even from things and people they love in order to act courageously. When courageous soldiers, law enforcement officers, or firefighters go into dangerous situations, they don't even think about their own lives, knowing that they might die in the service of a greater cause. When you detach yourself from something it does not mean that you cease to value it. It just means that if you were to lose that thing, you would still be okay with yourself. So, for example, you may totally love the car that you drive. You appreciate its engineering, and you're exhilarated by its power. You even enjoy the admiring glances you attract wherever you go. The crucial question is: if you lost it, for whatever reason, would you be okay with yourself? If you would be okay, then you are detached from it, even though you enjoy owning it.

We vary in how attached we are to the things we possess. It even extends as far as relationships. You might be involved in a precious relationship that you treasure more than anything. However, as engaged as you are in this relationship, if it were to end, it is possible that you would still be okay with yourself. That is engagement without attachment. When you are willing to lose what you have, even what you treasure, you are free to act courageously. When heroic soldiers go into battle, as much as they intend to protect themselves in every way they can, they are still willing to sacrifice their lives, if necessary. This gives them the freedom of courage, the freedom to "do the right thing even in the face of certain defeat without promise of reward or salvation."

This is one of the differences between people who operate by their ego, who define themselves by what they have, and people who operate by their sense of self, who define themselves by who they are and who they could become. People who define themselves by what they have lose their sense of self as soon as what they have is diminished or lost. They cannot be courageous, because they are enslaved by what they have. This includes position, status, and power. So, clinging to their status, they are reluctant to risk it even to do the right thing. Seldom will they sacrifice popularity for honor. They certainly will not be able to display their vulnerability and thereby risk their status by genuinely apologizing for something they have done.

Think of the biblical image of David and Goliath. Goliath is the massively powerful giant who instills fear in the entire countryside. David is small in physical stature, but a man of noble character and great spiritual stature. Goliath comes to the battle fitted out in almost impervious armor. David prefers to be free of cumbersome armor, and in his vulnerability he manifests his courage. When we feel afraid or insecure, we tend to cling to structures, to power, and to emotionally defensive methods like withdrawal or cynicism. But these are strategies of our ego rather than expressions of courage. Emotionally courageous people don't need emotional armor.

Even if we have a position of power and from time to time need to draw on that power for our effectiveness as a leader, we need not be *attached* to our power. If we can remain detached from it, we will never sacrifice our integrity in order to preserve our power. We will be willing to display vulnerability when necessary, and we will be quick to show accountability. An apology is often core to assuming responsibility, and most people think "I am sorry" is one of the hardest things to say. When we are detached from ego, status, and power, though, it is not difficult at all. Apologizing does expose our vulnerability, but courageous people with a strong sense of self find no difficulty in exposing their vulnerability.

An apology is not the only gesture that exposes vulnerability and requires courage. There is another phrase that is equally difficult to say, but it cannot be omitted in building a foundation of trust and communication, and it can unleash a generosity of spirit and generate enormous value. The phrase is simply: "Thank you."

CHAPTER FOURTEEN

UNLEASHING GENEROSITY

Generosity should be the engine room
of every business.

A CANADIAN PHILANTHROPIST was being honored at a dinner in Toronto. The speeches were as glittering as the crystal chandeliers and as glamorous as the fashionable women attending the elegant occasion. The honoree himself spoke about his accomplishments with a disarming modesty. When his brother spoke, he told the audience that he was about to share with them a little-known secret that he believed, more than anything else, was responsible for his brother's spectacular success. He said, "I need to share something with you about my brother. When he was a very young boy, our father asked him what he wanted to be when he was big. 'A philanthropist,' he said. 'Why?' our father asked him. He answered, 'Because I have noticed that all the philanthropists we know are very rich.'"

The audience laughed. But in reality the wisdom of the

(then) little boy was profound. Our adult eyes see philanthropy as the outcome of wealth. His fresh young eyes experienced the world differently: he assumed that wealth was the outcome of philanthropy. And he was right, because generosity drives business, and the lack of generosity is what, almost inevitably, kills what might otherwise have been a great business.

Generosity lies at the very core of all business. A business needs to treat its customers and its shareholders generously. Businesses aim to give their customers more value than the cost to them for their products, while generating a more-than-satisfactory return for their investors. And businesses hope to do this without exploiting their employees, vendors, and creditors. When possible, good businesses also aspire to make a contribution to their communities and to the sustainability of their environments. It is true that business gets something back, and from the perspective of our instinctual defensive operating systems, that would seem to be why we are generous in the first place. But we have a spiritual core, too, a heroic calling that wants to make a difference to others.

People often hold back from giving because they fear that others will exploit their generosity. This is why so few companies I know include generosity among their values. People can only feel free to act generously when they trust that others will reciprocate their generosity and not exploit them. Sadly, such a level of trust does not often exist in corporations, and this robs their shareholders of vast value.

Just imagine an organization that really did have generosity as part of its *corporate soul*. Imagine having employees who always made sure to give the utmost value to their employers. Imagine managers who made sure that they gave employees more recognition than they expected. Imagine putting customers first to such an extent that the entire organization is focused on how to please them and give them far more than they ever anticipated. And imagine having customers who valued the company so much that they supported it, even when it was not the cheapest.

There are companies like that, and there are leaders who have built cultures of generosity that translate into premium returns. How have they done this?

Removing the Fear of Exploitation

If we truly trusted that others would always give us back more than we invested in them, we would never hold back on our generosity. There would be no need to.

Great leaders create cultures of generosity simply by removing the fear of exploitation. Fear and mistrust block the channels of generosity in much the same way that they block communication, the other channel for the free flow of human energy. We tend to hold back from giving generously and unconditionally when we fear that others will take advantage of us. When we fear exploitation, we don't trust others with our boundless generosity. We are circumspect with giving out compliments, sometimes even to our spouses and partners, because we don't want them to take us for granted. When we fear exploitation, we withhold our love, material generosity, and even our ideas and intellectual generosity. If we truly trusted that others would, in one way or another, always give us back more than we invested in them, we would never hold back on our generosity.

Sometimes we hold back on generosity without even realizing it. For example, when you compliment someone, it makes a greater impact to address your compliments to the person rather than to the job he or she did for you. "You are an amazing person, and I feel privileged to have you on my team" feels much more affirming than "You did an amazing job, thank you." "You are an amazing wife; I am the luckiest man in the world" strikes a much deeper chord than "That was an amazing dinner, Honey." Yet, as you become conscious of it, you will notice how difficult it is for most people to actually compliment the person rather than the job, both at work and at home. The reason is that we fear making ourselves vulnerable.

I was coaching Carl, the vice president of HR in a large bank, on this very idea when his assistant, Trish, came into the room to give him some items she had prepared for his imminent overseas trip. Trish seemed to be a timid but highly competent woman and had clearly gone beyond the call of duty, anticipating Carl's every conceivable need and providing for it. Carl was visibly moved. I winked at Carl, indicating that this was a good time for him to try the new approach to complimenting people. "Trish," he said, "you are a rare and remarkable individual. I must have done something very worthy in a previous life to deserve a woman like you on my team." I was thrilled...that is, until Trish responded. This is what she said: "Remember that at evaluation time, Carl!" Carl looked shattered. "That's why I don't like being so generous with my compliments," he said later. "It raises unrealistic expectations in the other person."

Carl feared exploitation, and his one venture into his uncharted territory of generous compliments backfired on him badly. The irony is that if Trish simply would have thanked him and reciprocated with a similarly generous compliment, he undoubtedly would have remembered this, as well as all the other things at which she excelled. But Trish sabotaged her own reward by taking advantage of Carl's generosity.

Still, Trish taught me something very valuable that I have since shared with all my clients: to instill a culture of generosity, you must first ensure that your organization has embraced a culture of appreciation and reciprocation. People embrace a culture of appreciation and reciprocation when they feel uncomfortable being indebted to others. Reciprocation is the way people acquit themselves of material or moral indebtedness to others.

When there is a culture of appreciation, people feel the need to reciprocate. Sometimes we reciprocate just by saying thank you in a genuine and heartfelt way. If we consistently reciprocate and consistently show people authentic appreciation for what they do, we demonstrate to them that we will never take them for granted and never exploit their generosity. When people feel that you are not comfortable with feeling indebted to them and that you always find a way to reciprocate or show appreciation, they will continue to act generously toward you, secure in the knowledge that you will never take advantage of them or take them for granted. This is how relationships are built. Someone makes a gesture and the other reciprocates. Each time we try to do a little more for the other than he or she did for us. Each time trust grows and the genuine connection flourishes.

Everyone Is Indispensable!

Appreciation is not just a social law. It is a universal, natural law. In religion and spirituality, it is well recognized that showing appreciation attracts the universe's abundance and God's blessing. Sincerely appreciative people radiate their thankfulness to strangers as they walk down the street. They radiate it to family, colleagues, and customers. And as people radiate appreciation, others, thirsty for appreciation, are drawn to them and want to help and support them in every way they can.

We are wired to help people; we just fear being taken advantage of. So, when we see people who truly value our generosity and know how to show it, we give of ourselves abundantly. The opposite is true as well. When people feel undervalued, their channels of generosity shut down.

I am sure you have heard managers say that no one is indispensable. They do this to make people feel insecure and motivate them to improve. If, like Frederick Winslow Taylor or Douglas McGregor's X-Theory managers, we see people as mechanical beings motivated only by self-interest and their instinctual drive for survival and security, then saying that *no one is indispensable* might work to motivate them, or rather to scare them into performance. But this mantra does nothing to inspire the soul. On the contrary, it undermines people's sense of uniqueness and their capacity to make a difference.

At their soul level, people want and need to feel that they are trusted, valued, and able to make a difference. People are wired to try not to disappoint those that trust, respect, and value them. Making people feel valued and indispensable doesn't diminish their effectiveness, it increases it exponentially. When people feel trusted and valued, they bring their souls, their passions, and their creative, heroic drive to work, making a far bigger difference than anything we might have expected of them. Telling people that they are indispensable doesn't mean that you or your team could not survive without them; it simply means it would be different without them.

All people, provided they bring their souls to work and not just their bodies, add an ingredient to the team's energy and dynamic that no one else can. If we want people to bring their souls to work, then we as leaders need to be ready to nourish those souls. People feel spiritually nourished when their life has meaning, and when they feel honored by others. Telling people they are dispensable does not give them meaning, nor does it honor them. It diminishes their sense of worth and triggers their defensive instincts. They shut down, and we get less from them. Knowing how to say "thank you" sincerely attracts generosity in abundance in ways that nothing else can.

How to Say "Thank You"

The art of an effective *thank-you*, like any good communication, is not so much in the words as in the feeling you evoke in the other person. The Hebrew word for "thank you" (*todah*) appears often in the Bible and comes from the same root as the word for confession. In every thank-you there is an implied confession: "I do not feel deserving of what you have given me or done for me." Clearly, if you believe you are entitled to what the other person did for you or gave you, you would have no need to say thank you, other than as a superficial courtesy.

A meaningful thank-you is only appropriate if you believe the person did something for you over and above what you deserved. If this is the case, the feeling you want to evoke in the other person is one of your own humility, of appreciation for that person and his or her gesture, and of the certainty that he or she will not be taken for granted. It is difficult to say thank you, because it exposes a level of vulnerability that we are trained to hide from others. It shows that we need others, that they did something valuable for us, and that we feel in some way indebted to them. This is why only secure people with a high sense of self-esteem and little ego truly convey a sense of gratitude to others in a way that makes them feel honored.

Leaders of character set the tone in their organizations by going out of their way to genuinely thank everyone who does anything for them, from the doorman to the CEO, and by insisting that the people in their team do the same. These gestures of character are a leader's key to their success. Try taking the risk of doing generous things for people around you; things that are valuable to them but perhaps don't require a lot from you. And watch the response. You will be pleasantly surprised to see new levels of engagement and commitment from others as your own human greatness is reflected in them, and your team begins to pulsate with soul.

Creating Value from Generosity

Intangibles that cost you nothing can touch people's hearts, increase their energy, and inspire them to give more of themselves.

Consider two married men, Branden and Ricardo, both in severe trouble: they both forgot their wives' birthdays. When Branden suddenly remembers, he summons his assistant, writes a check for a thousand dollars, and pens his wife a birthday note with an apology, inviting her to spend the thousand dollars on anything she pleases. He asks his assistant to have it delivered to her immediately.

Ricardo handles the crisis in a different way. He leaves his office as early as he can and goes to two separate florists in different parts of town to buy the specific flowers he knows his wife adores. He then goes to his favorite card shop, chooses paper in which to wrap the flowers and a beautiful card on which he writes a heartfelt, albeit rather amateurish, poem to her. He reserves a table for dinner at her favorite restaurant and rushes home with the flowers that he has arranged and wrapped for her himself. His total expenditure on the occasion is less than $250. She opens the door when he gets home; he falls to his knees, takes hold of her hands, and begs her forgiveness for having been so wrapped up in himself that he forgot a very special day in *his* life: the day his wonderful wife was given to the world.

You are sure to realize that in most cases Ricardo scores more points from his wife than Branden does from his. This is because generosity is not about the cost to the giver, but about the value to the receiver. A precious diamond has no value to a man stranded on a desert island; a barrel of water and some food would be a far more generous gift to him. To Ricardo's wife, the thoughtfulness and the effort demonstrated how he values her more than the thousand-dollar check Branden's wife received. So, in purely economic terms, Ricardo converted thoughtfulness and caring into more than $750 of financial value!

People often value intangible things more highly than they value tangible equivalents. We will often pay a lot more for the same item if it comes with pleasant intangibles, like care and dignity. Think of premium restaurants, world-class hotels, and boutique fashion stores. People value and pay for fine service and for ambience. Different people value different things, and if you care about someone you make the effort to learn what he or she values most. Aim your generosity at things that are valuable to *them*, and the value they receive will far exceed the financial cost to you.

It works in exactly the same way with employees, and with customers for that matter. People's paychecks are very important to them, and so are their bonuses. This is because, apart from the fact that people have financial needs, a tangible payment indicates employers' willingness to share some of their wealth with the people who helped them generate it. However, paychecks are not the be-all and end-all. People value other things, too, and in some ways they value them as much as or more than their paycheck. They value being recognized and appreciated, they value a measure of autonomy, they value being treated with respect and dignity, they value work that is meaningful and that makes a difference, they value being cared about as individual human beings and not just as business assets that produce revenue. And all these things, so valuable to them, come at zero cost to you.

Intangibles like these that cost you nothing, touch people's hearts, increase their energy, and inspire them to give more of themselves. Freed from the fear of exploitation, they respond with their own nearly unconditional generosity. Unafraid of backstabbing in the workplace and knowing that you place their interests first, they focus all their attention and energy on your customers rather than on protecting their own turf. Your intangible zero-cost investment in your employees and your teams translates into tangible revenue and premium returns. Isn't that a no-brainer? Of course!

Yet so few leaders in business do this consistently or well. In fact, these intangibles are so uncommon in business that when managers begin to operate this way, employees are at first cynical and suspicious of them. It can take them a while to begin to trust the genuine nature of a leader's generosity and caring.

So if it's a no-brainer, why do so few business leaders adopt generosity as a way of creating value? Because unlike all other activities of management that are focused on people, things, and activities outside the manager himself, generosity starts from the inside out. For generosity to come across as genuine, leaders need to be great human beings; authentic, evolved, humble, and willing to expose their own vulnerability.

Vince Colarelli of Colarelli Construction in Colorado Springs, one of the *Inc. 5000* fastest-growing companies, is one such leader. "We need to be vulnerable about ourselves and place the care and custody of our relationships before ourselves," he explains. To do this, leaders need to trust themselves enough to trust the people they lead. They need to see people not as instinctual creatures battling selfishly for their own survival, but rather as heroic angels willing to make sacrifices for things they believe in, in order to make a difference. People respond to emotional nourishment. Leaders need to understand how the feeling of being valued and respected nourishes people just as much as food and shelter do.

Great leaders have the character and humility to focus on making others feel valuable and important rather than seeking approval and popularity for themselves. "People are interested in what you think of them, not what they think of you," Dave Lockton, chairman of the board of the Lockton Companies, the world's largest privately held independent insurance broker, told me. Great leaders have the humility to request help rather than issue directives, to show appreciation, and to be quick to apologize. Great leaders operate in their own creative, heroic system and not in their instinctual, defensive mode, and this powers their success in business and beyond. We can be heroic even when under attack, when our very survival is challenged by circumstances beyond our control, or when other people do things that trigger our defensiveness. Even in these situations, we are still masters of our own actions and can choose how we wish to respond: instinctively or heroically.

The Avocado and the Acacia Trees: Responding to Crisis

Like any other organism, humans crave security, but we can achieve it either by defensiveness and selfishness, or through generosity and contribution.

A few years back, I went hiking through a relatively wild part of the African jungle. The guide who accompanied my party told us how to escape in the event that a charging rhinoceros or territorial lion confronted us. He warned us—only half in jest, I suspect—that he would be more inclined to save the lion or rhino than to save one of us. "Lions and rhinos cost a lot of money; you guys are probably well-covered with life insurance!"

With that in mind, I found my heart beating faster every time I heard a rustle in the long yellow African grass. Every movement in the distance took on the appearance of a pending attack by some ferocious beast. But nothing exciting happened. Instead, the guide began to teach us something about the indigenous fauna we were walking through.

I noticed something odd about two acacia trees we passed: one of the trees had hardly any thorns, whereas the other, right next to it, was quite thorny indeed. Our guide explained that a rhino had probably rubbed its horn on the one acacia tree, and the tree, "thinking" itself under attack, grew thorns to defend itself. After a bit of rummaging around the tree trunk, he actually found rhino hairs on some clearly damaged spots of the tree's bark. He saw my surprise and explained that many trees react to threats, each in their own way. This is why there is an old wives' tale that you should drive nails into the bark of an avocado tree to stimulate its fruit production. When the avocado tree feels threatened, it grows many more avocados than it otherwise would, to ensure the survival of its species.

It suddenly struck me that there are two ways to respond to threat: the acacia way or the avocado way. You can respond to threats by getting aggressive, thorny, and defensive. Or, you can choose to increase your value by becoming so productive and contributive that no one could or would want to harm you. Avocados are naturally programmed to react one way and acacias the other. Animals are programmed, too. But humans have the benefit of choice. Like any other organism, we crave security, but we can achieve it either by defensiveness and selfishness, or through generosity and contribution. When we, using our creative, heroic operating system, lead by our stature and not our status; when we access our own greatness and the greatness in others, we inspire others to be open and to give of themselves, too. The results follow.

As leaders, you influence the way the people around you respond, whether as prickly acacias or generous avocado trees. As you show generosity to people by valuing and appreciating them, you inspire them to be generous in their responses to you, too. When we put ourselves out and trust others, they respond by becoming more worthy of our trust. Showing appreciation and generosity is the most effective way for people who are secure enough with their own stature to inspire others to perform extraordinarily.

The Canadian philanthropist was right in his youthful observation that philanthropists are wealthy. Philanthropists are wealthy because they are generous, not the other way around. They treat people generously and appreciatively long before they become wealthy. Their appreciation of people attracts the generosity of others. They quickly build teams and organizations of people who, sure that they will never be exploited, all want to give more than they take. A generous culture is a low-cost investment that produces high-value results. It is one way to convert the intangible strengths of great people into success that is tangible and measurable.

CHAPTER FIFTEEN

TRANSFORMING INTANGIBLES INTO GOLD

Identifying people's deep intangible needs
creates opportunities for product innovation and
sometimes even for new industries.

INTANGIBLE ASSETS such as culture, intellectual property, leadership competence, and reputation add a lot to a company's worth. Although it is difficult to measure the value these intangible assets add to a company, various methods have been developed to try to do so. One simple method of measuring the economic value of a company's intangible assets is to determine its ability to outperform competitors that have the same or more tangible assets.[58]

Intangibles can translate into even more value when they are also used to add to the customer experience. Think about what happens when you apply intangible values like appreciation, generosity, humility, and dignity to the way you view and interact with your customers. What might that do to your sales and profit margins? What might happen if you sought not only to give meaning and purpose to the people who work for and with you, but also sought to satisfy these same intangible needs in your *customers*?

We tend to view customers as people that have a need for *things* or *services,* but people will often pay significantly more if those things or services also satisfy their deeper, intangible needs and desires. Consider how much more some people are willing to pay for a first-class or business-class seat on a flight when a discounted economy-class seat would get them to the same destination in the same amount of time. The extra cost is not always justified merely by the additional space and better meals and service. In the same way, people will often pay more for a brand-name fashion item than they would for a similar piece of generic clothing.

As a young commodities trader, I was once sent by my company to negotiate a deal with a large petrochemical company in Europe. I had to take a long overnight flight to get to the meeting the next morning. Knowing my company's frugal policy of economy-class flights for everyone, including the chairman, and especially conscious of my youth, I fully expected to find my seat booked in coach. The day before I was due to leave, I met the CEO, Rudolph Raphaely, in the corridor.

"I assume you are traveling *first,*" Mr. Raphaely said. He saw the delighted surprise on my face. "I thought company policy was economy," I answered. He took me aside and explained to me how challenging it was going to be for me, a young man, to meet with senior counterparts in a major multinational corporation for a difficult negotiation. "I want you to walk into that meeting feeling like a king, not like a piece of cargo. You'll travel *first* this time."

The reasons that people travel first-class go beyond the extra space and better meals. They fly first- or business-class to feel dignified while they travel and to feel rested when they arrive. Worn down by day-to-day challenges and the chores of life, people sometimes forget the importance of their own humanity. Occasionally, they want to feel like royalty and will pay a lot to restore their sense of self-worth. Dignity is intangible, but it is something that all people crave and value, and for which they will pay a premium, if they can. Identifying people's deep intangible needs creates opportunities for product innovation and sometimes even for new industries.

When Howard Schultz founded Starbucks in 1987, he satisfied more than people's desire for a cup of coffee, and he did so with an idea far more innovative and far-reaching than good customer service. He satisfied a craving in people's souls: their need for community. He "pioneered the concept of the third space experience: the place between work and home where people can spend time"[59] and feel connected to others, all for the price of a cup of coffee. He understood that by satisfying this intangible need, he could get customers to pay more for a cup of coffee than they ever had before. And they did.

Coffee is the tangible part of the Starbucks offering and it has to be consistently good. But the intangible component of its offering is what people really pay the premium for. In a lonely world, they value the sense of community provided by the Starbucks experience—its ambience, the charisma of the baristas, the language they have created, and much more. Again, the *corporate soul* of Starbucks reflected Howard's own passion for people and his values.

Later, the company wanted to institutionalize the Starbucks experience and run it independent of Schultz. They allowed him to take a "backseat" in 2000 and relinquish his position as CEO. Competitors began to replicate the Starbucks experience, forcing the company into the volume game that ultimately eroded the very qualities that originally defined the company. In 2007, Schultz sent out his now famous Valentine's Day memo to Jim Donald after Starbucks shares had dropped 20 percent in four and a half months due to intense competition from McDonald's and Dunkin' Donuts.[60] "We have had to make a series of decisions," Schultz wrote, "that, in retrospect, have led to the watering down of the Starbucks experience, and what some might call the commoditization of our brand."[61]

Starbucks, recognizing the potential death of the brand's soul, began to experiment with a radical new model. It rebranded a few stores in Seattle, dropping the Starbucks name and giving each store a localized feel. The first is known as 15th Avenue Coffee and Tea. It sells espresso from a manual machine rather than the automated type found in most Starbucks stores, offers wine and beer, and hosts live music performances and poetry readings to give off more of a "community" vibe. This alone, however, was not enough to give Starbucks back its sparkle. Schultz returned to Starbucks in 2008, to take back the leadership reins and give the company back its soul.

Using your own soul to connect with your customers and satisfy their intangible cravings is not unique to the food and airline industries.

I once worked with a large retail bank that, although very successful, was struggling to differentiate itself in its market. The conventional strategy and competitor analysis approach led it to become more and more like every other bank. It was persuaded that retail banking is a commodity, and only operational efficiency could differentiate it. We at Lapin International didn't agree. We wanted to know what *value-drivers* were core to the bank's leadership and use them to discover the Bank's true essence and corporate soul.

Using our *Spiritual Fingerprint* methodology, we discovered that nearly every member of the twenty-one-person executive team at the bank shared *humanity* and *dignity* as core *value-drivers*. We then took the team through an "empathy exercise," during which they probed deeply into the hearts of their customers, identifying what intangible needs they had that were not met by other banks. The executive team identified that, with the move toward automated efficiency and staff reduction at customer interfaces by all banks, the banking experience had become purely transactional and had lost the human touch that customers craved.

For most people, money issues are charged with emotion and often with stress. The majority of retail banking customers feel unimportant to the mammoth institutions with whom they bank. They perceive banks as servants of the corporate community and wealthy individuals—sometimes at the expense of the "little people." The bank was losing an opportunity to nourish its customers with dignity at the moment they needed it most. The reason they had previously missed this opportunity was because they had never associated a quantifiable number with the value of dignity. In addition to the tangible offering of efficient banking services, the executive team decided that an authentic human touch gave customers what they needed most: a bit of dignity.

This team reached its conclusion without sending out a single survey or questionnaire. They found the answer to their question in their own hearts, in much the same way that Apple chooses not to do any market research before it designs a new product.[62] When you build product innovation on customer research, you are likely to come up with products that are similar to those of your competitors, because customers answer everyone's surveys in the same way. When you use your *corporate soul* to build an offering that is authentic to you and that connects to the souls of your customers, no one else can compete with you.

After our session, the bank changed many of its customer-relations processes. For example, it encouraged employees to connect with their customers in their own unique way, provided that the customer was treated with dignity. They did not fall into the trap of mechanizing customer interactions as many companies do to ensure standardization. Keihin Electric Express Railway Co. of Japan, for example, uses SmileScan, a software program developed by Omron Corp., to check the smiles of 530 employees each morning in order to "improve our services and make each customer smile."[63] Do you suppose that conveys an authentic experience to the customer? The bank took a wiser path. It articulated its higher purpose as an organization and shared it with the employees, trusting each one to implement it in his or her own unique and authentic way—as long as the outcome was dignity. This is what they formulated:

"We reclaim for all our customers and clients the warm, personalized experience that has been lost from the financial services industry. We recognize our customers fully at their moments of contact and endeavor to build authentic, mutually beneficial relationships. By affirming our customers' dignity we uplift the quality of their lives."

They did not use this statement in their marketing material and it never became a slogan. They used it internally to guide the architecture of their operating model, the development of their people, and their measures of performance. We estimated that if this people-centric philosophy generated a ten percent improvement in customer loyalty, the result would yield nearly one hundred million dollars per year in increased cross-sales savings on new-customer acquisition and reduced customer churn. They subsequently exceeded this goal.

The success of this strategy depended on two factors: firstly, it was born out of a value that was common to the leadership's *Spiritual Fingerprint* and was therefore authentic to them; and secondly, it was designed to satisfy a deep, intangible human need in their customers. This kind of authentic *inside-out* strategy is hard for a competitor to copy, and in their case no competitor has.

But what happens when more than one company in the same market and industry connect with their customers' intangible needs? What happens is that each attracts more of the customers that need their specific offering and that will therefore be more loyal to them in the long term. The bonds of each with their customers deepen, each creates more business opportunity with their existing customers and also attracts new customers with those same needs, and the pie gets bigger. As Southwest's Kelleher attested: "In California, for instance, where Shuttle by United invested millions of dollars to win a piece of our business, we maintained our 50 percent share of the market—but are now carrying many more passengers than we did three years before."[64]

With the application of intangible concepts like purpose, authenticity, and *corporate soul*, companies are proving again and again that tangible results ensue.

The Pie Gets Bigger

Neither of the two companies we were working with could imitate the other because each was fiercely authentic to itself.

We were once consulting to two competing investment banks

at the same time. Even though they were both serving the same markets they were both comfortable that there was not a conflict in this situation because they knew that our *inside-out* approach to strategy would help them to further differentiate themselves from their competitors, rather than eating away at each other's market share. This is precisely what happened. Each investment bank had a unique soul, and using their corporate souls we helped them each to identify different intangible needs in their clients. We encouraged them to see their clients not as faceless corporations or business units but as an individual or set of individuals. They both identified the chief financial officers of large private sector corporations and government agencies as their clients.

The first bank was of the view that these CFOs at times feel a little intimidated by the bright young investment bankers who call on them. Often these bankers are much younger than their CFO clients and are usually earning much more money than they are. This bank had recently experienced a "near-death" crisis. Despite the gung-ho attitude often associated with investment bankers, this particular team of smart bankers knew how it felt to be scared and insecure. They believed because of their own experience they could empathize with their clients' insecurities more easily than their competitors could. They believed that instead of eclipsing the egos of their clients with their own financial acumen, they should rather aim to build their clients' esteem and enhance their stature within their own companies. So they identified the intangible contribution they bring to their clients as the following:

> *Our ability to simplify financial complexity enhances our clients'*
> *confidence and stature. Our trusting relationships are built on our*
> *integrity and deep commitment to understanding and empathizing*
> *with our clients' unique needs and risks.*

The second investment bank, on the other hand, believed that the CFOs it serves are generally bored with their corporate lives and are a little envious of the glamour that the investment bankers seem to enjoy. So they identified stimulation, prestige, and recognition as some of the intangible needs they could satisfy in their clients. Their strategic purpose read as follows:

> We win our clients by inspiring them with energy, intellectual stimulation, market insights, high-level networking, and smart financial thinking. This, together with our premium brand and our personal attentiveness, enhances our clients' prestige and their sense of recognition.

Same industry. Same market. Same time. Yet notice the difference in emphasis in the way each bank has chosen to satisfy its clients. Each built its intangible offering on its own *corporate soul* and on the deep human needs each saw in their clients. We worked with each of the banks to design the cultural architecture that would best deliver these intangibles. They hired different types of people and trained and developed them in different ways. Neither could imitate the other, because each was fiercely authentic to itself. Interestingly, both businesses exceeded their stretch budgets by more than 20 percent. They transformed the intangibles of their strategic purposes into material value for their shareholders. When leading with soul, you don't have to compete just to get a bigger piece of the pie. Inevitably, you actually create new and bigger pies, no matter what market or industry you are working in, provided you keep in mind that shareholder wealth is the *outcome* of business, not its purpose.

CHAPTER SIXTEEN

THE PURPOSE
OF BUSINESS

*A business's higher purpose is to make a
valuable contribution to the well-being of people.*

DOES A BUSINESS exist to maximize the wealth of its
shareholders (in which case it sees customers and employees as just a
means to achieving that end), or does a business exist to serve the needs
of its customers (the result of which is that investors get returns and
employees have jobs)? Put more simply, is the purpose of a business to
make profits, or is profit the measure and outcome of a business that is
successfully and efficiently satisfying the needs of its customers?

Roger Martin, Dean of the Rotman School of Management at
the University of Toronto and named by *The Times* of London and
Forbes magazine as one of the top fifty management thinkers in the
world, takes a strong view on the subject. He demonstrates the "tragic
flaw" in the belief that the purpose of a corporation is to maximize

shareholders' wealth.[65] From 1976 until the end of 2008, the relentless focus on maximizing shareholder wealth delivered compound annual real returns to the shareholders of S&P 500 companies of 5.9 percent. This, Martin argues, is a poor comparison to the 7.6 percent annual returns delivered between 1933 and 1976, when shareholder wealth was not the focus of corporations in the U.S.

So what is a corporation's purpose if not to make money? *A business's higher purpose is to make a contribution to the well-being of people, the value of which yields an acceptable return on investment.* Contribution is the purpose; *profit* is the outcome; it is the measure of the corporation's success.

Michael Beer, the Cahners-Rabb Professor of Business Administration, Emeritus at the Harvard Business School, conducted a study of CEOs on the basis of two criteria: the company they led had to have performed in the top half of its industry for a decade before the inception of the study, and the leader had to have demonstrated evidence of a high commitment to culture. His findings were that:

> *The CEOs were quite different in personality, background, and leadership style. But they were similar in what they saw as the purpose of the firm. They shared the view that a firm has a larger purpose than simply profit and increasing stock price, though they were all laser-focused on profitability and saw it as essential to achieving their larger purpose for the firm. They had a multi-stakeholder view of the firm as opposed to a shareholder view. The purpose was to add value to employees, customers, community, and society—not just shareholders.[66]*

It was a moment of personal crisis that brought Ron Cain, CEO of TMSi Logistics in Portsmouth, New Hampshire, to the understanding of his own business's higher purpose. When he heard that his partner and mentor of many years, John Van Tome, was to retire, he told me how lost he suddenly felt. The company was at a pinnacle of success at that point and suddenly, alone at the helm, Ron realized that he would have to take his company to places it had never been before without his mentor by his side. He started by drawing on the principles that John had taught him over the years. The first was the need for *corporate purpose*. Ron told me that he figured there had to be a higher purpose to what they were doing than just making money.

> *"We really never had higher purpose holding everything together. Based on my own personal values, I decided I wanted to build an organization that puts others first and that moves others to think that way too."*

By articulating a *corporate purpose* for his business that went beyond just making money, Ron identified a cause for which he was passionate, because it resonated with his own beliefs and values, and he inspired those around him with the same passion for that cause. *Personal Purpose*, he realized, could not be divorced from *corporate purpose*.

"Questioning my *Personal Purpose* and what our *corporate purpose* is, was the point at which I stopped being lost," he told me. But this was not just about belief and purpose. The idea of a higher *corporate purpose* intersected with economic success. In 2009, *Inc. Magazine* recognized TMSi as one of the two thousand fastest-growing companies in America for its three-year sales growth of 208 percent, even through some of America's hardest economic times in recent history. TMSi has continued to grow at a rate in excess of 25 percent per year since then.

TMSi's logistics offering was hardly unique. There are many good logistics companies, but a logistics company that is on a genuine mission to inspire people to put others first is unique. The tangible commodities that most companies offer their customers are not unique. Purveyors of commodities are in a constant race with their competitors to provide the newest products or services and to protect their ever-eroding profit margins. A unique value proposition achieves premium margins in ways that a commoditized offering cannot. The uniqueness of a value proposition emerges when you embed an intangible quality into your offering, a quality that your customer deeply values.

There are some intangible offerings, however, like customer-service excellence that can be replicated by nearly anyone in your industry. How, then, do you secure the uniqueness of your intangible offerings? When the intangible components of your offering are born out of your *corporate soul* rather than out of its easily-copied operational processes, then your offering will remain unique. This is because no competitor has, nor can have, *your* corporation's soul.

Most companies start with a tangible product and then try to build a valuable, intangible quality into it. Google[67] did it the other way around. Google's founders, building on their own deep beliefs and passions, started with little more than a *corporate soul*, and a brilliant intangible concept, which at first they had no idea how they would monetize. Google still provides its extremely valuable, but intangible, offering to its customers, free of charge. Google also had to find a tangible component to its offering for which customers would pay; otherwise, its model could not have been sustained.

From the very beginning of Sergey Brin and Larry Page's

spectacular journey to success, the purpose of Google was not to make money, but to make all of the world's information freely accessible and useful. This purpose is at the core of Google's *corporate soul,* and they never once deviated from it; it is more important to them and their organization than anything else, including money. When, in the late 1990s, Google desperately needed their first injection of venture capital funding, they set as a non-negotiable condition that no investor could gain control of their company.

The reason for Brin and Page's almost fanatical insistence on retaining control had nothing to do with ego. They demanded control of their business because they understood that if investors controlled the business it would be driven by money and no longer by their intangible ideal. Google's founders were willing to sell Google shares to investors, but not Google's soul. To Brin and Page, the purpose of business—at least their business—is to make a worthwhile contribution to the world, not to make money. Money is just an outcome of their valuable contribution. Without so much as a business plan, Google attracted the attention of the foremost venture capital investors of the time, John Doerr of Kleiner Perkins and Michael Moritz of Sequoia Capital. They were attracted by Brin and Page's sense of purpose, and in 1999 each invested $12.5 million into Google, astonishingly leaving all control with the founders.

Everyone, including Doerr and Moritz, wondered how Google planned to make money from free information. At first Brin and Page weren't too sure themselves! Danny Sullivan, a *Los Angeles Times* reporter and later an Internet consultant, affirmed that the pair had no interest in becoming wealthy. Nevertheless, they needed to create a sustainable business in order to fund their higher purpose. Because Brin and Page believed that ad-funded search engines are "inherently biased towards the advertisers," and that this would compromise their relationship of trust with their users, ad funding did not seem an acceptable strategy for them.

Brin and Page needed a tangible adjunct to their intangible offering of free information, something for which people would willingly pay. Their solution came in the form of text-only ads that were triggered by users' specific search requests. The advertisements would supplement and enhance the search, thereby serving the interests of the search users. Because advertisers were getting sharply targeted audiences who had already "bought in" to the ad, they would pay for the ad rather than for a skewed outcome of the search results.

Google clung to its uncompromising principle that it would never bias search results. Sullivan talks of their dedication and seriousness about wanting to do the right thing. Advertisers funded the continued provision of free information to the user. Google started making money, and lots of it, from steadfastly pursuing the purpose of its business and by consistently living according to its own soul rather than by the expectations of investors. Google changed the world forever by providing free access to all information; that was its purpose. Money was the outcome of doing it with stunning efficiency and earth-shattering brilliance.

Just because Google provides meditation classes on campus does not mean the company has a soul. But its *corporate soul* is evident in every part of the company: its founders' beliefs, passions, and values, and even its business strategy. Google's tenacious adherence to the principles embodied in its *corporate soul* has generated untold innovation and wealth.

Larry Page and Sergey Brin built Google to make the world's information freely available. Herb Kelleher molded Southwest into an airline that would democratize the skies. Bill Gates founded Microsoft to revolutionize the way the world obtains, stores, and manages information. Walt Disney wanted to make people happy. These leaders and their shareholders made huge fortunes in the process, but their purposes were something much bigger than the wealth of their shareholders.

Like Sergey Brin and Larry Page, all leaders can find within their own belief systems and the souls of their company, a unique way to make a difference in the lives of their customers. When you do this, your customers commit to you because they identify with the things you stand for, they admire your *corporate purpose*, and they value the intangibles they crave that only you can provide.

CHAPTER SEVENTEEN

FINDING YOUR COMPANY'S SOUL

When a company has soul, the most
innovative "how-tos" emerge miraculously from
its "why"—and set it apart.

IF SATISFYING your customers' intangible needs is so important to a differentiation strategy, how do you determine what those needs are? Customer research and surveys don't teach you how to differentiate. Your competitors conduct these same studies and get the same information you do. With the same data you are using, they design products that are the same or similar to the ones you would design. We've learned that knowing your customers' deeper needs— the needs that only you can satisfy—must come from within you rather than from external data collection.

Building your differentiation strategy is an inside-out process; it starts with your own core beliefs and those of your leadership team. It comes from discovering your *corporate soul*, the higher purpose of your company, and how to use this to satisfy your customers' intangible needs and to address their deeper insecurities. You will want to know not only *what* product your customers want from you, but also, *why* they want it. Armed with this knowledge and understanding, you have an advantage that no one can take from you. To get to this point though, you'll need to answer some questions.

First, there are the basic questions you address every time you sit down to a strategic planning session, such as *what* your company does, *how* and *when* it does it, and *where* it aspires to go. But these questions are just previews to the one question you really need to know the answer to. The missing question is "*Why?*"

Why are you in this business and why is your company here? What is the higher purpose for which your organization has come into being? Your company's existence is no accident of circumstance; it is here to do something no other organization can do.

Albert Einstein apparently said that if he could ask God one question he would ask Him *how* the universe began, because the rest is all math. But upon later reflection, he said, "I would ask Him *why* the universe began, because then I would know the meaning of my life." Answering the *why* question in a clear way gives meaning to your work and soul to your company. When a company has soul, the most innovative "*how-tos*" emerge almost miraculously from its "*why*"—and set that company apart.

What is the soul of your company or the team you lead? What is its higher, unifying purpose? How do you articulate it? How do you nourish and sustain it? Do you know the souls of your customers and what their intangible cravings are? Do you know how to provide for the intangible cravings of your customers in ways others cannot?

These questions should sound familiar. You discover your company's higher purpose in a similar way to the way you discovered your own in Chapter 6. When you discovered your own *Personal Purpose*, the reason for which you believe you were put in the world, you didn't look at what you wanted to accomplish; you looked at who you are, what your *Spiritual Fingerprint* is, what your capabilities and passions are, and most importantly, who the people or entities are that could derive the most benefit from your specific contribution. To discover your *corporate soul*, you must go through a similar process.

To uncover your company's purpose, its soul, answer three questions: What are your company's *capabilities*? What are you and your leadership team truly *passionate* about? And who, exactly, are your company's *primary customers*?

A *capability* is the most valuable contribution, both tangible and intangible, a corporation can make to its customers using its unique portfolio of assets. A corporation's *primary customers* are the segment of people or entities that can derive *the most* value from its contribution. Many other people and entities will benefit from the corporation's contribution, too, but the *primary customer* is the one the corporation relentlessly focuses on while designing its offerings and strategies.

What are your differentiating capabilities?

As an organization, you have many strengths and assets. You have tangible assets like real estate, equipment, and the products you manufacture or sell. You also have intangible assets like brand reputation, intellectual capital, culture, and customer intimacy. Many other companies have similar assets, but few, if any, have the same unique portfolio of strengths and assets that you have, especially with respect to intangible. The nature of your unique portfolio of strengths and assets is key to identifying your capabilities.

A capability is different from a strength or an asset. A capability is what you can do for your primary customer *using* your strengths and your assets. Ask yourself what difference you can make to your primary customer's life. Why would they want your product or service specifically? Seek the deeper reasons if you can.

Going back to the Southwest Airlines example, their assets include a uniform fleet of only 737s, a secure network of routes to most high-traffic U.S. destinations, and a team of people who are passionate about making others feel good. Utilizing these assets, one of Southwest's capabilities is to provide lower-cost no-frills travel to people who won't mind the airline's simplicity because they are being treated well and having fun.

Take an example from a different industry: Warren Buffet's Berkshire Hathaway's assets include vast cash reserves, a sterling brand, a brilliant investment analysis methodology, and a proven investment philosophy. With these assets Berkshire Hathaway can identify and seize medium to long-term growth opportunities for their shareholders that others cannot.

So, what are *your* company's capabilities? What can you do for others using your unique portfolio of assets that competitors cannot easily do? Start off with an inventory of your company's tangible and intangible assets and its strengths, highlighting those that are more unique. Include everything that comes to mind, but articulate each one in the clearest, narrowest way you can. Instead of saying "a fleet of aircraft," say "a fleet of single-model aircraft that can be more efficiently maintained and turned around than the fleets of competitors who service a variety of different models." Instead of saying "two thousand employees," describe their skill sets and strengths, too. What stands out about your employees and differentiates them from the employees of others in your industry?

Your culture is an asset, too. Describe some of the differentiating qualities of your culture that could benefit your customers. What about the intellect of your people and any intellectual property your company owns? Think of some unique skills that differentiate your teams—their agility, their resilience, the degree to which they are empowered to make decisions at lower levels, or their ability to connect well with others, and so on. All these qualities are assets that your company possesses.

Now, considering your list of strengths and assets, ask yourself: What can we do for our customers with these assets? How can we change their lives for the better, and with the greatest impact? What are some of their deeper needs that we could satisfy with our product or service, or with the way we deliver our products to them? These are your capabilities, and you are likely to generate a list of them. Lay them aside for a while and proceed to the next step.

Who is your primary customer?

You would think companies should know who their customers are, but often they don't. Agreeing who the *primary* customer is sometimes takes executive teams hours of work and generates the most vigorous debate in our workshops. This debate usually triggers a very new way of looking at their business and often leads to profound product innovation as well as innovation in operational process and organizational structure.

Think of a hospital. Are its primary customers the patients who are treated there, the insurance companies who pay, or the physicians? Different hospitals may answer this question differently, depending on their capabilities. Are a newspaper's customers, for example, the readers who buy the paper or the advertisers who provide its revenue? Is the reader just a means by which to bring visibility to advertisers, or do advertisers enable the newspaper to efficiently provide information to its primary customers, its readers? Or think of a franchising operation: are franchisees the customers of the franchising company, or are the consumers of each franchise its primary customers? Is the franchisee just a distribution and delivery vehicle to bring products and services to consumers?

Of course, patients, physicians, and insurance companies all benefit from hospitals, and readers and advertisers both benefit from newspapers. The question, though, is which set of people derives the *most* value from that specific entity's *unique* portfolio of capabilities? When a company designs its business model and offering, it should think of all its customers but focus its offering on only one customer set, its primary customer. Assuming its customers are arranged like a target, the primary customer is the one that sits in the bull's-eye.

A company's primary customer may not be its biggest, but it will be the customer ready to pay the highest premium for the company's product. This is because the primary customer gets the most value from the company. When considering who exactly your primary customer is, there is no right or wrong choice. However, the business strategy and nature of your offering will vary depending on the *primary customer*, on whom you choose to focus.

Paradoxically, *the narrower your focus of primary customer, the wider your total net of customers is likely to be.* Apple, for example, does not try to be all things to all people. It designs its products with very specific kinds of customers in mind. This has enabled Apple to focus on an extremely deep intangible need in that customer-set. Because the need Apple satisfies is so deep, it is almost universal, and therefore, although it focuses on the few, it appeals to many. Apple still has a relatively small share of the total PC, laptop, and mobile phone market. But the premium its intangible offering commands has made it the most valuable company in the world.

Let's go back to the Google example. Because Google is absolutely clear about who its customers are and is committed to them, its leaders resisted the temptation to follow other search companies, many of whom biased their searches in favor of advertisers. Google's primary customer is the user of the search engine, whereas other search engines regard advertisers as their primary customers. For Google's competitors, the search engine is a strategy by which to draw customers to advertisers. This is very similar to the way many newspapers use their news articles as a strategy to bring an audience to their advertisers, who are their true customers.

Google was committed in its view of the search user as its primary customer and remained loyal to the needs of users even after it started to accept paid, targeted advertising. Google's purpose is to make all the knowledge in the world easily and freely accessible. Clearly, its primary customer is the search engine user. Google's vigilance against the seductive power of advertisers to attract revenue has allowed them to remain true to its customer. They remind themselves of the danger of this seduction every day with their playful but serious "*don't be evil*" motto.

Articulating passions

Passions are the strong feelings within us that distinguish us from one another. Similarly, the passions of an organization's leaders distinguish that organization and give it energy. Your organization's soul is, to some degree, molded by your personal passions and values, and those of your leadership team. What are you truly passionate about?

What excites you? What activities seem to energize you, rather than drain your strength? What would you want to spend your time doing if you neither had a job nor needed to work? It will help you to revisit your *Spiritual Fingerprint* for this part of the exercise. Make sure to weave your own passions into your company's purpose statement. You will energize your organization without tiring if its work is something you are passionate about.

Articulating purpose

In the final step of articulating your company's purpose, revisit your primary customer set and your capabilities. In considering your primary customer, try to focus on the actual individual who is likely to make the choice to use your offering. Have real people in mind rather than faceless corporations or business units.

Next, using your human capacity to empathize, put yourself into your customer's shoes and try to imagine what it is like to be him or her. Try to feel their insecurities (we all have them). Remember the two investment banks that identified different insecurities in the same customer, insecurities that each felt uniquely positioned to address? One of them highlighted the customers' feeling of being intimidated by investment bankers' acumen and knowledge; the other identified their sense of boredom and aspiration for glamour and excitement at work. Now, combine your particular capabilities and passions in a statement that describes how you can address your customers' deep-seated intangible needs and help them overcome their insecurities.

As was the case for Google, deciding who your customers really are and how you can address their intangible needs and aspirations will influence the design of your competitive advantage and the nature of your intangible offering. This, in turn, will impact the cultural architecture you select, because it is a corporation's culture and its soul that deliver the intangible components of its offering to the customer. Discovering your corporation's soul and the purpose of its existence can also power its transformation.

CHAPTER EIGHTEEN

PURPOSE AS A TOOL
FOR TRANSFORMATION

*Knowing the higher purpose of your business and the
deeper differences you can make to the lives of your customers can
transform even excellent companies into extraordinary ones.*

A PHOENIX REBORN.

Phoenix International is the largest and one of the fastest-growing privately held international freight and forwarding companies in the United States. Bill McInerney, a former Peace Corps volunteer in Somalia, schoolteacher, and insurance agent, founded it in 1979. Bill is a man of passion and soul, and he used his passion to imbue Phoenix with a culture of service and caring for employees, which has always been an important element of its success. But the world was changing, and Bill, who saw the changes coming, appointed Stephane Rambaud as Phoenix's progressive new CEO.

Based in the American Midwest, Phoenix's focus had always been eastbound freight from Asia to the USA. This trade lane began to show signs of shrinkage, particularly in the economic downturn of

2008–2009, while intra-Asian trade lanes, Asia-Europe trade lanes, and westbound trade lanes kept growing. Stephane was concerned the company was not well positioned, structured, or culturally oriented to exploit these new opportunities optimally. To make it worse, Asian competitors had begun to open offices in the Midwest and could potentially erode Phoenix's dominance in that area. The Chinese were taking on contracts at prices American companies could not meet. They threatened to commoditize freight, thereby challenging American pricing models. Phoenix was beginning to see these developments in its financial results. Stephane asked my firm to work with him and his team to move the company into the future.

Seeking to articulate their *corporate soul*, the Phoenix team deeply probed the company's purpose. First, they identified the set of individuals who benefit most from Phoenix's unique offering as the VP of logistics, a purchasing manager, or an import manager in any company with a need to move containerized product overseas. Many of these mid-level managers in their client companies have limited expertise in the complex field of international logistics and can at times feel overwhelmed by their organization's complicated supply chain. Logistics or purchasing managers usually wear many hats and work in high-pressure environments. Their work is often underappreciated and not fully understood. They have high levels of responsibility, but do not always receive the recognition they deserve for the important role they play and the contribution they make.

Identifying the intangible needs of Phoenix's real human customers as well as its own capabilities and the passions and *value-drivers* of its executives, the team articulated the new Phoenix purpose as follows:

> With *passionate commitment, we simplify and customize the international shipping process and information flow. We connect deeply*

with our global customers to understand their world and, with knowledge and expertise, position them to master their complex logistics processes. This gives them the confidence and security to succeed.

Phoenix had never thought of its customer as a single individual in a client company, nor had they considered that their contribution to that customer is so much more than a high-quality freight service. They had never thought about the difference they could make to their customers' lives and how they could help them overcome their own insecurities by providing them with the confidence and security to succeed. This "confidence to succeed" became the core of Phoenix's intangible offering.

This intangible difference is what now makes Phoenix a desirable partner in the eyes of export managers when they select a forwarding agent. Phoenix's purpose is not merely to provide superior service; many good forwarders give good service. Their purpose is also about creating a human connection and responding to the aspirations, insecurities, and deepest needs of their customer. Doing this will be central to the soul of Phoenix International if it remains faithful to its strategy moving forward.

To fulfill its *corporate purpose*, Phoenix needed to transform and set new plans in motion. It needed to build the technology platforms to deliver a customized international shipping process and information flow. It needed people who could connect deeply and use their significant knowledge of international freight logistics to help their customer, the export manager, look competent and feel confident. Phoenix began to rapidly build the appropriate technology platform and to modify its training programs. Leadership began a process with us to train their managers on the company's purpose so that they, the

235

managers, could focus on further deepening their human connections with customers.

Phoenix decided to adapt its culture and performance measures to focus on longer-term customer relations and not just on the immediacy of the next deal, as it had done in the past. The company planned to apply leadership greatness principles to improve their capability for forging deep and trusting relationships globally. In this way, Phoenix intended to expand from being a U.S.-based company to becoming a global freight forwarder, significantly increasing its intra-Asia and Euro-Asian traffic. Very soon after our work with them, Phoenix again turned in record results.

A Feel for Fashion

Transformation can only deliver meaningful value if it endures. Over the years the Lapin International method and process has helped new and tenured leaders not only to discover and articulate their company's corporate soul, but also to embed it into the company's DNA. Once embedded, a company's soul manifests authentically in everything it does from its management culture and media communications to its processes and structures. Embedding a company's *corporate soul* into everything it does makes the soul of the company less dependent on the leader's charisma and ensures the endurance of that soul even after the CEO departs.

Truworths International, a large fashion retailer, used our process to completely transform itself. When the company found itself caught in a conundrum of imitation and commoditization, Michael Mark, its CEO, broke the cycle to set Truworths on an unprecedented trajectory of growth and success. This is how he did it.

Michael is one of the most highly regarded fashion retail CEOs in the world. He overflows with exuberant energy, which, together with his quick wit and confidence, can make him seem abrasive to some of the people who work with him. It is almost eerie to watch Michael walk into one of his stores. He appears to be taking a whiff of the store's atmosphere; he senses its energy, its appearance, and its sounds. In seconds he makes a comment to the store manager, putting his finger on some change that needs to be made. Retail is in his blood, and he inspires his whole company with his enthusiasm.

I got to know Michael when, more than a decade ago, Truworths suddenly started to lose market share. In an almost panicked reaction, his team began to copy whatever their competitors were doing. The spiral only worsened; merchandise had to be heavily discounted, margins shrank, morale suffered, and Truworths began to hemorrhage talent.

Working with Michael and his team, we helped them to think about their industry in ways no one else had and to move into market space that was unoccupied by their competitors. They questioned their purpose as an organization and they asked themselves why people are willing to pay a premium for fashion. Which of people's insecurities does fashion address and how does that make them willing to pay so much more for brand-name fashion than an equally good item of clothing without a label? What they determined is that the intangible yearning of fashion buyers is to boost their confidence and project an aura of success. Yet they often lack knowledge of global fashion trends and the ability to blend their fashion successfully. Truworths found its purpose:

We help young, fashionable customers look attractive and successful and feel enthused with confidence. And the way we achieve this is by enticing them into the most exciting, visually appealing "real" and virtual retail environments, where they can shop effortlessly for an innovative and adventurous blend of color, fabric, value, and fashion styling in accordance with the latest international standards.

Michael proceeded to infuse this purpose into everything Truworths did: the way it purchased, merchandised, managed people, advertised, and designed its customers' unique experiences, from colors and music in the stores to lighting in the fitting rooms. Truworths had a soul, and its customers and employees could feel it. As a result, its return on equity, in excess of 50 percent, has continued to defy market analysts. Its growth of over 20 percent per annum has now been consistent for more than fifteen years and it hasn't stopped moving forward.

Michael's competitors could not replicate his model because there was such a perfect match between his own passion, Truworths' soul, and the intangible needs of its customers. This match is the key to the success of *inside-out* strategic thinking. Michael attracted people onto his team who were driven by values similar to his. Like Richard Branson did at Virgin, Michael infused Truworths' *corporate soul* with his own beliefs and passions and those of his team; no one else has Michael's soul and no other company has Truworths'.

Truworths did not stop at articulating its purpose. We also worked with Michael and his team to build a set of *value-drivers*, the building blocks of its new culture, with which it could deliver on Truworths' purpose. Deep, intangible human needs cannot be satisfied just by the effectiveness of a company's operations and the efficient application of its resources. Truworths excelled in these qualities, too. But in addition to operational effectiveness and efficiency, Truworths also designed and built a very specific culture. Truworths' *corporate soul* was spread across the entire company in all its geographical locations and business units, so that every part of the company could deliver the intangible benefits that Truworths promised its customers.

In Troubled Times

Like the avocado and the acacia trees in Chapter 14, when our security is at risk and our future is uncertain we sometimes feel threatened. In these situations, we can choose to default to our defensive operating system and, like the acacia tree, grow thorns and become harsh, aggressive, and nasty. Alternatively, instead of shutting down or chasing our attackers away with our fear-driven aggression, we can respond heroically. Like an avocado tree, we can increase the value of the contributions we make so that no one will want to damage or destroy us.

Like the avocado tree in Chapter 14, both Phoenix International and Truworths responded to market and competitor threats with growth strategies born out of their respective *corporate souls*. When things are tough, great leaders make sure that they never compromise their own values or the souls of their organizations. By respecting their customers' vulnerabilities and insecurities, they nourish not only their physical needs but also their deeper human and spiritual cravings. They care for their employees so they in turn will care for their customers. They leave their competitors to grow thorns like acacia trees with which to defend themselves. After the hard times, the companies that have responded with extra growth—companies with soul—come out on top.

All this seems straightforward enough. But what happens when a *multinational* company needs to articulate its *corporate soul* across cultures? Will the employees in China be able to understand and express it like their counterparts in North America? Can and does it still have one *corporate soul* or many? Can young people from a new generation identify with the *corporate soul* of a business led by much older people? Can leaders use one management language and philosophy to inspire many cultures and generations? These questions touch on the beauty and the idea of the *corporate soul*; an idea whose power is at once intimate in its depth and universal in its reach. Part Three takes this idea further.

THE NEXT ERA
OF LEADERSHIP

Taking the Corporate Soul Across
Continents, Cultures, and Generations

CHAPTER NINETEEN

CULTURAL INTELLIGENCE

*Culturally intelligent leaders are the leaders
of the future, and their companies will be
the success stories of tomorrow.*

PEOPLE IN foreign countries, from different cultures in your own country, and even within your own company understand that you will not always appreciate or practice their cultural norms. They make allowances for our ignorance, just as we do for people to whom our culture is foreign. However, when it comes to universal values like dignity, trust, and respect, very few people anywhere make allowances for cultural difference. All people always expect to be treated with dignity, no matter what culture they come from. The challenge is that different cultures view some words, attitudes, and gestures differently, and an unintentional wrong move can injure their dignity and erode their trust. Cultural intelligence is knowing how to uphold the dignity of people and quickly build their trust irrespective of their culture, faith, or nationality. This is particularly pertinent when doing business in emerging economies.

Conducting business successfully and forging enduring partnerships in emerging economies will power the next wave of growth for multinationals. U.S. companies recognize that as successful as their management methods have been for them in the past, they can no longer force "the American way" on their Asian or South American counterparts. As the economies of many emerging countries become immensely powerful in their own right, they are less inclined to have the U.S. dictate to them how to do business, even though the American market is still so important to them. American companies with subsidiaries in other countries are also encountering greater resistance to directives that are counter-cultural in those countries. Mastering cultural intelligence however, goes way beyond overcoming the challenges of differences between cultures. It offers a new and superb opportunity for economic advantage. I call this the *arbitraging of cultural differences for economic advantage*.

Arbitraging Cultural Difference for Economic Advantage

We did business at a price and at terms far more favorable to us than I could possibly have negotiated by any conventional means.

I learned about arbitrage in my very first job as an international commodity trader where my responsibility was trading for metals and minerals, and later for energy. Arbitrage is the practice of taking advantage of a price difference between two or more markets. Commodity trading in those days was not about sitting in front of a computer screen or designing complex mathematical formulas to capitalize on minute market inefficiencies. Our job was to use our relationship-building skills with producers and consumers globally to discover differences in the value of a given commodity between one country and another. However, the most important part of our work was not just to spot the value-gaps, but also to leverage these relationships, widen them, and arbitrage them to our advantage.

In 1975, Simco Cable, a small copper wire manufacturer in the town of Rasht in Northwestern Iran, entered into a joint venture with the large Swedish communication company, LM Ericsson. This joint venture grew Simco's capacity 100-fold virtually overnight. Recognizing the opportunity and having secured a source of raw copper in Africa, I went to pay a visit to their CEO at that time, Yusuf Esfahani (name changed to protect privacy). Unknown to me was that Mr. Esfahani was a respected leader of the Moslem community in Rasht and quite extreme in his religious beliefs. My office in Tehran advised me not to call on him myself, and that if I did, I would need to hide my connections with Israel and any hint of my Jewishness. Failing to do so, in their opinion, would not only destroy any chance of business but could also trigger an unpleasant or possibly violent incident.

Still in my twenties and not very wise, I decided that since I was the product specialist and the most qualified person in our company to negotiate the deal, I would not delegate my role. I would also not change anything about how I presented myself but would just be authentic. I proceeded to his plant in Rasht. At the security gate they called to his office, and by the time I drove up to the main entrance, a tall, imposing man dressed in a crisp, white thawb (an ankle-length robe) and keffiyeh (a traditional headdress), was waiting to meet me. He strode up to my car, opened my door, and pulled me right out of the car. Trembling in fear, I was convinced I was about to be knifed by a crazed zealot. But the opposite was the case. Yusuf embraced me and, referring to our common Abrahamic ancestors, addressed me as his cousin. He led me into his office and assured me that we were going to have a long and prosperous relationship. Thus started a warm, personal friendship and a long and profitable business relationship.

By being true to myself, I had unwittingly connected with Yusuf's core value-driver—trust. Yusuf, like many people with trust as their core value-driver, could not establish a meaningful relationship with an individual who was inauthentic. He accepted my difference and my relatively poor knowledge of his culture. But he would not have accepted my being inauthentic, because authenticity has nothing to do with culture; it is a universal value. By guarding my own authenticity—even at some considerable risk—and making myself vulnerable, I had laid the foundation of trust on which we could both later build. Consequently we did business at a price and at terms far more favorable to us than I could possibly have negotiated by any conventional means. I learned that just as you can arbitrage market differentials for advantage, so can you also arbitrage the differences between people's cultures and values for mutual economic advantage. You do this by appealing to people's core *value-drivers* and satisfying the intangible needs emanating from this core. This costs you nothing but could be worth a fortune to the other person. This idea became foundational to my philosophy of Cultural Intelligence.

Cultural Intelligence is an advantage not only for multinationals. Doing business domestically also requires more Cultural Intelligence than ever before. Many of the people you employ are likely to be from very different cultural backgrounds than yours. Your customers are probably diverse, too, even those who live nearby. As you engage more meaningfully with them, you will want to ensure that your *corporate soul*, while authentic to you, resonates with them, as well. In a global, multicultural economy an organization's *corporate soul* has to align not only with the beliefs and values of the executive team, but with universal beliefs and values as well.

Great leaders are culturally intelligent. They discover and articulate a *corporate soul* for their business that can be embraced universally. They build trust quickly with diverse foreign cultures and forge the most progressive trading alliances with people and businesses in foreign countries. These are the leaders of the future, and their companies will be the success stories of tomorrow.

Eureka! A New Model for Communication

By crafting one universal language that honors all cultures, we can speak to any person in the world in ways that leave him or her feeling valued and worthwhile.

The Three Culture Model is a quick and easy way to understand what builds trust in any culture and what undermines it; what commands respect and what destroys it. Instead of learning a different management language for every culture, *The Three Culture Model* provides you with a single, universal language that without fail inspires people to give of their best, irrespective of their cultural background. I developed this model many years ago and have used it around the world, training executives in the finance, mining, retail, and manufacturing industries to improve efficiencies and increase productivity. In Chapter 20, you will learn how we used it to help Fortune 500 and other companies improve their negotiating effectiveness in emerging economies. We have even used it with the U.S. Department of Justice to help them develop strategies to fight hate crime and terror.[68] Having shared this model with so many of my clients in the past, I would like to now share it with you and tell you how it all started.

The miracle happened on the first day of a workshop I was running for a large global mining group, Johannesburg Consolidated Investment Co. Ltd. (JCI), founded in 1989 by the famous British entrepreneur Barney Barnato. I was working in a remote part of South Africa at a time when racism was flourishing and apartheid was alive and well. Management throughout the entire country was white; labor was black. There was no love lost between these two groups.

The workshop delegates were the most diverse group I had ever worked with. Pieter, a bespectacled engineer in his fifties, was an autocratic manager who represented the extreme right wing of the political spectrum in the room. He was unabashedly racist and ultra-conservative in his outlook. Jeremiah represented the other extreme. He was a worker with no formal education. He was young, but his physical stature and natural confidence gave him the presence of a born leader. He was a left-wing trade union activist and loathed men like Pieter. Pieter, on the other hand, didn't loathe Jeremiah at all. He merely dismissed him.

At the start, Pieter and Jeremiah regarded me with equal mistrust, as did most everyone else in the room. I later learned that Pieter assumed I was a left-wing liberal academic, and Jeremiah decided I was a capitalist tool of management helping them to further exploit the workers. I was neither. I was a consultant hired by JCI to demonstrate my then new ideas on how to fuse diverse cultures into focused teams of explosive human energy.

Addressing this obviously hostile group didn't just scare me; it absolutely terrified me! Apart from concern for my physical safety and my ability to manage the tensions in the room, I was nervous because so much depended on the outcome of this experiment. Could we really build a management philosophy and language capable of bridging schisms between political, educational, cultural, and social extremes? Could I inspire trust and command respect across cultural and generational chasms even if I was not expert in those cultures? More important, would this group of people even give me the chance to try, or was the level of mistrust too high? Could I captivate both Pieter and Jeremiah, and thereby win them all?

Some hours into the day Pieter began to get noticeably fidgety. He needed to say something. I gave him the floor knowing there was a good chance he would spark a riot with some ill-conceived and possibly racist comment. But he didn't. He stood up and began sobbing like a child. "Why, when I was young, did no one teach me the value African culture brings not only to our business here in South Africa but to people all over the world? Why did no one help me access this information? How could I not have known it is possible to speak in a language that demonstrates respect and builds trust across all cultures? Why, even though I have lived in Africa all my life, have I had absolutely no appreciation for the way black African people see the world?" he began. He proceeded to talk about his shame and ignorance and of how different his life could have been. There was silence in the room as he sat down again. Hunched and crestfallen, he looked down, avoiding everyone's astonished stares.

Then, without asking for anyone's permission, Jeremiah stood up slowly and deliberately. He paused dramatically for a few moments, looking around the room before he began to talk. His features appeared softer than they had been until then, his gaze optimistic.

The group's attention was focused on him. All I could hear in the room was my own loud heartbeat as he began to speak. In slow and broken English, he said, "Today, I am proud of my company. For the first time, management has hired a consultant who can talk to me as if he, too, is a black man. Thank you." This was the miracle I had wished for.

I was stunned, silenced, and humbled by the openness and raw humanity of these two men on such opposite sides of the human spectrum. "Thank you, Jeremiah," I said. "However, I believe that there is no such thing as 'talking like a black man'—or a white man, for that matter. By learning how to combine the different principles of respect we can borrow from each culture to form one universal language honoring them all. In this way we can speak to any person in the world in ways that leave them feeling valued and worthwhile. You and Pieter have both just taught us that this is possible. Thank you."

I felt like Archimedes must have felt when, after discovering the principles of specific gravity while in his bath, he ran out into the street naked, shouting, "*Eureka*! I have found it!" Eureka! I had indeed found the secret, and it worked. I called it *The Three Culture Model*.

The Language of Sipho

The Three Culture Model came to me as an epiphany only a week before my workshop with Jeremiah and Pieter. I had taken a trip into the African bush for some rest and inspiration. I arranged a nature hike each morning with a wise, elderly African tracker named Sipho. Each morning we would leave the camp early, while it was still dark and cold. Slowly, the wild countryside would begin to fill with the sounds of morning life as we made our way into the veldt. One particular morning, while stopping for a flask of coffee, Sipho asked me why I appeared so troubled. I told him I was searching for the reason why African people seem to be much less productive than their counterparts in other parts of the world.

Looking me straight in the eye, he said simply, "The reason is because '*they*' do not know how to talk to '*us*,'" and he turned away from me. Recognizing "*they*" referred to *management*, I questioned him further about what exactly he meant. I learned that in African culture there is hardly anything so discourteous as to give another person a directive, especially if the other person is older than you. "Our managers are not our fathers or our tribal chiefs, and we are not in the military. Why do they bark orders at us as if we are barely human?" Sipho asked me.

"How then," I responded, "in your culture, would a manager tell a subordinate what to do in a way that doesn't offend him or her?"

Sipho sat down across from me on a tree stump and explained, "Imagine I was your boss and needed you to make a clearing right here in the bush. This is how I would ask you to do it. I would invite you to sit down and would talk to you about your family and other matters of personal interest. Then I would say, 'David, I have a problem. I need to clear the bush. Do you think you could help me do this?' You would never allow me, your superior, to do the work. Instead, you would tell me not to worry about it, and take care of it yourself. When you give orders, people obey you out of fear, with little energy and no enthusiasm. When you ask for their help, they jump to serve you."

I explained to Sipho that in business there often isn't time for conversations like these to happen each time we issue a directive. But I continued to reflect.

A few days later, I was at the airport. A stranger leaned over to me and, explaining he wasn't feeling well, asked if I would mind helping him with a glass of water. I hurried to my feet and got him a drink. Then, making sure he was feeling okay, I bade him farewell and boarded my flight. Sitting on the plane, the penny dropped. I realized if the stranger at the airport had issued me a directive—"Get me a glass of water!"—I would not have responded, at least not positively. Like Sipho, *I was happy to help, but I was not willing to obey.* I realized Sipho's discomfort with directives is something we all share. The difference is that in Western cultures we have allowed our abhorrence of autocratic directive to be diluted for the sake of efficiency, which for us is of higher value than human dignity. Sipho's culture has preserved the value of human dignity as inviolate.

In business, we follow orders because we accept this as the efficient way to communicate and get things done. But there is another reason why we follow orders in business, no matter how abruptly they are given: fear. Managers control so much of what is important to the people who report to them, these people cannot ignore their managers' commands. We do what we are told. We obey, often just to avoid the consequence of disobeying, not necessarily because we believe in the meaning of the task and the value of our contribution. Managers are seldom trained to convey to people why the task is important in the bigger picture or to explain where it fits into the corporation's purpose. This is a perfect example of how we so often manage people by the power of our *status* rather than with the personal authority of our *stature*. We compel people with the threat of force rather than convincing them of our cause and inspiring them with our intellectual power and the authenticity of our values.

When we give people orders rather than asking them for help, they respond out of fear. When people act out of fear, responding to the threat of consequence, they act only with their instinctual defensive operating system. They bring little or nothing from their

Compelling compliance by force of status.

heroic, creative systems to their work. Their activity is mechanical, just enough to cover their backs; it is not inspirational and rarely produces innovation. Managing by fear and implied threat cannot access the deeper human spirit; it does not touch the place within us that generates our energy, nor the soul in us that is responsible for our uniqueness. Business cultures in which people efficiently respond to directives, but are void of inspiration or a higher purpose, are soulless cultures. The cultures of businesses with a *corporate soul*, however, are saturated with human dignity, thereby bridging all cultural chasms.

When we ask others for help, we honor their dignity and make them feel valuable and worthwhile. If we order them to do something, it makes them feel like a dispensable instrument of our system. This is true for people from Africa, Asia, or anywhere else in the world. Sipho's lesson is universal.

This idea that issuing orders rather than asking for support is counterproductive applies even more in times of financial stress. When people are worried about their financial survival, their behavior is driven by fear rather than passion, and they instinctively, albeit unintentionally, instill fear in all those around them. Yet it is in hard times that we need human ingenuity, passion, and innovation more than ever. We need people who are inspired by their leaders to help their companies do more with less and generate more revenue from fewer resources. In hard times, great leaders are even more valuable than they are in good times.

In Western business, driven as we are by deadlines and efficiency, we are often reluctant to invest quality time to formulate longer but more effective communication. Rather, we articulate our directives in crisp, clear language, using as few words as possible and as little time as possible. We ensure obedience by implying, either overtly or covertly, the consequences of noncompliance. There is a veiled threat in every command.

In business, we have an unspoken contract with one another to allow mutual "abuse." We address each other in ways we would never permit in our day-to-day lives. African culture never entered into that contract; and nor should we.

In my research, I have discovered that one quality common among great CEOs is a deliberate mindfulness to avoid giving people orders, except in emergencies. Leaders of character power their success by asking people for their support and engaging them in the purpose of the task rather than by telling them what to do. Even when there is an urgent need for a quick and terse directive, they appreciate the potential damage such directives could cause to people's sense of worth. They repair the damage later by explaining the need for the way they spoke and apologizing for their abruptness. They are secure enough within themselves to expose some vulnerability and turn to others for help. In this way, they make others feel honored and valuable rather than like cogs in an industrial wheel.

This brings us to another phrase that, like "thank you" and "I'm really sorry," is very difficult to say but generates untold value at no cost at all. The phrase is "please help me," or just "please." The word *please* can be said in a way that shows much more than just common courtesy; it can express a deeply sincere and undeserving need. Even when we ask others to do a job for which we are paying them, it is appropriate to use the word *please* as an expression of undeserving need. This is because, as Rick Jackson, CEO of Jackson Healthcare, said to me, every employee is a "volunteer" who chooses to work for you rather than for someone else. The words *please* and *plead* have the same etymological origin.[69] *Please* really means: "I *plead* for your help." When you plead for someone else's help, you make them feel needed and valued. It makes them feel alive and full of purpose. It gives them the sense you cannot manage without their help, and this gives their life meaning.

This is one of many simple ideas I shared with a team of global purchasing executives from a *Fortune 100* company when I worked with the heads of their Pacific Rim businesses at a retreat in Macau, not far from Hong Kong. We found that, like African cultures, most Asian cultures also reject the idea of giving people orders rather than eliciting their help in a respectful way, even in business. Like African people, many Asian people are also offended at being told what to do rather than being invited into a collaborative exercise. Merely having seniority doesn't give people the right to order others around, and giving orders certainly isn't the best way to ignite people's passion.

For Sipho, human dignity is an inviolate principle, as it is for many Asian people. Although in the West we often sacrifice the value of dignity at the altar of efficiency, we still value dignity and crave it. The idea that a terse directive issued in a nonemergency situation is a violation of dignity is a universal truth, not one indigenous to Africa alone. African culture has preserved this universal truth in an unadulterated form, whereas in other parts of the world it has become diluted.

Every culture has preserved a body of great universal truths in an unadulterated form. The secret to cultural intelligence is to access these universal truths and fuse all of them into a new language of interpersonal conduct that inspires powerful responses from all people, irrespective of their cultures. Imagine if in the West, like in Africa, we asked each other for support rather than issued directives. Imagine the goodwill and energy we could create!

Before our very eyes, the American, European, and Australian executives we were working with in Macau began to gain the trust and respect of their Asian colleagues. They were starting to adopt the language of Sipho, the language that all of humanity speaks. It is understood in business and at home. It is understood amongst friends and amongst strangers. Except in emergencies, people resent being told what to do, even when they comply. They inevitably respond with enthusiasm, however, when they are asked to help. This enthusiasm translates to an ultimately more efficient response from people than you might get by issuing a brusque order.

If you measure efficiency by the length of your communication and the time and effort it takes, then using Sipho's language is inefficient. If, however, you measure efficiency as the effectiveness and speed with which a request is carried out to completion, you will see that Sipho's way is more efficient. It pays to invest a little more time and effort up front in speaking to your associates. When you make a request, include your measurable expectations as you normally would, but phrase your directives as requests, so that your team members feel needed and valued.

Employees and team members, like all of us, are wired from birth to please others, and generally they will. There is no need to threaten them with consequences. People engage with much higher energy when they do so out of a desire to contribute and perform, rather than out of a fear of consequences. If we manage people with dignity and respect instead of fear, we will bring out the best in them. Does this mean there will never be employees who take advantage of us? Surely there will.

Catherine Timmons, VP of human resources at PCI Gaming, a Poarch Creek Indian-owned resort in Alabama, decided it was undignified to keep signed records of verbal warnings to employees.

"These should be informal conversations, dignified coaching and mentoring opportunities, not sessions of fear and managerial intimidation. By keeping the meetings informal we have a greater chance to turn employees around and improve their attitudes and productivity. I know that here and there our failure to document verbal warnings will land us in trouble. I am ready to face that if it happens, because the advantages are so much greater than the risks."

Catherine is fortunate to be backed by her CEO, Jay Dorris. Jay is a leader who values the principles of *Lead by Greatness* and uses them.

So far, Catherine has hit no problems, and throughout the 2008–2011 recession, PCI Gaming did exceptionally well, with unprecedented levels of employee engagement that powered its phenomenal growth.

We know how to take calculated risks with millions of dollars of investment capital. We know we win some and lose some, and we aim to win much more than we lose. We don't expect zero loss. In the area of leadership, we need to be willing to take some risks, too, and show a degree of trust in people until they prove us wrong, even though we know we will experience disappointments along the way.

Sipho opened my eyes to the energy and brilliance we can unleash in people if we make them feel respected, even as we push their boundaries. The combination of pushing boundaries while at the same time showing respect is the key: push people's boundaries and challenge them to ever-greater heights, but do so in ways that leave them feeling dignified and valuable. Sipho's simple lesson makes it so much easier. Don't tell them; just ask them.

CHAPTER TWENTY

CULTURAL DIFFERENCE

Diversity is about how differently people see,
not about how differently they look.

PROBING THE RICHNESS of the universal truths treasured by different cultures, I learned that people from different cultures don't always look different, but they do always see and experience the world in different ways. The way a person from one culture experiences an event could differ significantly from the way a person of another culture experiences the same event. Different people see the world through different lenses. Every individual does. But culturally, there are some universal truths.

When we make assumptions about people based on their appearance, we often draw incorrect conclusions. There are many Asians whose values, and therefore the prism through which they experience reality, are more aligned with the West than with Asia. Certain elements of Japanese culture are more akin to German culture

Seeing life through different lenses.

than to other Asian cultures, even though to Westerners, Japanese people look more like Chinese people than like Germans. There are customs in regions like southern Spain and Italy that more closely resemble some African cultures than other European cultures. How people look tells you nothing about how they see, and how they see is what you want to know.

In order to align your communication and gestures to other people's cultural perspectives, you will need to understand how different cultures experience our words, our gestures, and us. Words or gestures that inspire trust in one culture can cause suspicion and mistrust in others. For example, in the U.S., looking a person in the eye generally indicates a level of openness, and failing to do so arouses feelings of mistrust. There are many other cultures where it is disrespectful to look an older or more senior person in the eye; it is seen as brazenness and arouses feelings of mistrust.

So what is one to do when encountering someone from a culture one doesn't know—look the person in the eye or avoid eye contact? The answer lies in learning an easy and authentic language of universal dignity so people feel respected whatever culture they come from, whether or not you look them in the eye or are fluent in their customs and traditions. To master this language of universal dignity it is helpful to understand the three primary lenses through which we all experience our lives, and how each culture uses these lenses in varying proportions. This is what makes each of them unique and different.

Three Cultural Lenses

People of different cultures all admire and idealize perfection. They differ only in how they seek it.

In researching what differentiates people, I learned more about what makes them the same than what makes them different. This is particularly so when it comes to their beliefs and values. None of the tens of thousands of people I have met and worked with in over thirty different countries has bad values. I have explored the values of criminals in prison, of illiterate workers in Africa, CEOs and PhDs in the U.S. and Europe, and religious leaders in the Middle East and Asia; they all share the same good values. Each of them would like their children to be honest, upright, contributive members of society, who in turn will raise good families themselves.

Another interesting observation is how so many people of different cultures admire and idealize perfection. But people differ in how they seek and often demand perfection. It is helpful to think of the people you know in one of three different categories. The first category includes those people who look for perfection in objects and structures. The second contains people who believe perfection can be found only in specific ideological models. The third category comprises those who seek perfection in their relationships with others.

Think of people you know who are fanatical about the perfection of objects. They demand perfection in their living environments, their

Structural: Inspired by the technology more than the music.

technology, their organizational and engineering structures. They feel insecure if they are not functioning within a clearly defined structure. They like society to be structured and to them social status says more about your position in society than any other criteria such as character, wisdom, or personal stature. Courtesy and the observance of social norms are more critical than the free expression of honest opinion. They expect zero defects in technology, and prefer even *people* to operate according to predictable rules. They find it hard to operate amid any form of chaos. You might think of these people as *structural* people. Structural people enjoy structured music and art and associate with people who are part of their social milieu.

Then there are people who are far less concerned about the perfection of objects, structures, and technology than they are about faithfulness to the "perfect" ideological model. It may be an economic, psychological, or religious model. They are purists and will not accept a compromise or adulteration of the model. People like this are sometimes intolerant of those with different beliefs. Religious fundamental extremism (within any religion) is a clear example of this category of person. But there are also academics, for example, in scientific, economic, or psychological fields, who are equally intolerant of theories that conflict with their own beliefs. These people we'll refer to as *ideological* people. Ideological people enjoy religious music, or music and art from the romantic period, and feel comfortable with people who share their beliefs.

People are my most valuable assets.

Ideological adherence trumps human kindness

The third category consists of people who are laid-back about structural and objective perfection, and are not obsessive about their own beliefs. To them, the quality of relationships and feelings are more important than structure, technology, outcomes and ideologies.

Loyalty before competence.

Perfection is not about what things look like nor is it about the ideas they represent. Perfection is about what something feels like. They want to feel good in relationships; they value loyalty and family. They enjoy rhythmic music and earthy art because they can relate to them in ways that are sensory rather than clinical or intellectual. It is helpful to think of people in this group as *relational*.

Friendship before safety

It is dangerously stereotypical to simplistically think of every person or of a nation or ethnic group as belonging to just one of these three categories; this is not so. Rather, for the purposes of this discussion, consider people and nations to be made up of these three orientations in differing degrees. Some are heavily structural and much less ideological or relational. Others may be predominantly relational and less structural and ideological. No nationality is composed exclusively of one of these cultural perspectives.

Classifying and Stereotyping

Just as individual people often seem to fit more into one of these categories than into the others, so it is with national cultures. There are just too many cultures in the world for the ordinary person to try to identify and understand each of them. It is helpful to classify the world's cultures into more manageable groups, provided one doesn't fall into the trap of stereotyping. Stereotyping is usually negative and occurs when one's impression of an individual is based on often superficial and even misinformed assumptions about the group to which he or she belongs. Stereotyping is particularly limiting when one is unable to accommodate individual variances in people that transcend their group affiliations. Notwithstanding these limitations, there do seem to be some cultures that are more structural than others, some more ideological, and others more relational.

If you were a foreigner about to make your first business trip to both Germany and the USA, I might advise you to use first names in your social interaction in the U.S. and more formal last names in Germany. Is this stereotyping? Well, yes, I guess in some ways it is. Would it still be helpful? You bet it would. It would provide you with a starting base. You would learn that the use of a first name in one culture is seen as friendly and warm, whereas in another culture it could be seen as disrespectful. Using this example, we might say that in the social arena, German people are culturally more prone to be structural and Americans more relational.

Once you became a little more familiar with each culture and got to know individuals within them, you would quickly learn how to relate both to Americans and Germans as individuals, and to understand the many exceptions to every stereotypical rule. The rule, however, would have been a good starting point.

By understanding the three primary cultural dimensions and how they play out in the different nationalities of the world, it will become easy to appreciate the unique angle from which those nationalities generally view life. We will also learn how to develop a single "language" that speaks with equal relevance and respect to all the cultures of the world.

A nation whose culture has a strong *structural* dimension is more left-brained: analytical, quantitative, and rule-based. It values outcome more than process and seeks perfection in the objective world: in science and technology, in structure and order, in systems and engineering. This culture builds awesome structures, both in the engineering and the organizational sense. It is formal and lives by policies, procedures, laws, and rules. People of this culture think in a more linear fashion. It manages people in a similar way to how it manages things. It motivates people with mechanical performance-management systems of reward and consequence.

Status in this culture is a function of position, wealth, and power. In business, people could be treated as mere factors of economic input and statistics of economic consumption. "People are our most important asset" is a phrase used to demonstrate management's belief in the humanity of employees, but in fact, by classifying people with other business assets like factories, real estate, and capital, it indicates how little management recognizes the uniquely human value of its employees. In reality, most businesses with a predominantly *structural* orientation see people as costs, to be reduced to a minimum whenever possible.

The dehumanization of people into numbers could pose a risk of inhumane cruelty if this culture were to exist in its pure form. (However, remember that no nationality or ethnic group is 100 percent *structural* in its cultural orientation, but is always made up of a composite of all three orientations.)

Cultures with a strong *ideological* orientation reject the perfection found in objects, systems, and organizations. Like the ideologically oriented individual, the ideological culture seeks perfection in a model. The model in which they seek perfection could be God, the Bible, the Koran, a philosophy, a religion, or an ideology. This culture is principle-driven rather than technology-driven. It attaches more value to principles and virtue than to measurable tokens of success. It seeks perfection in ideas and models from whose principles it never deviates.

Those cultures strong in the *relational* dimension seek perfection in the sensations and feelings engendered by the intimacy of relationships. For them, relationships need to be warm and intense rather than formal and structured. They value relationships and feelings over money, structure, principles, or ideology.

National cultures, though they are composed of each of these three cultural dimensions, differ from one another in the degree to which any one of these perspectives is dominant. So, in German culture the structural dimension may be stronger than the others, whereas in the cultures of the south of Spain and Italy the relational dimension might be more dominant. Many factors are responsible for these cultural differences, but much of what makes us different, both as individuals and as distinct nations, stems from our DNA. DNA is responsible not only for the way people from different nationalities look, but also for the way they see and experience the world.

Since the mix of cultural dimensions differs in almost every country, it helps to be competent in the dominant cultural dimension of the countries in which you work and live. Consider how competent one should be in each of the three cultural dimensions—structural, ideological, and relational—to be successful in each nation. This analysis is based on thousands of responses we get in workshops around the world, with special weight given to how people from these nationalities have rated their own cultures. These analyses entail no judgment, nor is it valid to compare one with the other. For example, two nationalities that focus mostly on the structural are not necessarily equal in their structural excellence. It is helpful only in that it gives a sense of the relative importance placed by each of these cultures on each of the three cultural dimensions.

How important is it, for example, to be socially popular versus technically proficient? How important is it in a particular culture that you buy into a nationally shared vision and ideology? Each nationality is a little different in these respects. In our workshops, I have asked thousands of people of various nationalities to classify their countries based on *The Three Culture Model*. This list, in a very simplified way, summarizes the general responses we received:

Northwestern Europe (Switzerland, Northern Germany, Belgium) – a strong structural emphasis, with less focus on ideology or relationship.

Middle East – Very strong emphasis on ideology, little on structure, and moderate on relational (although this is changing in some of the fast-developing Gulf regions).

Mediterranean Countries and South America – Very strong relational, somewhat ideological, and less structural emphasis.

Sub-Saharan Africa – Very high relational, low on both ideological and structural.

China – Moderate to strong emphasis on structure, medium on ideology, and very high on relational.

India – Moderate structural, medium ideological emphasis, and very high relational.

Russia – Low on structural, moderately ideological, and high on relational.

It is interesting to see how strong so many of the developing nations are in the relational dimension. One can see, for example, how China and sub-Saharan Africa could become natural strategic allies, something that is, in fact, playing out geopolitically at this very time. China is using its relational competence to create alliances in Africa based on the structural know-how it brings to Africa in return for mineral resources. Neither allows ideology to get in the way.

The USA, with its very structural approach to business, is finding it tough to compete with the relationships being built between China and Africa. One might have expected South Africa to be a more natural ally of its northern neighbors, but South Africa has a strong ideological component in its cultural mix that most other African nations do not. The battles for and against apartheid were ideological battles, and Nelson Mandela's rainbow nation-building idea was an ideological revolution, too. The rest of Africa defines itself more by its multifarious tribalism, a relational dimension rather than an ideological one. South Africa's strong ideological dimension could prove to be a handicap in the leadership role it should be playing in pan-African cooperation.

The United States: Its Strength and Its Complexity

The United States is probably more diverse in its way of life than any other nation in the world.

When we ask participants in our workshops to rate the U.S., we fail to get consensus. Even when the participants are Americans, the ratings for America are all over the place. The reason for this confusion about the U.S.'s dominant cultural dimension might be that the United States does not stand out in any one particular cultural orientation; all three are equally important in American life.

For over a century, the U.S. has led the world in the areas of business and technology, namely the structural areas. It is also ideologically influential far beyond its own borders, and Americans are generally very quick to form personal connections and create and sustain relationships, even when these relationships are not deep. To really succeed in the United States, it is important to understand all three cultures. To succeed in the U.S., one needs to master its corporate and institutional systems, be current with technology, and be focused on measurable deliverables. But this is not enough. One also needs to align with the American ideal of democracy and freedom (both economic and political), and one must be good at building partnerships, relationships, and networks. In the sense that you need all three cultural orientations in equal measure to succeed in the U.S., it is probably more diverse in its way of life than any other nation in the world.

The diverse nature of American life manifests itself in quite a unique way. Instead of blending the different orientations into one all-encompassing culture, the U.S. has evolved into three different domains, each with its own dominant cultural orientation: 1) business; 2) the constitutional and legal systems; and 3) the social and entertainment arena. Businesses in the U.S. are almost entirely structural in their values, the constitutional and legal systems are almost entirely ideological, and the social and entertainment arena is almost entirely relational. Interestingly, it is almost as if U.S. culture has allocated a dedicated capital to each of the three cultural dimensions. New York is heavily structural in its orientation, and structural competence is key to success in New York City. Washington, DC, is much more ideological, and Los Angeles strongly relational. Moving from one of these cities to another would be almost as culturally demanding as emigration from another country!

Can You Trust Americans?

The way American life has become compartmentalized into separate structural, ideological, and relational sectors confuses non-Americans and sometimes even undermines their trust in the U.S. This is precisely what happened when Neil, a newly appointed senior VP at a UK executive recruitment agency, made his first business trip to New York. On the flight, Neil found himself seated next to an American businessman, Seth. Neil normally keeps to himself when he travels, but on this flight Seth struck up a conversation with him. In no time, Neil felt as though he had known Seth forever. At the end of the flight, Seth invited Neil to give him a call in New York so they could get together, and he said he would introduce Neil to some of his contacts in the city. A few days later Neil called Seth, but could not get past his assistant. He left voice mail messages that were never returned. Eventually, calling just after the receptionist had left, Seth picked up the call himself. At first, he barely remembered Neil. Then he apologized for being too burdened with work commitments to get together. "But give me a call next time you're in New York," he said to the deflated Neil.

Somewhat confused, Neil went downstairs to the bar in his hotel for a drink. A little later, to Neil's surprise, Seth walked into the bar with a friend. He came up to Neil and again warmly connected with him as if nothing had happened only a few hours earlier. He felt even more confused. *Does this man ever mean ANYTHING he says? I could never do business with someone like Seth*, he thought to himself.

But Seth was not untrustworthy. In each compartment of his life, Seth is consistent and predictable. He would never back down on an agreement in business. There are rules in business, and Seth plays by the rules. He uses his time with an eye on efficiency, and while in business mode he is curt with people who are not part of his business world. Even his wife and family experience his abruptness when they call him at work. They are used to it and accept it. But Neil was not used to it and could not accept it. In Neil's world, Seth invited him to call and he ought to have given Neil the time and attention he had promised.

In Seth's world, that wasn't a promise or even a genuine invitation. If it were a serious business invitation, they would have agreed up front on a time for the call. The offer was a relational courtesy, like saying "see you later" to someone you know you will probably never see again in your life. In the U.S., the rules in the relational compartment are different from the rules in the business compartment. It is acceptable to be a little dishonest in the relational compartment, for the sake of social courtesy. It's called diplomacy in the relational world. The same behavior in the structural world of business would be considered disingenuous. In the structural world, unlike the relational world, people hold each other to their commitments. Most people who are part of the American business culture know this. But Neil was not American and did not understand it at all. The experience fractured their connection, which bewildered Seth.

"Why did that guy cold-shoulder me?" he asked his companion after Neil got up to leave the bar. "We had such a good conversation on the plane over from London a few days ago. He seemed to be a really nice guy. Why did he behave so peculiarly tonight? Did you see the look he gave me?" In Seth's world, he had built a relational connection with Neil, not a structural or business one. He had not been unfaithful to that relational connection and had no intention of being unfaithful to it in the future. What had caused Neil to suddenly sever that connection?

That night Neil called his wife in the UK and told her of his strange experience with the "flaky American." Seth also talked to his family at dinner and told them of his baffling experience with the "cold Englishman." Neil and Seth each believed in honesty and both valued trustworthiness. These two Caucasian males looked quite similar, but the way they experienced the world couldn't have been more different. And the way they viewed trustworthiness was different, too.

You may have a Neil and a Seth on your team. You may be a Neil or perhaps you're married to a Seth. How do you build trust between people for whom trust has such different meanings? If you have a multinational corporation with trustworthiness at the core of your value system, how do you use your value system across cultural boundaries to build trusting relationships?

Cultural Intelligence: The Business Case

Had we understood the different lenses through which each of us saw the same event, we could have saved both our companies millions of dollars.

By arbitraging cultural intelligence for advantage, you can win deals that might otherwise have eluded you, and you can optimize the value of deals you have already won. But you can also lose deals and erode value if you are culturally deficient—as I myself once was.

I was negotiating the long-term supply of coal to a very large chemical and petrochemical manufacturer in Taiwan. The negotiations were long and protracted. Every time we reached agreement on a particular item in the contract, our discussions were elevated to the next level of management, where we seemed almost to have to start over from the beginning. Eventually we agreed on everything, and were meeting with a large team of executives, including the president of the company, for "the signing" of the contract. After many flattering pleasantries, the president went through each major item of the contract and thanked his team and us for the agreement we had reached and for the generous way we had accommodated all of their requirements. I felt relieved for the first time in weeks—that is, until the president said, "There is just one item left that we cannot accept: your price." At that point, I felt misled and betrayed. I picked up my papers and left for the airport. I had done my best to meet their demands and had pressured our coal suppliers down to the lowest they could possibly go, but even this did not satisfy my Taiwanese counterparts—who, until that moment, had never indicated any problem with the agreed price.

Many years later, I realized how I could have managed things very differently and won an enormous contract for my company and our suppliers. My intentions were honorable, but my tactics were void of cultural understanding. I had done the best I could to come in at an acceptable level, and was up-front with them that this was the very lowest price we could go—any further concessions would need to be made in other areas of the agreement. I assumed a global company of that size would appreciate our openness and our being unwilling to enter into a bargaining session over the price. I had regarded price as a purely structural detail and handled it structurally. Taiwan, however, is a much more relational culture, and to many people there, price is not merely a contractual detail; it also has a relational dimension. My counterparts simply assumed I had left a little margin to give away at the end, as a gesture of goodwill and as a way to enable the president to bring some value to the table, even though he only joined the negotiations at the end. The relationship was as important to them as the price, and they felt I disrespected the relationship and the president of their company for the sake of a few cents per ton of coal. Both they and I felt a loss of trust for the other and a feeling of having been disrespected. We each saw the same event through two very different cultural lenses: I through a structural lens, and they through a relational one; and this cost both our companies millions of dollars.

When we do business strictly in a structural way, we use only one currency—structural currency. We can only negotiate around measurables like price, delivery time, quality, and quantity. Other cultures value other "currencies" even more than money. They are willing to make a sacrifice on price or quantity, if they feel a values alignment or an authentic relationship. When we adopt a more globally acceptable cultural language and use "currencies" from other cultures, we increase our chances of reaching agreement and resolving conflict. The improved efficiencies are significant. We saw this with Yusuf Esfahani and with Sipho in Chapter 19.

Dignity was so valuable to Sipho, authenticity and trust were important to Yusuf, and in a business capacity, money is valuable to me. These differences in values bring an opportunity for arbitrage— an opportunity I missed in Taiwan but took in Iran. By investing some time and thought in Sipho's desire for dignity, and framing my directives as requests for help and not as commands or demands, Sipho would give me much greater productive output than he would give to my competitors, who do not understand his cultural differences. Likewise, by taking the time for open and authentic conversation with Yusuf and risking my vulnerability to establish my integrity, I negotiated better terms with him than my competitors could. By recalibrating your measurement of efficient communication not by the length of the message you give, but by the effectiveness and speed of its execution, you will find that you can arbitrage cultural differences, with the result of significant gains in total efficiency and considerable financial savings.

The economic advantage of cultural intelligence goes beyond negotiating with foreign counterparts; it also applies to managing your own teams, especially when they are spread across the globe. Can you build one universal culture for a global company that still allows for its different nationalities to feel at home, trusted, and trusting of its management?

CHAPTER TWENTY-ONE
CULTURAL ARCHITECTURE FOR A GLOBAL ECONOMY

Just as in the case of individuals, corporations
can share the same values,
but have different Spiritual Fingerprints.

EVEN DOMESTIC companies operating in one American city need considerable cultural intelligence to manage the subtleties and complexities of the cultural diversity of their employees and customers. This is especially true for global companies operating in many different regions.

Technobrand Electronics, Inc. (names changed to protect privacy), is a U.S.-based global company. Chuck Branden, its CEO, championed a values exercise throughout the organization, hoping to create within the company a consistently high-performing culture. But the cultures in his operations in China and Saudi Arabia differed radically from the culture in the U.S., and he wanted to understand why.

Technobrand had spent a lot of time and money developing and communicating a unified set of values. They finally agreed on four:

- Excellence in Efficiency
- Respect
- Trust
- Recognition

Chuck asked my firm to help them determine why, despite all the work they had done on values across the company, there was not only a range of disconnected cultures in each of its operations, but there also seemed to be a high level of mistrust.

We conducted a study to determine the *Spiritual Fingerprint* of the operations in each of the countries in which Technobrand operated. We found that every culture in each region was built on the same values, the corporate values chosen by their global head office in the US. However, just as in the case of individuals, corporations can share the same values, but have different *Spiritual Fingerprints*.

After applying our method to map the organizational *Spiritual Fingerprint* at Technobrand's U.S. head office, the following emerged:

Chuck was a turnaround wizard and a relentless driver of efficiency. He had implemented the well-known Six Sigma process of quality improvement with resounding success. His team knew that, if necessary, almost anything (within the bounds of the law) could be compromised for the sake of excellence in efficiency. Excellence in efficiency could not be compromised for any reason. The way to earn Chuck's respect was to deliver results and to continuously take costs out of the system. Speed of delivery and accurate execution was essential at all times.

Put into words, the U.S. *Spiritual Fingerprint* would read:

We are uncompromising in our expectation of excellence of efficiency in the way we deliver our offering. We will only hire and promote people who are passionate about excellence and efficiency and who show a track record for achieving it. As an organization we only respect people who deliver efficiency and this builds our trust in them. Once we trust people we will recognize them, knowing they will not take advantage of our generosity.

We found a very different culture in Technobrand's Chinese operation, although it was founded on exactly the same values as the U.S. head office. Key to the difference was that the Chinese regarded respect as the non-negotiable core value-driver. Management in China only expected people who felt trusted and respected to deliver efficiency. They took upon themselves the responsibility to create an environment of respect and trust so that efficiency would result.

The *Spiritual Fingerprint* of the Chinese operation would read:

We are uncompromising in our expectation that the people we employ show respect for one another, for their supervisors, and for the company. We hire and promote people whose families we know and respect and who show respect to us, because those are the only people we trust. We believe that if our people feel respected, they will deliver the highest standards of excellence and efficiency, for which we will reward and recognize them generously.

Then we analyzed the culture at Technobrand's Saudi operation. For a while, the head office had been concerned that the Saudi management team was favoring members of the Moslem community and were not showing respect to the resident American managers. Their *Spiritual Fingerprint* explained the reason why. It also explained why the Saudi team was willing to reward people even before they had performed. They trusted their employees implicitly.

Put into words, the *Spiritual Fingerprint* of the Saudi operation read:

We only hire and promote people whose values we know and trust. These are people who will make sacrifices for the same things we would, and we truly respect them. Because we trust and respect our people, we will invest in them, knowing that the more generosity we show them, the more they will deliver to our standards of excellence and efficiency.

The Saudi culture emphasizes ideology, so trust is at their core. They do not feel comfortable with people they cannot trust from the beginning. In their case, that means people with the same values and beliefs, members of the same religion. This is non-negotiable for them. China is a relational culture and so their core is respect and dignity; everything else flows from that. The U.S. business environment is focused on efficient delivery; it is structural in nature and will not trust or respect people who are not delivering.

You will immediately see the cultural tensions between these three regional offices of the same multinational corporation. In the American model, the business imperatives of excellence and efficiency override every other ethical consideration. Respect and trust are as vitally important to Americans as they are to people in China or Saudi

Arabia. But for the American team, trust and respect are the *outcomes* of excellence and efficiency. They were perpetually frustrated with the regions that were willing to show respect and trust for people who had not yet proved themselves. To the Chinese team at Technobrand, respect and trust are core *value-drivers*, a fact that many Western companies doing business in China often fail to grasp.

Jacko Maree, CEO of the Standard Bank, told me how he gained this insight about the Chinese and applied it early on in his partnership negotiations with ICBC (Industrial and Commercial Bank of China). Curious about how trustworthy Chinese counterparts had proven to be in multinational partnerships, he asked his friend Ken Lewis, then the chairman, CEO, and president of Bank of America, about his experience with Chinese financial institutions after their acquisition of a stake in China Construction Bank. In a sentence or two, Ken shared an invaluable insight with Jacko that helped the Standard Bank and ICBC consummate their proposed deal. He explained that in his experience, provided the Chinese counterpart felt they were in a true, mutually beneficial partnership, they would prove to be at least as loyal and trustworthy as anyone else in business. As partners, Chinese business partners expect that each is as interested in the other's success as they are in their own. If they feel the other partner is an adversary trying to optimize his own interests at their expense, they will also adopt an adversarial attitude to protect themselves in the relationship. "If this happens, you will lose their trust and respect," Ken explained.

Technobrand Electronics was experiencing the same phenomenon. Their Chinese operation needed to have respect and trust as the foundation of their relationship. Once they received the respect they desired, they would deliver efficiently and gain recognition. This was hard for the American operation to understand.

We worked with the leadership at Technobrand to help them move to a place of comfort by allowing each of their global entities to use the company's values in ways that are indigenous to their own cultures. We explored what that would mean and how it would look at each location. We painted the cultural landscape that each entity would develop and how those cultures could function within the universal cultural architecture that Technobrand had designed. The key was to ensure that everyone across the globe understood that Technobrand was a business and its ethical responsibility was to deliver returns to its investors in a way that always upheld its values. Leaders everywhere in the world would be held equally accountable both for their results and also for *the way* in which they achieved them.

Technobrand was able to become a successful multinational company, with each geographical location developing its own culture without compromising or distorting the company's global *corporate soul*. Relationships improved as trust increased, and the resulting efficiencies were substantial and measurable.

Cultural Architecture for Talent Advantage

Measurement and structure alone do not inspire people to be creative and heroic; big ideas and authentic relationships do.

The way U.S. culture has become compartmentalized into three separate parts—a structural business culture, an ideological political culture, and a relational social culture—can play out with some disruptive social consequences. However, it does allow for companies to become as innovative with cultural architecture as they are with products and processes.

Ratchettech, Inc. (names changed to protect privacy), for

example, is a large company that prides itself on its nondiscriminatory hiring and HR practices. Howard, Ratchettech's CEO, was perturbed that employees from minority groups did not seem to experience cultural tolerance while working for the company. For this reason, many talented people left the company.

We worked with Howard's team, and as we did so it became clear that, deep down, despite all their platitudes, many executives at Ratchettech did not really believe diversity was a good business (*structural*) practice. They believed it was easier to achieve efficiency in a team made up of people who shared similar cultures, education, and social background. Nevertheless, despite their reservations about the case for diversity in business, they followed a strictly equal opportunity code of practice, because they genuinely believed it was "the right thing" (*ideologically*) to do.

Take Elizabeth, a talented senior executive at Ratchettech, slated to become the next CEO. Ratchettech showcased Elizabeth as an example of how they had successfully removed the glass ceiling for women in the company. But Elizabeth told us in an interview that she was receiving professional coaching to learn how to act more like a man. "We accept all cultures and genders and embrace them, but once they join us they have to think, feel, and act like white American males," she said. "Is that really diversity?"

Many employees talked about how the informal social network at Ratchettech was totally segregated, and how the male, WASPish old-boys club made the real decisions and was generally impenetrable to women and minorities. The Ratchettech Way—the company's guiding principles and the foundation of its culture—had been designed a long time ago by a group of Boston-educated white men, and it had worked well for Ratchettech for decades. But it was the reason why talented minorities, at first attracted to Ratchettech for its equal-opportunity reputation, were disengaging from their work and leaving the company in droves.

As successful as Ratchettech had been, the Ratchettech Way was also the reason why the company was not keeping up in the innovation race—so vital for its future market share. Diverse teams may not always be the easiest and most efficient to manage, but they are the most innovative and the quickest to challenge the status quo. The Ratchettech Way discouraged challenge, and despite its hiring policy, the company was becoming culturally and educationally bland; it was losing its edge. This is why Howard was worried.

Ratchettech was operating in cultural compartments. In its business it was uni-culturally structural. In its hiring and HR practices, it was ideological, and its ideology was equality. And in its networking systems it was relational; longtime personal connections were more important than professional merit. This made it easy for someone from a different culture to get hired, but difficult to fit in at the company without considerable adjustment to the Ratchettech Way.

We were careful not to tamper in any way with Ratchettech's relentless focus on measurable results or the way it evaluated itself and the people who worked for it. Measurement is, by definition, structural, and it should always remain so. But there is a difference between the way you *measure* results and how you *achieve* them. You measure results with structure and numbers, but you achieve them through people; measurement and structure cannot inspire people to be creative and heroic. In a purely numbers-driven environment, people often operate out of instinctual defensiveness, doing as little as necessary to hit the number targets and covering up their mistakes to avoid consequences. Big ideas and authentic relationships are what inspire people.

People are inspired by a higher *corporate purpose* that resonates with their own beliefs and values and by the authenticity of the people they work with. An inspired workplace is one in which all three cultural dimensions function in harmony: people connect with relational competence, they set targets and budgets with structural competence, and they work toward a higher ideological goal, a *corporate purpose* that unites them.

Ratchettech was an efficient company, but not an inspired one. It was a well-structured company, but it had no soul, and both Howard and Elizabeth knew this. We encouraged Ratchettech to remain strictly structural in the way they budgeted and measured, but to build a competitive strategy out of an inspiring higher *corporate purpose*—which we helped them formulate—a purpose that was authentic to the *Spiritual Fingerprints* of the executive team. We also taught them how to embrace relational competence as part of their management philosophy and their customer retention strategy. By infusing an authentic ideology (purpose) and a relational component into what was once an exclusively structural culture, Ratchettech found its soul, and people like Elizabeth now felt inspired and "at home" in the company.

After we reset the culture at Ratchettech, people with strong relational orientations, irrespective of their gender or nationality, all felt free to use their own characters and qualities to deliver results while acting in accordance with Ratchettech's universal values. Elizabeth told me that after this shift in the company, she was able to be more emotional, sympathetic, and genuine, whereas before she was playing an inauthentic role to get ahead. Now she is respected both for who she is and for the results she delivers.

Hiring diverse people doesn't just mean hiring people that *look* different; it means hiring people that see and think differently. Diverse teams generate new ideas that set your company apart from its competition. But for diverse teams to flourish, you must nourish them with a culture that encourages each person's authenticity and contributions. You should lead them as holistic beings that incorporate both defensive operating systems that desire security, and creative and heroic ones that aspire to greatness. To lead in this way, you and your managers should access your own human greatness, believe in the inherent greatness of others, and seek to unleash it in the diverse people you lead.

All of this will not only give you a leadership edge; it will give you an edge when it comes to recruitment and retention. But in the last few years, recruiting and managing the new generation has introduced fresh challenges. Often, people think of and talk about the new generation as spoiled kids who feel entitled, want immediate gratification, and are only in it for themselves. But if you think of the human energy at Google, Facebook, and hundreds of smaller companies made up mainly of the younger generation, you'll quickly realize this is simply not true.

When poorly led, the new generation *does* act entitled and *does* seek immediate gratification. But when led by people who "get" them and know how to respond to them, they blossom and will take your company places it could not go without them. But how do you do this? How do you attract the new generation? Once you recruit them, how do you engage them? And if they are really good, how do you keep them? Unlike previous generations of entry-level employees, it is not sufficient to "attract, motivate, and retain" this generation. You need to *captivate their imagination.*

CHAPTER TWENTY-TWO

NEW LEADERS FOR A NEW GENERATION

*Unlocking young people's energy will
transform your team, propel your business,
and be personally exhilarating for you.*

WELL-DIRECTED, talented young people in your business can help accelerate your journey into the future and help you leapfrog from yesterday to tomorrow. Ideally, you want droves of brilliant young talent craving to work on your team because your *corporate soul* resonates with them, because they feel inspired by your higher *corporate purpose* and are energized by your mentorship. You need young people who will joyfully help you build your organization and keep it at the cutting edge. Young talent should tweet on Twitter about how yours is the best place for people like them to work. Your talent should be beyond the reach of avaricious headhunters, and your competition should be scratching its head in wonder at what you have built and how you did it. You and the people who work for you should love coming to work, and the whole place should pulsate with passionate energy.

This is how it *will* be if you captivate the imagination of your young talent. Unlocking young people's energy will transform your team, propel your business, and at the same time prove to be personally exhilarating for you.

To captivate young people's imagination and release their exuberant energy, you will also need to:

- Understand the Internet generation
- Build a different culture from the one you have
- Forge a new kind of relationship with your team members

The Internet Generation

The gap between older people today and the generation born after the early 1980s is qualitatively different from any generational divide before.

How often have you heard managers (and parents) complain about the new generation? Perhaps you find yourself complaining about them sometimes, too. Many experience the new generation as their toughest managerial task yet. They say things like: "they're so entitled;" "they're only interested in money—what they can get, not what they can give;" "they don't know the meaning of hard work or loyalty;" "it's as if they're from another planet."

Well, in some ways they *are* from another planet, and this makes the current generation gap far more complex and challenging than any before it. This is because the gap between people born after about 1983 and those born before is different from any generation gap that has ever existed. Every adult generation in history has felt a gap between themselves and their children's generation. Our parents complained about our sense of entitlement and lack of discipline, as their parents did about them, and so on. But the gap between older people today and the generation born after the invention of the Internet in the 1980s is different from any generational divide ever.

As challenging as the young generation is to older managers, today's young people do want good leaders. They want role models. They crave leaders who portray competence and humility. They admire people who lead not by the status attributed to them by others, but by their own human greatness. Vince Colarelli of Colarelli Construction told me about his own leadership philosophy: "Good leaders today are guys who can be vulnerable. Humility is about allowing yourself to trust yourself and others, to be vulnerable, to put yourself in the hands of others."

Tony Hsieh is a brilliant leader of the new generation. At twenty-six he was appointed CEO of Zappos, a then struggling online shoe retailer. Just ten years later, in 2009, it sold to Amazon for $1.2 billion. Tony emphasizes the role of humility in his company: "One of our values is to be humble, and that is the one that trips us up most during the hiring process. There are a lot of smart people out there that are also egotistical, and for us it is not a question, we just won't hire them."[70]

Planet-E and Planet-S

Once upon a time, new generations were separated from their predecessors only by age and experience. Eventually, young people would grow up to be much like their elders. Not so today. This new generation, unlike others before it, will not grow up to be like their parents. There will in fact never again be people quite like the generation born before 1983. Today's gap between generations is more than generational; it's cultural. A child in Houston, Texas, for example, could have more in common with his or her peer in Beijing than with his or her own parents. As in the case of diverse cultures, both the new and the pre-Internet generations have huge contributions to make, but we ignore the generational culture gap at our peril.

People born prior to the Internet Age tend to think primarily in tangible terms. They think in real constructs and use rationally linear processes for building those constructs in the proper order. The new generation is more at home with the intangible. Many of them think more easily in abstract and even exponential terms than they do in concrete terms. Of course, there are older people who excel in the abstract and exponential, just as there are many young people who do not. So, instead of talking about it from an age and generation perspective, we will simply refer to intangible, exponential thinkers as the people from Planet-Exponential, or Planet-E; and tangible, structural thinkers as coming from Planet-Substantive, or Planet-S. We all are made up of part E and part S. However, it is helpful to consider that, generally, those people born before 1983 are stronger in Planet-S attributes and those born later tend toward Planet-E.

President Obama's election was a good example of a Planet-E campaign, although he himself was born long before 1983. He was forty-seven when he was nominated, but his campaign was built on the exponential capability of mobilizing the support of millions of people at minimum cost. He knew using technology and appealing to the values and vision of Planet-Es would make it easier to raise millions in small contributions (from both younger and older people). This system would not have worked in any of the previous elections, when almost every political contribution needed personal, face-to-face contact. New business models are no different in how, using technology, they exploit incremental amounts of revenue into exponential growth. This is the world in which Planet-Es are at home. So what is so special about the 1980s?

The late 1980s are the cut-off point for the old generation because it was then that Sir Timothy Berners-Lee, a British computer engineer and MIT professor, invented the World Wide Web (based on the Internet developed ten years earlier by Vinton Cerf). The Internet is much more than a work tool. As we have adapted the way we think and work to the Internet, it has shaped the way our minds, and in some ways even our personalities, work. The Internet has impacted everyone, but especially those who did not know life before it: people born after about 1983.

People born after 1983 tend not to feel as constrained by physical limitations as many older people do. Marc Prensky[71] claims that this generation has "not just changed incrementally from those of the past…a really big discontinuity has taken place." They live in a conceptual world where ideas can generate more money more quickly than structures of material substance ever could. Their thinking is not bound by distance and geography. They know that the relationship between time and effort invested in a project and its measurable outcome is not correlated the way it used to be. It takes no longer to communicate with a million people than it does to communicate with one.

You'll notice the difference between Planet-Es and Planet-Ss in the ways they go about planning a new business. When young Planet-Es plan a business and think about what they can offer the market, they don't think about customers and products first. Mostly, their first thought is about technology platforms and how to use them for new business ideas. They develop business ideas based on technology platforms rather than using technology to help promote an "old-world" business idea. Generally, older Planet-Ss prefer to decide on their offering based on their own strengths and weaknesses and what they think the market needs. They then figure out how best to use technology to market and deliver their product. For Planet-Ss, the Internet is a communication and delivery tool. For Planet-Es, the Internet is their world.

To the Planet-E generation of exponential, abstract thinkers, a long and expensive college education followed by a career up the corporate ladder is not the only, or even the best, road to success. They know some young people—and have read about many more—who made quick fortunes by utilizing the exponential capability of technology. Many young people are full of bright ideas on how to do this. They know that only some will succeed, but they are willing to take a risk, figuring that they have little to lose and so much to gain. In a few weeks and with no funding, they can create a "global" business that years ago would've taken fortunes and decades to build. In five years, they can conceive hundreds of such business ideas. Nearly all will fail. But who cares? The cost is small, and if just one of them succeeds the rewards are beyond imagination.

Planet-Es think differently from Planet-Ss. They find it easy to hold more than one idea in their minds at a time. They can work with these different ideas at once and easily switch their attention from one to the other. They multitask with amazing adeptness. They can easily manage a face-to-face conversation, a text-message dialogue, and possibly a movie or video clip, all at the same time. This is not necessarily a form of attention deficit disorder. It is the way they function, and they can get bored doing only one thing at a time unless that one thing absorbs many different facets of their minds. Amazingly, educators are finding that young people concentrate better in classes if they are permitted to be doing other things, like listening to music and even occasionally checking their Facebook page or watching the odd YouTube clip while listening to the teachers! I am not recommending this model of education. It would probably be better if teachers became more adept at holding their students' attention and inspiring them, without needing to resort to extraneous diversions to avoid boredom. However, education *will* need to redefine itself as it becomes easier and easier for the students to access up-to-date information, some of which is more up-to-date even than what the teacher is speaking about that moment.

Multitasking leads to hyperlinking, another different way that Planet-Es acquire information. Hyperlinking is not just a way around the Internet. Hyperlinking has become the way members of the new generation think and connect ideas and information. It is the way they build knowledge and explore ideas. It is their path of mental and intellectual adventure.

Some older inhabitants of Planet-S feel unnecessarily threatened by Planet-Es and console themselves with the thought that Planet-Es are incompetent communicators. This is an oversimplification and not entirely accurate. They are competent and versatile at using today's communication instruments. They are also masters of social networking across cultures and geographies. Although often brief to the point of abruptness and sometimes unintelligible to many people from Planet-S, Planet-Es' communications sometimes reveal much more emotion and vulnerability than their parents used to show when they were younger. The anonymity and isolation offered by technology insulates them from many of the fears associated with exposing personal vulnerability, and so they feel less emotional risk when they open up, which they often do. A study by Professors

S. Craig Watkins and H. Erin Lee of the University of Texas at Austin published in November 2010, surprisingly finds "social media afford opportunities for new expressions of friendship, intimacy, and community," that in many instances extend into real life.

It is true some of the younger Planet-Es can be awkward and inexperienced in face-to-face communications. But with their vast experience of multicultural communication through technology, they can quickly learn to improve their face-to-face skills, especially with coaching from a more mature mentor.

It is probably safe to assume Planet-Es will not achieve the same depth, wisdom, and insights thoughtful Planet-Ss can when they concentrate all their mental energy on one thing at a time. But by combining the strengths of the new generation and the older one, the results can be phenomenal.

A New Culture for a Changed World

People are motivated by challenging goals, inspired by a worthy corporate purpose, and energized by fun. Companies with soul have it all.

Google, Facebook, and other companies like them demonstrate the power of Planet-Es when working in the right environment. These companies' cultures and management models are not right for everyone, but they have overturned some well-established management myths. For example:

- **Myth:** Young people today are in it only for what they can get, not what they can *give*.
- **Fact:** When inspired, Planet-Es are energized, focused, and very hardworking.

- **Myth:** Young people need to learn that work is not play; they can play after work, *but not on my time.*
- **Fact:** Work and play are not always mutually exclusive. When successfully *combined within a single activity, they can result in superior innovation and inspired performance.*

- **Myth:** They will need to learn how to manage corporate hierarchy; there are no *shortcuts.*
- **Fact:** In many cases, hierarchical structure and very large teams can now be *safely demolished.*

- **Myth:** If you give them an inch, they'll take a mile.
- **Fact:** In a trusting culture, you can provide some of the reward up front. *New generation employees reciprocate with even more energy.*

Inspiring the New Generation

People are motivated by challenging but realistic goals, inspired by a worthy, meaningful corporate purpose, and energized by fun. To really ignite the power of Planet-E, companies with soul motivate, inspire, and energize them with all three of these forces at once.

Planet-Es resist the idea that the bulk of their lives will be spent on something that is not aligned with a worthy ideology and not any fun to do. They are interested in the well-being of their communities, in bold philanthropic initiatives, and in issues of global concern like environmentalism and combating disease in poor nations—and they expect their companies to be engaged in these issues, too.

Introducing a dimension of idealism into a business goes

beyond delegating philanthropy to the VP of corporate responsibility. "Philanthropy no more canonizes the good businessman than it exculpates the bad."[72] A business with soul has a dimension of idealism at its very core. This idealism is articulated in its *corporate purpose* and drives its strategic choices. Bill Gates and Paul Allen didn't create Microsoft just to make money for shareholders. Their purpose was to change the world by making it possible to put a computer on every business desktop and in every home in the world, so that people and businesses could realize their full potential. Professor Robert Barro of Harvard University and a senior fellow at the Hoover Institution at Stanford University, calculated Bill Gates' contribution to society through his core business: nearly one trillion dollars: more than ten times his total planned (at that time) charitable donations.[73]

By discovering and articulating your corporate purpose, you will more easily attract and fully engage people (Planet-Es and others) who truly identify with what you are doing and with *why* you are doing it.

Corporate purpose, as we discussed in Chapter 12, is not just another mission statement, written but not lived. The new generation has no interest in that. People generally, and Planet-Es especially, trust leaders whose espoused beliefs are aligned with the values they live. They become disillusioned when leaders tolerate unacceptable behaviors from individuals in their organization just because they are highly productive. Jack Welch used to say that firing high performers who don't live the company's values was among the hardest things he had to do as a leader. Young people value that courage in their leaders.

Respecting the New Generation

Like Sipho, young people value dignity and respect in a business culture. Talented young people have other options open to them, and they will not work in environments in which they feel they are treated without dignity and respect. They do not accept that their youth is an excuse for older people to talk to them in patronizing or abusive ways. To captivate young talent, apply the same behavioral standards at work as you do at home, speak to colleagues and employees as you would to family and friends, and watch their trust for you grow.

Playing at Work

Children are at their most creative when they play, and so are adults. I have asked thousands of leaders around the world what they were doing when they got their best ideas. Only two have told me it happened when they were working at their desks. Generally, people are doing things entirely unrelated to work when they have their best and most innovative work ideas. Some are working out, some are running, driving, walking, or relaxing in bed. Many say their ideas come to them in the shower. It makes you wonder why, when we want more productivity, we tend to chain people to their workstations for longer hours, the one place where we know innovation doesn't happen!

To innovate you need both sides of your brain: the left brain—analytical and calculative—and the right brain—intuitive and artistic. This rarely happens when we are all work and no play. As long as it does not intrude on others' focus, allowing your people to have fun while they work can be a wonderful motivational tool, and it can inspire much higher levels of engagement and innovation. For Planet-Es, fun is like fresh air: without it they wilt. It is hard to have fun in an inflexibly structured environment. New generation talent flees from such companies.

Freedom from Rigid Structure

People who don't trust themselves look for structural support. If you don't trust your sense of balance, you'll hold onto something firm for support. If you don't trust your memory, you'll create a structural aid to prompt you. The same applies when we don't trust others; we impose rigid structure to support them. Legal contracts, for example, are (mostly necessary) structural supports for agreements between two parties who do not fully trust one another: the less we trust, the more rigid the contract. Corporate structures, performance management, and reporting systems are designed to monitor and control people we do not fully trust to deliver the desired outcomes on their own. Some structure is always necessary, but the degree of its rigidity is inversely proportional to the level of trust.

Like Douglas McGregor's Theory-X,[74] cultures with very hierarchical structures assume most people dislike their work and must be controlled and managed so that they will work hard enough. They assume that people prefer direction, dislike responsibility, and desire security above everything. Theory-X considers only one operating system in people, the defensive instinctual one represented in the lower reaches of Maslow's view of human needs. But we have rejected that as distorted because it fails to take into account the second operating system in people: the creative, heroic drive to make a meaningful difference to others.

More than anything, people want to be valued and recognized for the difference they make in the world. They want to be working for and with people they respect. They want to enjoy what they are doing. And through the contribution they make, they want to be able to provide for their families. They want order, but not control. They want to be inspired without being threatened.

When Planet-Es are working on something they are passionate about, they generally use their creative, inspired, heroic operating system, not their instinctual defensive ones. When their leaders at work channel their passion and give them purpose, they bring their heroic operating system into their work. When their leaders manage them with McGregor's Theory-X model, they use their work time to pursue their true passion and take every opportunity they can to follow their passion rather than their job. For years, their rejection of Theory-X has spurred them to abandon corporate careers in favor of Silicon Valley start-ups. There, some made fortunes and others did not, but the Silicon Valley revolution inspired untold innovation that continues to benefit every facet of modern life.

To create a culture that is hospitable to talented Planet-Es, question the need for every layer of hierarchy in your organization. Dismantle large units into clusters of small, self-directed teams and use structure to measure, not to lead. Take the first step by trusting the people you have hired to deliver what you hired them to do, and they will respond. Remember that people are wired not to disappoint those who place their trust in them. You will be more than compensated for any minor disappointments you might meet by your savings (through ridding your company of costly and inefficient bureaucracy), the building of trust, and the unleashing of human energy in your teams.

Rick Jackson, chairman and CEO of Jackson Healthcare, has helped conceptualize and develop more than twenty-five healthcare organizations. Although born long before the Internet Age, Rick is a Planet-E person at heart. He has been an entrepreneur since he was ten, and when he married at nineteen without a college degree, he realized he would have to start at the bottom to get anywhere. Jackson Healthcare has won countless awards for being one of the fastest-growing companies, being the best place to work, and pace-setting for private companies.

In talking to Rick about his experience with the new generation, he commented how in the past we thought young adults were just lucky to have a job. They were just glorified servants.

> "The new generation of associates is different. They have a forty-hour mentality. They want lifestyle even if it means less money. No careers today, only a way of financing their activities outside work. They don't see moving from one job to another as negative or disloyal. Trying to motivate people who don't seem to be motivated by traditional means is the challenge. So, we treat all associates as volunteers. They have chosen to come to work for Jackson Healthcare and spend much of their day with us. We have also adapted our business model to their values; for example, forty-hour weeks. I also believe in vacation, and we encourage people to take vacations. I believe in putting others first, as a parent would."

Assuming that all employees want to do a good job, Rick invests in them up front; he takes a chance on them.

Investing Up Front

The greatest surprises come from the people we take a chance on. As in other areas of investment, the reward we get from investing in people is proportional to the risk we take in backing them. Some relationships disappoint, just as some investments do, but just as we manage the risk of our business decisions rather than avoiding risk altogether, so do we take risks in human relationships that we can manage. Assuming the worst of people seldom inspires their best, especially with Planet-Es.

When you take a leap of faith, you invest in people up front and you build a bank of spiritual credit that honest people generally want to repay. Not only do they repay you, they often reciprocate your trust by giving back much more than you invested in them. They believe that you, too, will respond in the future; and so the relationship grows.

Investing in people does not mean giving them bonuses before they perform (although some companies have done that successfully, too). Google provides stunning perks for its employees: free gourmet food, on-site medical attention, massages, and much more. It selects employees, mostly Planet-Es who value these perks, respect them, and reciprocate. These perks are costly, but they yield so much more than they cost.

Not all companies can or should do what Google does, but we can all seek out our own ways to show our teams that we believe in them and trust them. We can invest in them in ways that are worth much more to them than what they cost us. We can demonstrate thoughtfulness of their needs. Then, instead of focusing on the few disappointments that are bound to come along, we should measure the whole spectrum of costs and benefits to our companies, and based on those measurements manage those costs and benefits going forward. Treat people like you treat investments; choose them well, nurture them, lead them, and watch them grow.

Forging New Partnerships

Perhaps for the first time in history, young people generally possess the competencies needed for success in the future to a greater degree than their parents do.

After learning to understand the Internet generation and building an appropriate culture in which to nurture it, the third strategy to captivate young energy is to redefine your relationship with talented Planet-E employees. In fact, we should probably no longer refer to them as employees, because the more talented Planet-Es are not really employable at all in the old sense of the term *employment.* Entry-level employment used to be based on a power equation where all the power was in the hands of the employer. The applicant needed the job and didn't have that many options. Not so anymore. At least in the minds of Planet-Es, they can make a living for themselves with nothing but a computer. In their minds, there are almost unlimited ways to earn a living. So they want more from their jobs than a wage. And since they are not as oppressed by choice limitations and a need of money, as job entrants used to be, talented young entry-level employees do not readily succumb to the power model of the old employment relationship.

Experience is no longer the determining factor it used to be; in fact, in some areas experience can be a handicap! Older people have less of an advantage over younger people than they once had. When the future was a linear continuation of the past, experience gave us an edge in handling the future. This was because, barring unforeseen disruptions, the past used to be a reliable predictor of the future. Now new and profound developments send us in different, uncharted directions so quickly that the past can no longer accurately predict the future. Experience is still, and always will be, important, but it is no longer as crucial as it used to be.

In many ways when it comes to the future, Planet-Es, even those with little experience, have a clearer vision of what tomorrow could look like than older people do. Clearly visualizing the quantum leaps that technology can facilitate, they are liberated from the restraints of structure and status quo that still govern much of Planet-Ss' thinking. Despite their youth, or because of it, consider engaging your Planet-E teams in strategizing and envisioning the future. Doing so will open up possibilities for new products, markets, and process innovations that will leapfrog you over your competitors and give you the greatest competitive advantage.

Take a moment to list some of the competencies that are most important for future success. Your table may look something like this:

COMPETENCIES	Planet S Competencies	Planet E Competencies
Flexibility/Adaptability		
Technology		
Comfort in Diversity		
Ability to Learn Chinese		
Innovation		
Imagination		
Energy		

Then, if you are over thirty-five (typically more Planet-S than Planet-E), rate the degree to which you feel competent in each of these areas (on a scale of one to ten, where one is grossly incompetent and ten supremely competent). Then using your opinion, do the same for the general competencies of talented under-twenty-five-year-olds (typically more Planet-E than Planet-S).

You may be surprised by what we so often see when we run this exercise with our clients: in many cases the numbers in the Planet-E column are higher than those in the Planet-S group. Perhaps for the first time in history, young people generally possess the competencies needed for success in the future to a greater degree than their parents do. This is not to say that people over thirty-five do not have a very important part to play in this equation; they absolutely do. There are many competencies that young people cannot possibly yet have and for which they need to access the wisdom of more experienced workers. However, unlike in the past, when experience tipped the balance of power in favor of older workers, it no longer does so. The power equation has been equalized. *Each generation has a component of success that is vital to the other.* Planet-Ss have the wisdom gained from experience, and Planet-Es have the imagination gained from technology and passionate exuberance gained from freedom. It is this new equalization that compels a different kind of relationship.

Lest Planet-Es think that they can get along just fine without Planet-Ss, try doing the same exercise with a different list of competencies. Just as agility, imagination, technology, and energy are important for the future, reputation and sustainability are important in a rapidly changing world. Consider the qualities necessary to ensure sustainability of an organization and to build its reputation. Some of

COMPETENCIES	Planet S Competencies	Planet E Competencies
Patience and a Sense of Timing		
Ability to Build Enduring Stakeholder Relationships		
Media Management		
Humility		
Willingness to Sacrifice Immediate Gain for Long-Term Reputation		
Readiness to Do What's Right, Even at a Short-Term Cost		

them might be: patience and a sense of timing, the ability to build enduring stakeholder relationships, media management, humility, a willingness to sacrifice immediate gain for long-term reputation, and readiness to do what's right even at a short-term cost. And who is more competent in these qualities, Planet-Es or Planet-Ss? Fill out the table and see for yourself.

This is not the first time there has been an older generation somewhat cynical about a bright, younger generation reputed to have the new-world knowledge needed to take organizations to new levels. Back in the 1950s, a friend of my father's, Rudy Hammel, founded and built his family business into a multimillion-dollar manufacturer and distributor of wholesale food products. In the 1960s, when MBA graduates were reaching the zenith of their celebrity status, Rudy was persuaded to hire a new breed of professional managers to replace his "old-style" entrepreneurial managers who had grown his business with him up to that point.

At first, Rudy was skeptical. Then he bought into the argument. At that time, globalization and information technology were posing new challenges and opportunities. He thought his "old-style" managers might indeed not be up to exploiting those opportunities and managing the challenges. He retired them all generously and replaced them with a new cadre of professional managers, mostly from Ivy League business schools. The company continued to grow. Shareholders were exhilarated.

But after a few years, the global economy was hit by its second recession in a decade and things took a sudden turn for the worse. It wasn't long before Rudy's company joined many others in an almost uncontrollable tailspin. Everything his managers tried had the opposite of their desired effect. Their business school case studies had not simulated these business conditions, and they were groping for ideas. So Rudy retired them all generously, too, and rehired his "old" management team. The company's almost instant turnaround into growth defied all trends. Rudy's shareholders were relieved. And so was Rudy!

Planet-Es today are very different beings from Ivy League MBAs of the 1960s, and Planet-Ss today are far better educated than Rudy's older entrepreneurs were at that time. Still, the lesson is clear: neither Planet-Ss nor Planet-Es can achieve corporate greatness alone. To successfully transition from the old world order to the new one takes a partnership. It takes a partnership of generations; of Planet-S and of Planet-E. It takes partnerships between people of diverse cultures, disciplines, passions, and talents. It takes partnerships between people whose wisdom is steeped in experience and those who can imagine a future that has no precedent in anything from the past.

From Employment to Partnership

Since they were five years old, competent Planet-Es have been mastering the technology that business needs. Irrespective of their age and *formal* experience, this gives them fifteen years of *effective* experience in a fast-changing field. With their level of knowledge, skill, and freedom of opportunity, organizations cannot think about Planet-Es in the same way they used to think of *employees*, *trainees*, or *subordinates*. Instead of thinking about them as employees, you must think of them as strategic partners in your enterprise from the moment they walk in your doors. Evaluate their potential based more on their talent and passion than on their credentials or experience. They are strategic partners because, unlike traditional entry-level employees, they come to us with a "commodity" that we need as much as they need the job we provide them, perhaps even more. By thinking of them as strategic partners, you can craft coalitions of collaboration with them, fully engaging them in your enterprise. Like partners, they work for you not because they are compelled by circumstances, but because they choose to.

The Partnership Is Two-Way

Planet-Es need Planet-Ss, too. When they experience their working relationship as one of partnership rather than one of hierarchical control, they value relationships with Planet-Ss highly. They seek out mentors and role models they can look up to. They want heroes in their lives. The heroes they seek are people whose authority comes from who they are as human beings and leaders, not from the position they hold or the money they have. They want to work for and be mentored by great leaders who are accomplished and confident, but also who have the humility to see the value young people can bring. Humility is rare, but it gives invaluable advantage to those who master it.

The Power of Humility

If business is a university of greatness, then dealing with bright, talented young Planet-Es is one of its most challenging and important classes.

Perhaps what makes the creation of strategic alliances with younger employees so challenging is that their success depends more on humility than on any other single character trait. Humility does not always come easily to successful leaders. If business is, as I see it, a university of greatness, then dealing with bright, talented young Planet-Es is one of that university's most challenging and important classes. This is because you can only engage brilliant young talent if you are willing to learn from them. Learning from people younger and less experienced than you requires a large dose of genuine humility and authentic greatness, qualities we are not taught in business schools or in the corridors of corporations.

Humility is not the opposite of self-confidence or self-esteem. Humility is the opposite of arrogance. It is surprising how easy it is for other people to see us as arrogant, even when we do not see ourselves as such, nor do we intend to come across that way. The reason for this is that people come across as arrogant whenever they feel internally insecure. When people feel insecure, they lean on the structures that support their insecurity; structures like power, status, or arrogance.

308

Instinctively, they put up barriers that keep others at a distance, fearing others might pierce the thin layers camouflaging their fragile egos.

Planet-Es do not relate well to egotistical people and they do not respect these barriers—they see right through them. Planet-Es want heroes, not power-hungry tyrants. They are attracted to people they admire, respect, and trust, and people from whom they can learn. The heroes that Planet-Es want to work for are ordinary people with ordinary fears and vulnerabilities, who overcome these weaknesses to do extraordinary things. They do not think less of you when you trust them enough to take down your defenses; they respect you more.

The truth is that it is not only young Planet-Es that do not respect status. Even the more conventional Planet-Ss do not really respect empty shells of status and power! Planet-Ss are schooled to show respect for position and authority, even when they see nothing truly worthy of admiration in the characters of the individuals they are supposed to respect. Planet-Es do not function that way. Like creative, playful, uninhibited young children, they are much more open about how they really feel, and they are not very good at being diplomatic and politically correct.

When interacting with young Planet-E talent, it is helpful to set age aside. See a powerhouse of idealism, passion, imagination, and creativity beneath the young, childlike package in front of you. See a young person who can help you take your organization to the next level. See someone who has many other options but has chosen to work with you. If these people stay with you, it will be because they admire your values and character, they value your mentorship, and they identify with what you are trying to accomplish. So, it is important to share these things with them. Include them in your vision and share your *corporate purpose* with them. Share your wisdom generously and never condescendingly. Seek their advice, and use them to keep you in touch with their generation. That is where your customer of tomorrow (if not today) will come from, and perhaps, in some cases, your boss of tomorrow, too!

I met Ronnie, a bright young CEO of a successful venture capital firm in California, as I panted up the steep slopes of one of the Red Mountains in Utah on a crisp early morning in the spring. He told me that in many of the companies in which his firm is invested, the CEO or founder is a twenty-something Planet-E who assembles a management team of thirty- and forty-year-olds. Firstly, this illustrates how aware Planet-Es are that experience is crucial. Secondly, it was illuminating to learn how Ronnie saw his role as a venture capital partner. Ronnie's role went far beyond identifying start-up opportunities in new technologies and applying capital to them to assist in their growth. Ronnie saw part of his role as a bridge between two generations, mentoring young CEOs who were learning to manage accomplished and senior people and coaching experienced executives who were learning to manage a complicated relationship with a boss half their age.

Both Planet Es and Planet Ss need humility to recognize the value in each other. Humility does not mean you should in any way underrate yourself. On the contrary, humility means you are secure in who you are and confident in what you have accomplished—yet, at the same time, you are humbled by the gap between your present self and who you could be. Humility is being careful not to underrate the contributions others do make and can make to your success. It is the capacity to learn from every other human being.

Seven Ways for Planet-S Leaders to Captivate Planet-E Talent

Here is a recap of seven fundamentals to help Planet-S managers lead a Planet-E team with greatness.

1. Their lack of experience is not a disadvantage. Innovation and technological imagination are rarer, and therefore more valuable, than experience. You probably have plenty of experience within your organization to support a bright, innovative young person who lacks it.

2. The employer-employee power balance has changed: you need them as much as they need you. So, even though you have authority and access to the purse strings, those are no longer effective management tools.

3. They respect you for your knowledge and experience, and most of all for your character. You, however, can respect them for their passion and talents, and value them for what they can contribute to your team.

4. There is no substitute for maturity and experience, but experience and future focus are often not found in the same individual. This is where partnership and mutual respect enter the picture. Planet-Ss and Planet-Es working closely together in a mutually respectful partnership will take your team into unmapped territory with the confidence born from experience and the excited energy of youth.

5. Young talent does not need to start at the bottom and work its way up. Identify the areas where young newcomers can use talents they possess despite (or because of) their inexperience, to contribute optimally to your team or organization. Then, place them where they can best contribute, irrespective of hierarchical norms.

6. It is okay to ask twenty-somethings for advice. Just as you don't mind asking your ten-year-old to show you how to use your smartphone or new digital camera, you can ask young people on your team about possibilities for technology in your business.

> They may also know more about your customers of tomorrow than any market research survey can tell you.

7. Treat every talented person who works for you, irrespective of age, as a valued volunteer.

Of course, authenticity is paramount. Young people are the perfect instrument panels to help you be authentic because of their tendency to provide immediate feedback. They are transparent enough to show you when you are connecting with them and when you are not. They have a disdain for pretense and do not hesitate to show it. When they recognize authenticity, though, they shine, and you will know it.

CONCLUSION
THE AUTHENTICITY DIFFERENCE

The only thing you can give your customer that competitors cannot
is an experience that is authentic to who you
and your company are at your very essence, in your soul.

ARTHUR KAPLAN was a doyen of the retail jewelry industry in South Africa. He started off as an ambitious young salesman in an upmarket jewelry store, eager to prove himself to his new boss. On his first day at work, a man approached him interested in buying a strand of ten-millimeter round cultured pearls. Such pearls have always been rare and extremely valuable. The sale was going to be an enormous coup for the new salesman. At today's value, the cost of the strand of pearls was well over thirty thousand dollars—a phenomenal sale for young Arthur. The customer said he would make the purchase if Arthur could justify the price of these genuine pearls compared to a nearly identical-looking strand of artificial pearls that would cost him no more than five hundred dollars. Arthur was quick to respond. "You are right. It is difficult for the untrained eye to tell the difference. But take two women out to a black-tie event. Give one the artificial necklace to wear and the other the genuine strand—and notice the difference in the way they walk!"

Authenticity is the only thing that can't be replicated. John Reinhard, Explorer-in-Residence at the National Geographic Society said: "There's nothing like seeing the authenticity of a real person. Replicas just don't have the same emotional power." People know authenticity when they see it, and they are willing to pay a substantial premium for the real thing.

Many companies in your industry probably offer the same products that you do, and many may do so with the same high quality, customer convenience, and service. Whatever innovation you introduce can be copied the next day. There is only one thing you can give your customers and other stakeholders that competitors cannot: an experience authentic to who you are and to the essence and soul of your company. Groups of people, teams, and corporations have a soul of their own. A company's soul is its spirit, its personality, its culture, and the values by which it stands. A company's soul is the reason why its customers stay loyal to it and why its best employees never leave it. When your customers' experience is derived from your *corporate soul*, it is authentic in the truest sense and cannot be copied.

When customers feel their interactions with your company are authentic rather than scripted, they experience the soul of your organization, connecting with you deeply in ways they don't with your competitors. When employees experience the beliefs and values of your organization authentically, they connect with your company in a profound way. It will take competitors more than salary incentives for employees or price reductions for customers to lure them away from you.

Customers and employees have deep intangible needs seldom fulfilled in their daily lives. You can satisfy these needs at no additional cost to you, and when you do, you nourish their souls. The benefits in market share, innovation, and customer and talent retention are tangible, measurable, and impactful. When your competitive strategy is built on the foundation of your *corporate soul* rather than on operational efficiencies alone, you will have won the competitive game. Even an online retail store can have a *corporate soul* that is worth billions. Tony Hsieh breathed a *corporate soul* into Zappos.com when it was struggling for survival and sold it for over one billion dollars ten years later.[75] Tony used soft input like values and culture (the foundations of the *corporate soul*) to build hard bottom-line output: shareholder value. "Our belief is that if we get the culture right, most of the other stuff, like delivering great customer service or building a long-term enduring brand for the company, will happen naturally on its own." He designed the cultural architecture of his company to reflect his own beliefs and passions, and that is what gives it soul.

Your *corporate soul* is the fountainhead of your company's authenticity, and for it to flourish your company must be staffed and led by people of character who exude authenticity. Authenticity is crucial to human greatness. This is something Tony Hsieh "gets." He stresses the importance of not hiding or holding back who you really are inside the office. "It is about being yourself in the office because…that is when creativity really blossoms and great ideas come out, which is what has driven our growth."[76]

A *corporate soul* cannot be invented or engineered, it can only be discovered. Leaders of character who possess qualities of human greatness discover their *corporate souls*, articulate them, and use them to build their uniqueness. You have it in you to be such a leader; one who is imbued with a sense of *Personal Purpose* and who sees your work as a vehicle through which you can realize that purpose. You see life and the world through the prism of your *Spiritual Fingerprint*. Everything extraneous to this becomes secondary, even irrelevant, as your priorities become plain. Life is simplified, and its choices are clear.

In this space of moral clarity, the pathways before you are bright and the places they lead to are where you want to go. Once you have identified your *Personal Purpose*, the higher purpose of your organization becomes manifest. By remaining faithful to your *corporate purpose*, you satisfy not only your customers' tangible needs but also some of the deeper cravings of their souls. You connect to people, whatever their culture, and are energized to make a difference.

The power of purpose is inestimable. Whatever the true purpose of your existence, if you stay faithful to it you will succeed. James Tobin brilliantly chronicles the story of the Wright Brothers in his book *To Conquer the Air*.[77] He compares their journey to fame with that of Samuel Langley, who was trying to build the first flying machine at about the same time. Langley, Tobin suggests, was pursuing achievement and fame, whereas Orville and Wilbur Wright were "afflicted with the belief that flight is possible to man," as Wilbur himself wrote in 1900, a belief for which he was willing to sacrifice everything he had, even his life. The Wright brothers had a purpose and they infected everyone around them with a passion for that purpose. Fame was the outcome of their passion, not its driver. On December 17, 1903, they succeeded in flying for fifty-nine seconds at an altitude of 120 feet, changing the world forever. Langley faded into oblivion.

Hundreds of phenomenally successful business leaders are, like the Wright Brothers, driven by their internal beliefs rather than by the desire for a specific economic outcome. These people, leading by greatness rather than greed, invest their passions in building their companies' *corporate souls*, not just their structures and processes. As in the cases of famous companies like Google, Southwest Airlines, and Starbucks, as well as smaller "unsung corporate heroes" like Gateway Group One, TMSi Logistics, and other privately owned companies I have mentioned in this book, the economic outcome flows, almost effortlessly, as a result.

I hope you, too, will engage in the journey of discovery of your own *Personal Purpose* and the higher *corporate purpose* for which you believe your team or company has come together. I hope you will see how, using the power of your own authentic beliefs, passions, and values, you can access your company's *corporate soul* and use it to satisfy the deep, intangible needs both of your employees and of your customers. The world needs leaders like you to transform the environments in which we work and live, and in which we generate our wealth. Leaders like you will create a new wave of economic growth.

Men and women who lead by their own greatness feel secure and unthreatened. They do not insulate themselves by projecting defensiveness when they are challenged; rather, they courageously open themselves to others, unafraid to expose their vulnerability. They act generously and build trusting connections with people. Such leaders consistently show the people around them authentic appreciation even for the little things they do. This assures people that their leader values their generosity and will not take advantage of them.

As you conquer your defensive instinct and increasingly act creatively and heroically, people will sense your quiet self-mastery.

They will witness your confidence and humility arising from the inner peace of your authentic living. They will experience the passion and focus that you convey. Like the stationary center of a turning wheel, you will exist as a center point of spirituality, the source of your company's ability to deliver results and create value.

Recognizing that your greatness lies in who you are, not in the power you wield, people will gravitate toward you, trust you, and follow you, and with abundant generosity, they will support your purpose.

This is a life of character.

This is living authentically.

This is how you *Lead by Greatness*.

LAPIN**INTERNATIONAL**

Lead by Greatness™

Lapin Consulting International, Inc. works at the intersection of strategy and leadership development to deliver bottom-line results to its clients.

Using *Lead By Greatness*™ methodology to build high performance cultures, we optimize human input and help our clients convert it into measurable economic output. Our proprietary process, customized to client needs, takes leadership to new levels of strategic thinking and execution effectiveness. With laser-beam precision, we penetrate the very *soul* of a company or team to uncover the blockages that prevent them from solving their most strategic and pressing business issues, helping them deliver extraordinary performance. Our results consistently unleash passion, employee engagement, and a unifying sense of purpose that power unrivaled growth. Our 20-year track record on four continents in multiple industries guarantees our clients' results.

Whether you are an influential individual in your community, or the leader of an organization, small business, or team, our expert *Lead By Greatness* consultants and coaches are dedicated to support you on your path to greatness.

Our consulting services are designed around three core offerings:

Strategic Innovation

Our proprietary methodology has led our clients to think about their business in ways they never had before and ways their competitors never will. The resulting innovation in their product, process, and structure has positioned them to consistently outperform industry norms.

Cultural and Generational Intelligence

This unique program has helped clients worldwide to turn differences between individuals, generations, and cultures into economic advantage.

Leadership Development and Coaching

Our flagship program, *Lead by Greatness,* has inspired leaders at all levels to spark innovation and deliver growth, while embracing ownership and accountability. Our process combines:

- **Interactive Workshops**—Our workshops challenge participants to explore new strategy and leadership paradigms and to build deep, authentic connections with others. Working in groups, participants learn new thought processes as they study both client-specific and global case study materials inside the classroom setting and beyond it. Often, participants use their learning to design a deliverable output that adds strategic value to the organization.

- **Facilitated Action Learning**—Participants learn to develop a culture of peer-to-peer coaching and knowledge sharing.

- **One-on-One Executive Coaching and Consulting**— Working either face-to-face or by phone, our team of licensed coaches helps executives master *Lead by Greatness* principles amidst their real time challenges.

- **Web-Based, Simulated Classroom Learning**—We leverage cutting-edge technology to deliver content cost-effectively to large groups of people or to those working at remote locations.

- **Assessment Instruments**—Our tools provide executive insight into existing organizational culture and leadership effectiveness, inform program design, and serve as benchmarks for individual and team development.

Take the next step to further the greatness in you or in your organization. Contact Lapin International for more information on our consulting and leadership development solutions, or join our team of certified consultants and coaches to help others hone their leadership greatness.

Visit us at www.lapininternational.com, email us at info@leadbygreatness.com, or call us at +1.310.444.9602.

ENDNOTES

[1] Ascentium has been ranked six times since 2005 by *Inc. Magazine* as one of the country's fastest growing private companies.

[2] Churchill, Sir Winston. *The Gathering Storm* (Mariner Books, 1986), 601.

[3] Formerly known as SBE, Strategic Business Ethics, Inc.

[4] In its series of over 30 *Institutes Against Hate Crimes and Terror*, held at the Simon Wiesenthal Center in Los Angeles.

[5] Quoted on Summit TV in August, 2008.

[6] Leviticus 12:1-3.

[7] Kelleher, Herb. "A Culture of Commitment," *Leader to Leader*. 4 (Spring 1997): 20-24.

[8] Ibid.

[9] Ibid.

[10] "Virgin Atlantic Profits Soar," *The Guardian*. May 26, 2009.

[11] Ogilvy & Mather. *The Eternal Pursuit of Unhappiness.*

[12] Collins, Jim. *Good to Great*, (New York: Harper Collins, 2001), 37.

[13] Williamson, Marianne. *A Return to Love: Reflections on the Principles of a Course in Miracles*, Harper Collins, 1992.

[14] Rabbi Menachem Schneerson, leader of the Lubavitch Hassidic Movement, December 11, 2008.

[15] Park, Alice. "The Happiness Effect," *Time*. December 11, 2008.

[16] Isaiah 45:18.

[17] Martin, Roger L. "The Execution Trap," Harvard Business Review. (July 20, 2010).

[18] Eliot, T.S. *The Rock*, (London: Faber & Faber, 1934).

[19] Farelo, António. A History of Fingerprints (Interpol, April 2009). Farelo is a fingerprint examiner for In-terpol's forensic support and technical databases.

[20] Sanhedrin 37a.

[21] Farelo, António. *A History of Fingerprints* (Interpol, April 2009).

[22] "It is in fact the intertwining of genetic and epigenetic factors which guarantee the uniqueness of each individual." Arnold B. Scheibel MD. "Embryological Development of the Human Brain," *New Horizons for Learning*, 1997. Dr. Scheibel is a professor of neurobiology and psychiatry at the UCLA Medical School in Los Angeles, California.

[23] Avot DeRabbi Nattan 5.

[24] $157 billion total asset base (December 2008) and a tier-one capital ratio of 10.7 percent.

[25] *Harvard Business Review*, July-August 2010.

[26] Babylonian Talmud, Avodah Zarah 20b.

[27] Babylonian Talmud, Hulin 7a.

[28] *Harvard Business Review*, July 22, 2010.

[29] Psalm 89:3.

[30] Interactive Advertising Bureau (IAB), May 13, 2010.

[31] Melloy, John. "Apple on Pace to Be Most Valuable Company... Maybe Ever," *CNBC*. July 21, 2011.

[32] Ibid.

[33] Cain Miller, Claire & Helft, Miguel. "Google Shake-Up Is Effort to Revive Start-Up Spark," *New York Times*. January 22, 2011.

[34] "Saving Starbucks' Soul," *Bloomberg Businessweek*, April 22, 2007.

[35] "Hewlett-Packard Co.," Notable Corporate Chronologies, Business and Company Resource Center, 2001, http://galenet. com/servlet/BCRC> (February 18, 2003).

[36] Steve Jobs: Apple's One-Dollar-a-Year Man. *Fortune*, January 24, 2000.

[37] "This 1998 Model Is Looking More Like a Lemon." *New York Times*, November 26, 2000.

[38] Ibid.

[39] This research took place in the 1990s, before the WorldCom and Enron collapses and the subsequent focus on corporate governance and the Sarbanes-Oxley regulations. We might

have received different responses had we conducted the same research today. The point, however, remains valid in illustrating the gap between those employees' values and their ethics.

[40] Enron 2000 Annual Report: http://picker.uchicago.edu/Enron/EnronAnnualReport2000.pdf.

[41] Taylor, F. W. *Principles of Scientific Management*, 1911.

[42] Geoffrey Colvin. "Managing in the Info Era: In the knowledge-based economy, workers will be valued for their ability to create, judge, imagine, and build relationships," *Fortune Magazine*, March 26, 2000.

[43] Maslow, A.H. "A Theory of Human Motivation," *Psychological Review*, 50(4) 1943: 370-96.

[44] McGregor, Douglas. *The Human Side of Enterprise* (McGraw-Hill Higher Education, 1960).

[45] Colvin, Geoffrey. "Managing in the Info Era: In the knowledge-based economy, workers will be valued for their ability to create, judge, imagine, and build relationships," *Fortune Magazine*, March 26, 2000.

[46] Pink, Daniel. *Drive: The Surprising Truth About What Motivates Us* (Penguin, 2009).

[47] Frankl, Viktor. "Self-Transcendence as a Human Phenomenon," *Journal of Humanistic Psychology* 6 (1966): 97.

[48] Darwin, Charles. *The Descent of Man*; Chapter V.

[49] Shemot Rabbah 52:2.

[50] Southwest Airlines 1999 Annual Report: http://southwest.investorroom.com/download/1999+Annual+Report.pdf

[51] Cohen, Allan; Watkinson, James; Boone, Jenny. "Herb Kelleher Talks about How Southwest Airlines grew from Entrepreneurial

Startup to Industry Leadership," *Babson Insight*, February 2005.

[52] Maynard, Micheline. "Southwest Airlines Posts a Fourth Quarter Loss," *The New York Times*, February 2, 2009.

[53] *Washington Post*, November 9, 2010.

[54] Haque, Umair. "Eudaimonics 101: America Needs a 21st Century Investment Plan," http://umairhaque.blogspot. com/2011/07/america-needs-human-potential.html July 25, 2011.

[55] Tzu, Sun. *The Art of War,* (Oxford University Press: 1971).

[56] Babylonian Talmud, Tractate Shabbath 55a.

[57] Adapted from Leon F. Seltzer's *Paradoxical Strategies in Psychotherapy*.

[58] Schultz and Raiton, "Knowledge As Intellectual Property," (2005).

[59] "A Cup of Joe for the Average Joe," *Focus.* http://sinekpartners. typepad.com/refocus/2006/06/a_cup_of_joe_fo.html, June 9, 2006.

[60] Ibid.

[61] *Starbucksgossip.com*, February 27, 2007.

[62] Steve Jobs, former CEO of Apple, discussed this in an interview with Betsy Morris, senior editor of *Fortune Magazine* in February 2008.

[63] *The Mainichi Daily News*, July 4, 2009.

[64] Kelleher, Herb. "A Culture of Commitment," *Leader to Leader.* 4 (Spring 1997): 20-24.

[65] *Harvard Business Review*, January-February 2010.

[66] Lagace, Martha. "Q&A with Michael Beer," *HBS Working Knowledge*, February 9, 2009.

[67] All of my information about Google in this chapter is garnished from the outstanding book by David A. Vise and Mark Malseed, *The Google Story* (New York: Bantam Dell, 2005).

[68] In its Institutes Against Hate Crimes and Terror, held at the Simon Wiesenthal Center in Los Angeles.

[69] http://www.etymonline.com/index.php?term=please

[70] Blodget, Henry. "Investing, Tales of the Valley," *Yahoo! Finance.* September 10, 2010.

[71] Author of *TEACHING DIGITAL NATIVES: Partnering for Real Learning* (Corwin, March 2010).

[72] "Microsoft: The End of Bill Gates Era," *The Economist* (June 26, 2008).

[73] *The Wall Street Journal*, June 19, 2007.

[74] McGregor, D. *The Human Side of Enterprise*, 1960.

[75] "Amazon Closes Zappos Deal," *TechCrunch.* November 2, 2009.

[76] Blodget, Henry. "Investing, Tales of the Valley," *Yahoo! Finance.* September 10, 2010.

[77] *To Conquer the Air* (New York: Free Press, a Division of Simon & Shuster, Inc., 2003).

ABOUT THE AUTHOR

DAVID LAPIN has earned the respect of global business leaders because of his unique ability to identify a business's most advantageous strategic opportunities and its hidden operational challenges while simultaneously unraveling the complex dynamics of the human spirit. This ability, combined with his uncompromising position on growing revenue and maximizing profit, places him in a category with other powerful international speakers, thought leaders, and organizational advisors.

The genesis of David's *Lead by Greatness* philosophy was the work he did with South Africa's greatest business and national leaders who, alongside Nelson Mandela, transformed the country into a vibrant new democratic economy. His groundbreaking work around the world has built self-driven, high-performing teams in environments of complex diversity. Founder of the South African Institute of Business Ethics, he was both the architect of the Code of Ethics for the first

King Commission on Corporate Governance and a regular columnist for *The Star*.

David, who lives in Los Angeles and Toronto, is also a rabbinic leader of international repute. He coaches, guides, and teaches business leaders, professionals, and educators throughout the world.

INDEX